TABLE OF CONTENTS

Chapter 1: Five Steps to Changing Bad Food Habits 7
To Build New Habits Understand the Cue, Routine, and Reward 7
5 Steps to Clean Eating 8

Chapter 2: Drink Abundant Water & Replace All Sugary Drinks ... 10
How *Not* to Drink Yourself Fat, Tired, and Insulin Resistant 10
The Magic of Water for Weight Loss, Brain Health, Mood, Energy, and Detox 11

Chapter 3: How Do I Get Enough Protein for My Macro Nutrient Ratio? 12
A Reminder: The Right Fat/Protein/Carb Ratio Will Keep You Healthy and Fit 12
How to Get Enough Protein from Plants 12
Doctor Recommended? 13
Healthy Plant-Based Protein Comes from Amino Acids 14
Toh-mato, Tomah-to, Aminos! 14

Chapter 4: How to Meet Your Nutritional Need with Just Plant Based Foods 16
You Can Fully Meet Your Nutritional Needs with Plants (No Animal Products Needed) 17
Plant Proteins 18
Plant Fats 19
Plant Carbohydrates 19

Chapter 5: Meet Your Nutritional Needs Without Eating Gluten, Soy, Processed Foods, and Alcohol 21
Let's Talk Gluten 21
Why Not Soy? 21
Replace Processed Foods with Something Better 22

Skip Alcohol, and Forget the Extra Calories (Among Other Deadly Health Concerns)..........23

Create the Right Fat/Protein/Carb Ratio to Truly Thrive..........24

Chapter 6: Eat Consistently and Optimize with Food-Based Nutritional Supplements 26

Why You Need to Eat the Same (or Similar) Foods Every Day 26

Why You Need Supplements Even When You Eat Clean 24

What's Causing Nutrient Depletion? 27

Why You Need Food-Based, Not Synthetic Nutrient Supplements 28

Food-Based Synergy 28

19 of the Best Food-Based Supplements 29

1. Magnesium 29
2. Zinc 30
3. B Vitamins (B6, B9, B12) 30
4. Tyrosine 30
5. Tryptophan 31
6. Plant-Based Omega 3s 31
7. Korean Ginseng (Panax Ginseng) 31
8. Glutathione 32
9. Choline 32
10. Turmeric (Curcuma longa) 32
11. Maca (Lepidium meyenii) 32
12. Luna Natural Sleep Aid 33
13. Nopal Cactus 33
14. ZMA 33
15. Ginger (Zingiber officinale) 33
16. Probiotics 34
17. Digestive Enzymes 34
18. Multivitamin 34
19. Vitamin C 34

Chapter 7: Follow an Intermittent Fasting Schedule Appropriate to Your Life's Flow 35

TABLE OF CONTENTS

Infographics 37

- 15 Foods For Carbohydrates 37
- 12 Foods For Fats 38
- 12 Foods For Proteins: Seeds And Grains 39
- 9 Foods For Proteins: Dips And Vegetables 40
- 8 Foods For Proteins: Nuts 41
- 13 Foods For Fiber 42
- 10 Foods For Vitamin C 43
- 13 Foods For Iron 44
- 9 Foods For Bone Health 45
- 10 Foods For Pregnancy Health 46
- 10 Foods For Gut Health 47
- 10 Foods For Immunity 48
- 9 Foods For Menstrual Support 49
- 12 Foods For Mental Health Support 50
- 9 Foods For Hypothyroidism 51
- 10 Foods For Heart Health 52
- 10 Foods For Liver Support 53
- 10 Foods For Sleep Support 54
- 11 Superfoods' Hall Of Fame 55
- 10 Foods For Hair, Skin And Nails 56
- 10 Foods For Healthy Eyes And Vision 57
- 9 Foods For Pre And Post-Workout Meals 58
- 10 Foods For Eczema 59
- 17 Foods For Inflammation 60
- 10 Foods For High Blood Pressure 61
- 10 Foods For Arthritis 62
- 12 Foods For Stress Management 63
- 15 Foods For Prostate Health 64
- 13 Foods For Budget-Friendly Shopping 65
- 11 Foods For Powerful Breakfasts 66
- 11 Slow-Cooked Dinner Ingredients For Cold Winters 67
- 4 Plant-Combos Tips For Spectacular Salads 68

PLANT-BASED HEALTH

TABLE OF CONTENTS

4 Plant-Combos Tips For Spectacular Salads	69
8 Foods For Losing Weight Without Hunger Pangs	70
11 Alternatives For Your Most-Craved Comfort Foods	71
11 Foods Children Will Love	72
11 Plants For Juicing And Blending	73
15 Foods For Meal Prepping	74
5 Egg Replacements For Baking, Breakfast, And Beyond	75
11 Sources Of Antioxidants	76
9 Purple Foods For Antioxidants	77
8 Orange Foods	78
7 Yellow Foods	79
11 Red Foods	80
17 Green Foods	81
5 Blue Foods	82
12 Non-Acidic Vegetables, Legumes, And Grains	83
8 Non-Acidic Fruits	84
10 Low Glycemic Index Foods	85
10 Foods For Nourishing Yourself After A Stomach Bug	86
11 Foods With Cancer-Fighting Properties	87
8 Foods For Sensitive Digestive Systems	88
11 Foods For Runners	89
12 Foods For Meat Cravings	90
7 Foods For Butters And Spreads	91
6 Spices: Benefits, Flavor And Uses	92
9 Leafy Greens: Benefits And Uses	93
9 Plant Milks: Flavor And Uses	94
8 Popular Seeds	95
9 Popular Nuts	96
17 Tasty Snacks	97
11 Sweet Treats	98
4 Faq About Turmeric	99
3 Faq About Apple Cider Vinegar	100

simple + optimum
core routines for extraordinary living

DOWNLOAD YOUR FREE BONUS:
simpleoptimum.com/bookbonus

TABLE OF CONTENTS

Stevia: Sweetener Without The Nasties 101

3 Faq About Garlic 102

**3 Faq About Ginger: The Miracle Root, The Top Benefits And
How To Harness Them** 103

4 Fabulous Funghi – Guide To Mushrooms And How To Use Them 104

11 Pretty Foods: Guide To Edible Flowers 105

**9 Reasons Why To Choose Plant-Based Diet - What Can It Do For
Your Body And Mind?** 106

18 Foods For A Home-Grown Edible Garden: Herbs, Veggies And Berries 107

10 Gluten-Free Whole Grains 108

5 Meal Ideas For Meat-Eating Guests 109

6 Meal Ideas For Meat-Eating Guests 110

**5 Tips For How To Use Herbs, Nuts, Vinegars And
Oils To Create Dressings And Dipping Sauces** 111

**5 Tips For How To Use Herbs, Nuts, Vinegars And
Oils To Create Dressings And Dipping Sauces** 112

7 Tips For Making The Transition 113

6 Ways How To Use Cooked Leftovers And Offcuts To Avoid Waste 114

8 Tips How To Prepare And Freeze Fresh Produce Yourself 115

7 Easy Ways To Use An Excess Of Stone Fruits During A Generous Harvest 116

8 Best Ways To Make The Most Of Citrus 117

10 Lower-Carb Fruits 118

**7 Ways To Use The Whole Vegetable Without Wastage:
Stalks, Leaves And Flowers** 119

**7 Tips For Maintaining Your Plant-Based Diet During
The Festive Season And Holidays** 120

What Are Nightshades? Concerns And Benefits 121

7 Cabbages - The Underrated Benefits Of The Humble Brassicas 122

**4 Tips For How To Use The Plants In Your Kitchen And
Garden To Make Your Own Herbal Teas** 123

**5 Tips For How To Use The Plants In Your Kitchen And
Garden To Make Your Own Herbal Teas** 124

9 Tips For Storing Fresh Product In Fridge Or Cupboard 125

5 Tips For Storing Fresh Product In Fridge Or Cupboard 126

TABLE OF CONTENTS

Chapter 8: The Two-Week Diet Plan and Grocery Shopping List 127

- 8.1 Breakfast Recipes 127
- 8.2 Lunch Recipes 132
- 8.3 Dinner Recipes 152
- 8.4 Dessert Recipes 178
- 8.5 Snack Recipes 181
- 8.6 Substitutes 183
- 8.7 Grocery Shopping List for the Two-Week Diet Plan 184
- 8.8 Saving Money While on the Vegan Keto Diet 187

Chapter 1: Five Steps to Changing Bad Food Habits

We're about to dive into the best clean-eating course you've ever put your hands on, but first, we need to talk about how you're going to create some life-changing and life-saving habits.

Just telling you that you need to change how you eat isn't enough. If it were that simple, everyone would already be eating like a God or Goddess. You are not average, though. You are beyond mediocre. You can change habits if you just tap into the psychology that causes us to do what we do, and "trick" your brain into making better choices.

To Build New Habits Understand the Cue, Routine, and Reward

All habits are formed based on a cue, routine, and reward. Charles Duhigg in *The Power of Habit* and other authors talk about this cycle of habit formation extensively. There are thousands of different ways to change a habit but the successful ones always utilize these 3 major processes in the human brain:

#1 The Cue (A triggering action) – This is usually a situation in which you feel tired, bored, sad, frustrated, or worn out from a busy day. Since you mention catching oneself as the cue stage as so important now and even later in

the book, consider adding two more common examples of cues so everyone can identify theirs.

#2 The Routine (The action you take repeatedly) – This can be a negative action or a positive action, but it's what you do most often. This can be smoking cigarettes and watching TV, or going to the gym and drinking green smoothies first thing in the morning. It's the things you do without thinking because they are *already* a habit.

#3 The Reward (A positive reinforcement of the action or routine) – This is the thing that temporarily makes you happy when you engage in an action. It keeps you from feeling bored, sad, frustrated, or unhappy. It may just keep your hands or mind busy, bring you a small amount of pleasure, or completely light you up.

The key to creating new habits is interrupting them from the *beginning* of the cycle – from the trigger or cue. This is when you feel the weakest and most vulnerable (but that's just a trick of your mind to keep the status quo).

If you wait until you are already mindlessly doing something that you always do, you're already in the habit itself. To create a new habit, you need to interrupt the cue, or at least be mindful of it. You then have a moment to choose to do something new.

FIVE STEPS TO CHANGING BAD FOOD HABITS

Once you are doing the new thing, you will want to reward yourself in a small way (sometimes just doing the new thing and feeling proud of yourself is reward enough). This will give you incentive to then do the same thing the next time you are about to engage in the previous habit.

As you read through the changes we suggest in this book, it is important to notice what your cues are for eating in ways that don't support your life's flow. It helps if you write them down. For instance, you may write down: "Every time I wake up, I go straight to the kitchen and make coffee, and end up skipping breakfast."

Your cue can be interrupted by having all the ingredients to make a green smoothie stocked and ready in the fridge, and by writing a note to yourself that today you are going to choose to eat cleaner. You can further put the note on the coffee machine so you see it when you wake up while you're still groggy and in your old habit. This makes it very simple for you to choose to make the green smoothie and celebrate that you just interrupted an old "cue."

Do this several times and your new habit will be to automatically make the green smoothies without even having to think about it. You will have created a *new* habit.

5 Steps to Clean Eating

Now that you know how to interrupt the habit cycle to make a new habit, let's look at five

steps you can take to create a clean eating habit:

1. **Drink Abundant Water**. Forget about sugary sodas or supposedly "healthy" sports drinks. Replace them all with water. Water helps to create a faster metabolism, helps flush toxins out of your body, and keep you hydrated which can also help you maintain a healthy weight.

2. **Eat Clean**. Skip hectic meals that you eat standing up or while in your car. If you pre-prep meals as we've suggested you can even take your lunch to a park and sit in nature while you develop new, clean eating habits. This will lower your cortisol (stress hormone) levels and make eating well an even more enjoyable experience. This also means starting each day with a good, clean, protein-packed breakfast so that you have the energy to eat plant-based, clean food the rest of the day, too, and won't be tempted by junk food due to insulin spikes and drops.

3. **Eat Consistently**. Eating the same foods with only slight variations every day will keep your nutrient density high, your calories on target, and your chances of succumbing to temptation low.

4. **Eat the Right Ratios**. Choosing plant-based foods that are high in healthy fats and protein will ensure that you stay fit,

FIVE STEPS TO CHANGING BAD FOOD HABITS

healthy, and full of boundless energy. Minimize carbs where possible.

5. **Eat nothing, regularly.** Giving your body a chance not to digest food and assimilate nutrients gives it an opportunity to do some serious house-cleaning and fat burning. Take a break from eating consistently to experience top-notch health.

Now that you know how to put new habits into action, let's get straight into the life-affirming, new clean eating habits you'll want to develop.

Chapter 2: Drink Abundant Water & Replace All Sugary Drinks

How *Not* to Drink Yourself Fat, Tired, and Insulin Resistant

The average American is still drinking way too many sugary drinks. Though beverage companies vowed to lower calories in their sodas by 2025, more than 4 years ago due to growing obesity and diabetes epidemics, those same drinks are still fueling a national health crisis.

Drinking soda, and sugary drinks is an insidious habit that was designed by Coke, Pepsi, and other drink makers to keep you addicted to their product. Only 0.2% of beverages made by these companies actually have lower calories now.

This is why some cities are passing tax bills to make sugar-sweetened beverages like sports drinks and fizzy sodas less appealing to consumers. An article written for the New York Times states, "Sweetened beverages are the single largest contributor to the obesity epidemic, scientists say, and that epidemic exacts a big toll, in both health problems and medical costs."

Sodas have such a high sugar content that they tax your pancreas, eventually making it unable to regulate your insulin levels. Just drinking 2 sodas a day can increase your chances of getting diabetes by 25%, but there are more health concerns you should be aware of, like these:

- Harvard Medical School has found that drinking soda increases the risk of kidney disease.
- The chemical colorings in soda like 2-methylimidazole (2-MI) and 4 methylimidazole (4-MI), that make it a caramel color, contribute to increased cancer risk.
- Soda dehydrates you, making it more difficult for your body to absorb nutrients from the food you eat or the supplements you take.
- Soda cans are lined with a highly toxic, cancer-causing substance called Bisphenol-A or BPA. This leeches into the drink, and then you consume it.
- A single can of Coca-Cola has around 17 teaspoons of sugar, 240 calories and provides you with ZERO nutrients. Even the "mini-cans" that Coca-Cola started to make contain 25 grams of sugar, and no nutrients. That's about the same amount of sugar as a candy bar.

Sports drinks aren't much better. They are touted as a way to quickly restore electrolytes, but you'd be better off drinking some coconut water which is full of potassium or simply eating a banana and drinking some pure water. Here's the problem with most sugary sports drinks:

PLANT-BASED HEALTH: DRINK ABUNDANT WATER & REPLACE ALL SUGARY DRINKS

- Gatorade and Powerade are about 6-8% pure sugar. They are also full of chemical colorings.
- They don't give you extra energy for sports. They just jack you up with sugar which will give you temporary energy and then cause a sugar crash that will leave you feeling depleted and even angry.

The problem with fruit juices is not as obvious but this is another culprit in the sugary drink dilemma.

When you eat a piece of fruit, it contains pectin and fiber. Fruit juices deliver fruit sugars directly into your bloodstream without the added benefit of fiber and pectin which act to *slow the absorption* of fruit sugars.

Many fruit juices also contain added artificial colors and chemical "flavor" packets, as are notorious in even orange juice so that they don't taste disgusting after sitting on trucks or store shelves for months at a time.

The Magic of Water for Weight Loss, Brain Health, Mood, Energy, and Detox

The magic of water for weight loss, brain functioning, mood improvement, physical energy, and effective detox is truly astounding.[1]

Water is one of the most prevalent elements in our bodies, and it is vital. When we drink ample water it does so many things to promote health, for example:

- It helps to prevent dehydration. When our cells are "thirsty" they can't get rid of toxins, and they end up being stored in fat.
- Drinking water helps us lose weight by revving up our metabolism.
- Drinking water helps us to burn more fat.
- Drinking water helps to boost athletic performance.
- Without enough water, our brains don't work as they should. Even mild dehydration has an effect on our memory and cognitive abilities.
- Drinking enough water can also prevent migraine headaches.
- Ample water prevents constipation and digestive issues.
- Staying hydrated keeps you happy and anxiety-free.

With all the benefits from drinking water, why would you want to keep drinking sugary sodas, sports drinks, or even fruit juice? To rev up your metabolism, mood and energy, you can just drink more water!

Chapter 3: How Do I Get Enough Protein for My Macro Nutrient Ratio?

A Reminder: The Right Fat-Protein-Carb Ratio Will Keep You Healthy and Fit

As we discussed in Chapter One, not only will you stay fit and energized by eating a plant-based diet, but knowing your correct fat-protein-carb ratio will really boost you toward God or Goddess status so that you can achieve all your goals with ease and efficiency.

The key to understanding a macro-nutrient healthy diet is this: It's not so much about how much fat, protein or carbs you eat, but rather the ratio or proportion of each macronutrient to the other two macronutrients in your diet, in terms of total calories. Each gram of fat has 9 calories, while each gram of protein and carbs has 4 calories each.

Though you may eat more carbs if you are extremely athletic, most of us eat far too many carbs and need to eat more plant-based protein and healthy fats.

Healthy fats tend to have more calories, so while they may be a larger portion of your fat-protein-carb ratio, they also provide

important nutrients, boost immunity, keep you full, and prevent you from binge eating on processed carbs and sugar.

Everyone's fat-protein-carb ratio will be slightly different but it will most often look something like this:

Average – Moderate Exercise	For Weight Loss	Super Active Lifestyle
Protein 30-40%	Protein 35%	Protein 30%
Fat 30% - 40 %	Fat 35%	Fat 20%
Carbs 10 – 20%	Carbs 30%	Carbs 50%

For the sake of fueling a healthy everyday lifestyle, your meals and snacks should be comprised as such:

40% of your calories should come from carbohydrates, 30% should come from protein, and 30% from fat. **Your macronutrient ratio will ideally be 40:30:30.**

How to Get Enough Protein from Plants

Before we dive into the current information available in science and medicine regarding

PLANT-BASED HEALTH

HOW DO I GET ENOUGH PROTEIN FOR MY MACRO NUTRIENT RATIO?

needs and sources of protein and amino acids for the average human being, let's clear up some fuzzy login on this topic.

There have been significant changes every year in what is presented by professionals as optimal nutrition for hundreds of years now.

Some of the more recent assertions heralded by medical professionals have been countered with zealous conflicting information. You are then left to sort through topics like these: the ketogenic diet, the paleo diet, the blood-type diet, the raw diet, the gluten-free diet, The Atkins diet (which is heavily meat-based), organic, vegetarian, vegan, nut free, alkaline, and the list goes on.

If you plunge into the literature on all of these diets, you'll find one thing in common. We all need essential amino acids for optimum health but they don't need to come from non-plant protein sources. The assertion that we "need" meat is simply unfounded in science.

Doctor Recommended?

Today there are distinct advantages in access to research and information about nutrition. There's also a reality to contend with that there is much unsubstantiated information on the internet, as well as outright fraudulent studies.

Many choose to seek the advice of their doctor to know how to eat. Unfortunately, most doctors have only a basic knowledge of nutrition, and recommend only generalities for common ailments such as diabetes or high blood pressure.

According to a study published by the Journal of Biomedical Education, "medical schools reported that they provide on average 19 hours of nutrition education." That's it. So your doctor has 19 hours of knowledge about an incredibly vast subject unless they've specifically dived deeper into the subject.

On the contrary, there are professionals who have spent between 56 hours to four years of postgraduate intensive study in nutrition and are Certified Nutritional Specialist, CNS, and Certified Clinical Nutritionist, CCN. Certainly consulting one of these professionals would be prudent.

By eliminating certain foods from a person's diet, scientists have systematically proven that animal products are not only inflammation-inducing and health damaging, but that we can get our essential amino acids elsewhere, without harming our health at all.

Ultimately, each human being is different and will require different nutritional needs, but let's address the need for amino acids head-on.

PLANT-BASED HEALTH | HOW DO I GET ENOUGH PROTEIN FOR MY MACRO NUTRIENT RATIO?

Healthy Plant-Based Protein Comes from Amino Acids

The question of how much protein is needed for each individual is variable. While the current RDA is 46-50 grams per day for the average sedentary woman and 58-63 for a similar man, there's obviously a lot more to it.

Age, sex, pregnancy, lactation and lifestyle play a significant role in what the proper intake is for anyone wanting to choose the perfect amount of protein.

Toh-mato, Tomah-to, Aminos!

Amino acids are known as the building blocks of protein. Of the twenty amino acids we need to grow and be healthy, nine are absolutely necessary as they are not synthesized in the body.

These amino acids and the required intake in mg/g of protein are histidine (11), isoleucine (13), leucine (19), lysine (16), methionine (17), phenylalanine (19), threonine (9), tryptophan (5), and valine (13).

It is true that animal products such as milk and eggs can provide more than enough of all nine of these alone. It's possible to get all of these from fruits and vegetables too.

Need aminos? Here are 9 amino acids that can be found in plants:

Amino Acid	Plant-Based Foods That Contain Amino Acid
Leucine	Seaweed, pumpkin, peas and pea protein, whole grain rice, sesame seeds, watercress, turnip greens, sunflower seeds, kidney beans, figs, avocados, raisins, dates, apples, blueberries, olives, and even bananas. You don't have to limit yourself to one of these. Aim for a serving of either seaweed, leafy greens, hemp seeds, chia seeds, grains, legumes, seeds, or beans at each meal to be sure you get enough high-quality plant protein.
Isoleucine	Rye, soy, cashews, almonds, oats, lentils, beans, brown rice, cabbage, hemp seeds, chia seeds, spinach, pumpkin, pumpkin seeds, sunflower seeds, sesame seeds, cranberries, quinoa, blueberries, apples and kiwis.
Lysine	Beans, watercress, hemp seeds, chia seeds, spirulina, parsley, avocados, soy protein, almonds, cashews, and some legumes (with lentils and chickpeas being two of the best).

PLANT-BASED HEALTH: HOW DO I GET ENOUGH PROTEIN FOR MY MACRO NUTRIENT RATIO?

Methionine	Sunflower seed butter and sunflower seeds, hemp seeds, chia seeds, Brazil nuts, oats, seaweed, wheat, figs, whole grain rice, beans, legumes, onions, cacao, and raisins.
Phenylalanine	Spirulina and other seaweed, pumpkin, beans, rice, avocado, almonds, peanuts, quinoa, figs, raisins, leafy greens, most berries, olives, and seeds.
Threonine	Watercress and spirulina have more of this amino than even meat. Pumpkin, leafy greens, hemp seeds, chia seeds, sesame seeds, sunflower seeds and sunflower butter, almonds, avocados, figs, raisins, quinoa, and wheat. Sprouted grains are excellent sources of this amino acid as well.
Tryptophan	Oats and oat bran, seaweed, hemp seeds, chia seeds, spinach, watercress, soybeans, pumpkin, sweet potatoes, parsley, beans, beets, asparagus, mushrooms, all lettuces, leafy greens, beans, avocado, figs, winter squash, celery, peppers, carrots, chickpeas, onions, apples, oranges, bananas, quinoa, lentils and peas.
Valine	Beans, spinach, legumes, broccoli, sesame seeds, hemp seeds, chia seeds, soy, peanuts, whole grains, figs, avocado, apples, sprouted grains and seeds, blueberries, cranberries, oranges, and apricots.
Histidine	Rice, wheat, rye, seaweed, beans, legumes, cantaloupe, hemp seeds, chia seeds, buckwheat, potatoes, cauliflower and corn.

You can get plenty of the building blocks of protein – amino acids – in an all-plant diet.

Chapter 4: How to Meet Your Nutritional Need with Just Plant Based Foods

What are you giving up in life because of the way you eat right now?

Aside from being fat, sick, and nearly dead, are you keeping yourself from achieving your dreams?

Can you spend truly quality time with your family?

Do you have the energy to exercise frequently and intensely?

Do you have the mental clarity to achieve greatness in your job or creative endeavors?

How about enough nutrition-based mojo to fuel just about any big goal you can think of?

There are myriad definitions of "eating clean" out there, so it's no wonder it can get a little confusing about how to actually eat to support your life and goals.

You already know that eating more leafy greens and drinking more water is good for you. That's universally accepted. However, with the mounds of science available, there's a little more to eating clean than just ordering a salad everyday and carrying around a water bottle.

A *truly* clean diet offers the following benefits:

- A healthy digestive tract
- More than enough energy to be as active as you want to be
- A boosted immune system
- Rare sick days, if ever
- An easily maintained body weight
- Balanced blood-glucose levels
- Balanced hormones and a healthy endocrine system
- A happy, positive outlook (good mood)
- And freedom from contributing to the Big Pharma/Big Food machine which will always make you sick, tired and fat

A truly clean diet is one that does not contain animal products, processed foods, GMO foods, sugar, gluten, alcohol, soy and food additives. It is primarily composed of plant-based products, with their own life force, and that is absolutely exploding with nutrients your body needs not only to *survive* but to *thrive*.

A clean diet doesn't remove something without giving you a much better option to put in its place.

PLANT-BASED HEALTH

HOW TO MEET YOUR NUTRITIONAL NEED WITH JUST PLANT BASED FOODS

It isn't about denying yourself delicious things to eat, but retraining your body and mind to crave things that will actually support your overall life goals: a lean and energetic physique, tons of energy, and a daily experience of joy.

Animal products, processed foods, GMO foods, sugar, gluten, alcohol, soy and food additives aren't going to kill you in small doses. But together, along with other unhealthy lifestyle choices like too much stress and not enough sleep, they are going to **rob you of the ability to be the very best version of you that you can possibly be**.

You Can Fully Meet Your Nutritional Needs with Plants (No Animal Products Needed)

There are some serious problems with animal proteins and what they do to your body and mind.

Once you understand these drawbacks and the ways that plant based eating can completely suffice, if not outdo animal-based eating in order to give you all the macro and micronutrients you need, you'll clearly see why switching them out one by one is in your best interest.

1. **Unlike plant protein, animal protein is lacking some really important stuff**: fiber, antioxidants, and phytonutrients to be specific.

Fiber does this for you:

- It helps you feel full so you don't eat as much and don't crave sugary or salty foods
- It helps to promote a healthy gut and balanced microflora
- It helps control blood sugar levels
- Reduces the risk of gallstones and kidney stones
- Helps with weight management
- Helps remove fungus and mold from the body
- Promotes heart health
- Reduces incident of many diseases including heart attack and stroke, diverticulitis (polyps in your intestinal tract), IBS, and more

Antioxidants like Vitamins A, B, C, D, E, Beta Carotene, and more do this for you:

- Lower your risk of infection by removing free radicals
- Slow the aging process
- Boost the immune system
- Lower oxidative stress from cellular metabolism, excessive exercise, stress, environmental toxins, radiation, pollution, and more

Phytonutrients are also incredibly beneficial. This includes many antioxidants but plant compounds have hundreds of additional benefits that act as antiviral and antibacterial agents, promote immunity, slow aging, stop disease, balance hormones, prevent cellular damage, and even boost your mood.

PLANT-BASED HEALTH

HOW TO MEET YOUR NUTRITIONAL NEED WITH JUST PLANT BASED FOODS

2. **Animal protein increases cancer risk.** When we eat plant protein, our bodies *don't* create more of a hormone-insulin-like growth factor called IGF-1. When we eat animal proteins, because they are higher in certain amino acids, the body *increases* its production of IGF-1.

   While this is an important hormone when we are infants and into childhood to help us grow, as we age, too much of it can actually cause us to age faster increase oxidative stress on the body, and cause insulin sensitivity.

3. **Unlike plants, animal protein increases inflammation.** Eating animal protein causes our bodies to have higher circulating levels of a substance that lines our blood vessels, called trimethylamine N-oxide. TMAO injures the lining of our vessels thus creating inflammation and oxidative stress.

4. **Animal proteins create an acid-state in the body.** Our bodies thrive when we are in a more alkaline state. Foods like meat, cheese, fish, dairy, and grains make us more acidic.

   In numerous studies, common diseases are overcome simply by changing from a more acid diet to a more alkaline one. Conversely, chronic acidosis leads to many diseases.

5. **Eating animal protein increases your risk for heart disease.** There is a lot of controversy around cholesterol and whether or not this single factor can lead to heart disease, but a study by Harvard found that L-carnitine found in red meat increases our chances of developing atherosclerosis (hardening of the arteries) because bacteria in our gut digest L-carnitine and turn it into trimethylamine-N-oxide (TMAO).

You can fully meet your nutritional needs with plants and not consume animal products. You just have to know where to get what you are "missing" when you don't eat meat, milk, fish, or eggs.

For instance, many plant-based foods have all the amino acids you need, but also contain the important nutrients listed above like fiber, antioxidants, and phytonutrients.

Plant Proteins

Complete plant-based proteins (those that contain *all* the amino acids we need that our bodies can't make on their own, including isoleucine, leucine, lysine, phenylalanine, tyrosine, cysteine, methionine, threonine, histidine, tryptophan, and valine) include foods like:

- Quinoa (contains 8 essential amino acids, and 3 additional)
- Mycoprotein (from mushrooms)

simple + optimum
core routines for extraordinary living

DOWNLOAD YOUR FREE BONUS:
simpleoptimum.com/bookbonus

PLANT-BASED HEALTH
HOW TO MEET YOUR NUTRITIONAL NEED WITH JUST PLANT BASED FOODS

- Rice and beans (contain all 8 essential amino acids and then some)
- Spirulina (contains all 8 essential amino acids)
- Nuts and nut butter (Brazil nuts are 8% protein, for example)
- Hempseed (contain 8 essential amino acids and 2 of the semi-essential)
- Chia (contains 18 of the 22 amino acids and also important fatty acids)
- Goji berries (contain all 8 essential amino acids but 18 total)

Plant Fats

Plant-based fats are usually much more healthy for us, as they contain the perfect ratio we need to sustain good health.

Just a few years ago we were told that saturated fat was really bad for us. Most fats were absolutely demonized.

Due to some pretty savvy marketing campaigns, we started eating more refined sugars and carbs, and our health took a nosedive in the process.

The truth is that we need plant-based fats for many reasons, among them:

- To promote better brain health and guard against neurological diseases like Alzheimer's and Parkinson's
- To feel full longer so that we don't overeat
- To control our blood sugar levels
- To lower bad cholesterol and triglycerides
- To reduce stubborn belly fat
- To improve our gut health
- To improve immunity
- And more

Plant-based fats are abundant in foods like:

- Avocados
- Cacao (dark chocolate)
- Nuts
- Coconuts and coconut oil
- Hemp seeds and oils
- Flax
- Chia
- Olive Oil

Plant Carbohydrates

Simple carbs are treated like sugar when you eat them. Most processed carbohydrates like breads, pasta, etc. also lack nutrients.

Plant carbohydrates like sweet potatoes, blueberries, bananas, etc. contain plenty of fiber, so while you are eating carbohydrates that would normally spike your blood sugar, the fiber in fruits and vegetables helps to slow the "sugar dump" into your blood when consumed in the proper proportions in your diet.

PLANT-BASED HEALTH
HOW TO MEET YOUR NUTRITIONAL NEED WITH JUST PLANT BASED FOODS

Fiber in a plant-based diet is paramount when you consume carbs because your body handles it differently than refined carbs like processed, white flour.

Fiber doesn't require insulin to digest as part of it passes through the digestive system without your body having to do anything to it.

Soluble fiber also reduces the absorption of carbohydrates which can lower blood glucose and insulin levels.

In one study, patients with type 2 diabetes who had sufficient dietary fiber, above the level recommended by the ADA, saw improved glycemic levels, decreased hyperinsulinemia, and lower plasma lipid concentrations.

Fiber also fills you up so you don't tend to eat as much, and can stave off hunger for longer periods.

Getting your carbs from fruits and vegetables instead of white flour provides a much higher nutrient density in your food and more fiber which controls hunger, blood sugar, and energy levels. It's just a much better way to go.

Chapter 5:
Meet Your Nutritional Needs Without Eating Gluten, Soy, Processed Foods and Alcohol

Gluten, soy, processed foods and alcohol are a no-go if you want to thrive, but don't worry! There are better plant-based options to replace them.

Let's start with a discussion about why each of these food choices may be sabotaging your ability to be the healthiest you possible.

Let's Talk Gluten

Gluten is a plant product. "So why can't I eat it, if it comes from plants?" You may ask yourself. While wheat is a plant, there is an increasing number of people who have gluten sensitivities.

Although some people have full-blown Celiac Disease which means that they usually have to abstain from gluten completely, other people have what is called non-celiac gluten sensitivity. Even people who aren't "sensitive" to gluten at all can still suffer from deteriorated health by eating wheat and wheat products.

Here's why:

Inflammation – Gluten increases gut inflammation, neuroinflammation, gut-brain axis signal interruption, and a greater incidence of brain fog and neurodegenerative disease. Even people who aren't sensitive to gluten specifically can experience increased inflammation if they eat foods containing wheat regularly.

Inflammation of the gut causes increased intestinal permeability. This is a fancy phrase that means the bacteria in your gut become irritated and can tear tiny holes in the lining of your intestinal tract, making you more susceptible to "leaky gut" and other diseases.

It doesn't stop there though. Wheat germ agglutinin, (WGA) a part of the wheat plant that is ground up into flour, can provoke an inflammatory response in our gut cells causing our natural immunity to become compromised.

This means that foreign pathogens will make their way into your bloodstream with greater ease and things like viruses and bad bacteria can make you sick.

Why Not Soy?

In Okinawa, where the lifespan of its people often exceeds the age of 100, soy is a staple food. (They also happen to eat a mostly plant-based diet).

PLANT-BASED HEALTH
MEET YOUR NUTRITIONAL NEEDS WITHOUT EATING GLUTEN, SOY, PROCESSED FOODS AND ALCOHOL

However, soy that you find in America and most other Westernized nations is not the same, and it can contribute to a number of health conditions.

In America, soy is grown by the billions of pounds primarily as feed for animals. It is drenched in pesticides and herbicides and is one of the top 7 genetically modified crops grown in the U.S. This means that the soy plant has been altered to withstand copious insecticidal spraying, chemical fertilizers, and other pests. It is Roundup ready.

Monsanto, the Big Ag giant that is responsible for GM soy and Glyphosate, the main ingredient in Roundup that is used across millions of acres of crops, was just forced to pay a man with cancer $289 million dollars.

He attests that the weed killer caused his illness, and he's not the only one. Thousands more people claim their lymphoma, testicular cancer, breast cancer, and other cancers are from eating genetically modified foods doused in herbicides like Roundup.

Soy, as it is grown industrially has also been linked to the following health concerns, even when it isn't genetically modified:

- Endocrine imbalances caused by the estrogen-mimicking effects of soy are experienced by those who eat it often. This can cause infertility, miscarriage, and other reproductive issues.
- Mineral depletion due to anti-nutrients present in the form of phytic acid (from phytates). These bind to important minerals that your body needs like zinc, calcium, and magnesium. This is compounded by the fact that glyphosate is also a mineral chelator, and almost all soy grown in the U.S. has been sprayed with it.
- Soy is one of the most common food allergens among the U.S. population, causing gut health problems, and more.
- Protein bars and protein powders made from soy isolates are obtained by a chemical process at very high temperatures which denature the protein.

If you are going to eat soy at all, it should be organic and fermented, to make sure it does not alter your gut flora, cause food allergies, and cause other health problems. If you eat fermented soy you can still get the nutrients and probiotic qualities of the food, without all the health dangers. Making sure it is non-GMO and organic is also imperative.

Replace Processed Foods with Something Better

When you saddle up to your dinner table, you don't usually think to yourself, "Hmm I'm starved. What chemical concoction can I devour that will satisfy this hunger?"

You may as well though.

PLANT-BASED HEALTH: MEET YOUR NUTRITIONAL NEEDS WITHOUT EATING GLUTEN, SOY, PROCESSED FOODS AND ALCOHOL

Processed foods are a chemical cornucopia of health-damaging, life-force depleting, hormone-wrecking, fat-making "stuff." They aren't food.

What we are served up by food manufacturers instead is something that resembles food, but that is concocted in a lab to be highly addictive so that we will think it tastes great and we want to eat more of it.

There are a few problems with this approach, though:

- We're more nutrient deficient than ever, causing food manufacturers to add back in the good nutrients that they've taken out.
- Animal welfare has been completely forgotten, even with "sustainable meat" practices. Most meats are still full of nitrates and other harmful additives like "artificial flavors" to make it palatable and storable for longer periods of time.
- Produce is picked before it is ripe and therefore lacks the full nutrient density that it should have. This is done so that it can be frozen and packaged, instead of us eating fruits and vegetables as they were meant to be consumed: fresh off the vine, bush, or from the ground.
- Chlorine solutions and ozone added to packaged foods meant to minimize bad bacteria damage our gut health.
- Food companies can claim that a food is "all natural, "or "healthy," or "low fat," even if it damages your health, isn't all natural, and still contains chemical additives.
- There are hundreds of food additives, hydrogenated vegetable oils (highly processed making them very unhealthy), "natural" sweeteners, fillers, preservatives, food dyes, colorings, and even stuff like embalming fluid (yes, the stuff they use on corpses) in our food, and no one is even certain how damaging the synergistic interactions of these compounds affect our health.

The general rule to follow is: If it has its own package, and is plant-based then eat it in its original form.

These foods are a product of nature, NOT industry.

Give up "fast food," "convenience food," and even "diet food" because it's all highly processed. Replace these foods with tons of fruits, vegetables, nuts, sprouts, and healthy fats, and you'll feel incredibly different.

This is called whole-food eating, and it is a big part of a truly clean diet.

Skip Alcohol and Forget the Extra Calories (Among Other Deadly Health Concerns)

Alcohol is not health-promoting, even with all the articles promoting resveratrol and a few

PLANT-BASED HEALTH: MEET YOUR NUTRITIONAL NEEDS WITHOUT EATING GLUTEN, SOY, PROCESSED FOODS AND ALCOHOL

other antioxidants that you can find in both beer and wine.

Though you could conceivably drink a very small bit of alcohol every day and be fine, the damage that the habit causes is difficult to overcome, even if we were just talking about the increased calories and swings in your blood glucose levels.

Alcohol does more damage than good, however, because it:

- Shrinks the frontal lobes of your brain
- Causes impaired mental clarity so that you make poor decisions
- Interferes with how your brain makes memories, even causing blackouts
- Damages your liver, your main organ of detoxification
- Causes fatigue
- Damages your heart when you drink chronically
- Increases your chance of developing cancer
- Increases inflammation in the body
- Thins your bones (causing osteoporosis)
- Impairs your sex life and can cause fertility problems
- Prevents your body from absorbing nutrients properly
- Can lead to diabetes

Understandably, people can find it difficult to give up alcohol altogether, but when you think of all the health benefits you are giving your

body by finding some delicious substitutes, why bother with an alcoholic drink?

Instead, you can try:

- Virgin and "mocktails" like grapefruit mock mojitos or a cranberry, rosemary and nectarine splash with seltzer water
- Herbal tea
- Fruit, mint or cucumber infused water
- Green juice
- Non-alcoholic ginger beer
- Blood orange and basil "soda"
- A kumquat spritzer
- And more

Create the Right fat-protein-carb Ratio to Truly Thrive

The next part of clean eating and eating to thrive, not just survive, is knowing the right fat/protein/carb ratio and why you need to give this any thought at all.

Now that you know what kinds of foods you need to eat, you need to know the proportions in which to eat them.

You don't have to go full keto (ketogenic) to stay healthy and vibrant but lowering your carbs and increasing your protein and healthy fat intake are ideal for fueling a high-powered life, keeping your weight at the perfect level, and reducing a host of disease factors.

PLANT-BASED HEALTH: MEET YOUR NUTRITIONAL NEEDS WITHOUT EATING GLUTEN, SOY, PROCESSED FOODS AND ALCOHOL

Of course, your specific ratio of fat-protein-carbs will depend on your lifestyle. If you are a marathon runner you're going to need more healthy carbs. Your ratio will look quite different from someone who does sprints, HIIT training or powerlifting, where short bursts of energy are needed rather than sustained energy. We all need a combination of the two, though, even if we aren't super athletes.

Let's assume that you are moderately to very active though, as you should be to live an optimum life.

If you aren't yet at this level of fitness, it is something you can work up to, even if you are overweight, tired and struggling with chronic inflammation, and other problems caused by a sedentary lifestyle.

No matter what kind of diet you consume, just lowering your calories and increasing your activity will help you lose weight. However, the right macro-nutrient ratios will support mental, physical and spiritual health. Since they are comprised of more plant-based healthy fats and plant-based proteins, they will keep simple carbs and refined sugars to an absolute minimum as well.

Some common healthy macronutrient diet ratios look like this:

Average – Moderate Exercise	For Weight Loss	Super Active Lifestyle
Protein 30-40%	Protein 35%	Protein 30%
Fat 30% - 40 %	Fat 35%	Fat 20%
Carbs 10 – 20%	Carbs 30%	Carbs 50%

You can use a macro nutrient calculator like this one to figure out the ideal ratio for you or consult a nutritionist to talk about your goals: weight loss, marathon training, to winning the next regional body building competition, etc.

A ketogenic diet for super-fast weight loss might look more like this:

Protein 35%	Fat 65%	Carbs 5%

The important thing to note is that healthy fat generally has 9 calories per gram while protein or carbs have only 4 calories per gram, so **the ratios are based on calories**.

You are now aware of what soy, gluten, animal products, alcohol, and caffeine can do to ruin your optimal health. You know that plant-based fats, protein, and carbs will set you free from the pitfalls of unhealthy eating, and the many diseases that inevitably would follow.

Chapter 6:
Eat Consistently and Optimize with Food-Based Nutritional Supplements

Why You Need to Eat the Same (or Similar) Foods Every Day

Eating consistently and keeping the food ingredients you eat every day similar is paramount for good health. With a million different foods to choose from it can seem odd to choose from a limited number of foods, but by keeping it simple and making just small tweaks to your diet along the way, you can prevent a shock to your system, digestive mishaps and inflammation. Consistent eating offers the following not-to-miss benefits:

- **You won't accidentally eat too many calories**. By eating a bowl of oatmeal with fresh blueberries and pea protein powder, a green smoothie, salmon and veggies and quinoa every day you'll keep your calorie intake consistent. Sauces, "flavours" and other "additives" in many dishes (even those advertised as healthy) are often loaded with hidden calories, chemicals, and sugars.

- **You won't suffer from decision fatigue**. Having to make too many choices about food every day is exhausting to your brain and is likely to make you cave in to temptation out of sheer frustration in having to make a choice, rather than stick to a simple menu that provides you consistent nutrition and calories. This also keeps you from the dinner-trap. You get to the last meal of the day and order pizza because it is too hard to figure out what heathy meal to cook. No bueno.

- **Meal prep is a breeze**. Eating the same or similar foods every week makes meal preparation super simple. You don't have to keep hundreds of different ingredients on hand. Therefore you can make the same sandwich, salad or bean casserole to last for two whole weeks.

- **You'll be less likely to gain weight**. Research has shown that the more food choices we have, the more food we tend to eat, and the more likely we'll be to gain weight.

Why You Need Supplements Even When You Eat Clean

Even if you eat a super clean diet, you still need supplements. Why? It's pretty simple. Food isn't what it used to be.

PLANT-BASED HEALTH
EAT CONSISTENTLY AND OPTIMIZE WITH FOOD-BASED NUTRITIONAL SUPPLEMENTS

Conventionally grown fruits and vegetables often have a third or half the nutrient density of the same fruit and vegetables grown in our grandparent's time.

The decline in nutrient value was noticed around 10 years ago, but it has likely been building since the dawn of modern agricultural mono-cropping.

A biochemist named Donald Davis from the University of Texas said that of 13 nutrients studied in fruits and vegetables tracked by the Agriculture Department from 1950 to 1999 in 43 different gardens, six proved to be declining rapidly:

- Protein
- Calcium
- Phosphorous
- Iron
- Riboflavin
- Vitamin C

That's just the beginning. More nutrient loss has been detected as well in additional studies.

What's Causing Nutrient Depletion?

We've dumped so many chemicals on our soil, we've altered the delicate soil microbiome that helps to grow healthy, nutrient-dense plants.

Fruit and vegetables are also picked super early so they can be frozen or shipped thus losing their highest potential nutrient density because produce that is picked prematurely doesn't contain its full value of antioxidants, minerals, and other important plant compounds that we need to be healthy.

Furthermore, when we started using chemical fertilizers, we disrupted the circle of life. Tiny bacteria and microscopic fungi that normally help a plant's immune system were destroyed, and superbugs, molds, and viruses became more prevalent.

The "good" critters in our soil, though microscopic, helped keep our plants healthy and full of nutrition. They are increasingly eradicated with modern farming and gardening practices (mostly non-organic).

Then add genetically modified organisms to the mix, and now we have chemical pesticides like Bt toxins, bred right into the plant itself, which negatively impacts our immune system, making the eating of once healthy plants, now dangerous to our health.

GMO crops are also known to chelate important minerals out of the soil, making it even less hospitable for healthy plants, and thus lowering their nutrient density.

The key thing to understand is that the antioxidants and phytonutrients that have benefited us since the time of the caveman, *also*

PLANT-BASED HEALTH: EAT CONSISTENTLY AND OPTIMIZE WITH FOOD-BASED NUTRITIONAL SUPPLEMENTS

help a plant defend against its own predators and sickness in the form of bacterial or fungal infections, boosting natural pest control, protecting against drought, and more.

Collectively our fruit and vegetable nutrition has declined dramatically.

Nutritional gaps are much more likely to occur now for these many reasons.

Why You Need Food-Based, Not Synthetic Nutrient Supplements

There are only 13 human vitamins:

A, C, D, E, K and seven B vitamins (thiamine (B1), riboflavin (B2), niacin (B3), pantothenic acid (B5), pyroxidine (B6), biotin (B7), folate (B9) and cobalamin (B12)), but that is not all we get from our food and drink.

We also have an opportunity to get minerals and hundreds of different plant compounds from what we eat and supplement, too.

When looking to close the gaps in your nutrition, you need to source food-based, not synthetic supplements to get all these nutrients.

Here's why:

Food-Based Synergy

Food-based supplements are synergistic. This means that they interact with each other due to a myriad of plant compounds that scientists still don't completely understand on their own, let alone how they work together.

Specific vitamins and minerals interact with one another increasing their effectiveness and bioavailability (how your body absorbs nutrients that it needs.)

You can see this synergy happen most obviously in lipids or fat-soluble vitamins. Just one example of this synergy in action can be seen when we consume an avocado. It increases the bioavailability of provitamin-A carotenoids, a vitamin found in a completely different set of plants like tomatoes and carrots, as well as Vitamins E and K.

Our bodies also tend to want nutrients in their natural form. This is often called their "biologically active version."

You can see this in a comparison between the consumption of Vitamin E made synthetically in a lab, and Vitamin E that is consumed in foods, or food based supplements.

Why is there any difference?

- Many synthetic supplements including Vitamin E contain eight possible stereoisomers, called all-rac-alpha-tocopherol.

PLANT-BASED HEALTH
EAT CONSISTENTLY AND OPTIMIZE WITH FOOD-BASED NUTRITIONAL SUPPLEMENTS

- Natural vitamin E contains 100% of the RRR-alpha-tocopherol stereoisomers which makes it more bioavailable and easier for your body to make use of.

There have not been a ton of studies comparing natural vitamins and their synthetic counterparts, but the ones that have been completed make it astoundingly clear—that the natural nutrient in its form intended by nature is the most helpful to our health.

With this greater bioavailability in natural vitamins and minerals in mind, let's now look at a few things added to some non-vegan, chemical vitamins and supplements:

- **Artificial (chemical) colors:** including FD&C Blue No. 1, Blue No. 2, Green No. 3, Red No. 4, Red No. 40, Yellow No. 5 and Yellow No. 6.
- **Hydrogenated oils:** usually from soybean oil and used as a filler so your vitamins sometimes don't even contain the nutrients or nutrient levels described.
- **Lead:** Highly toxic and cancer-causing.
- **Mercury:** A neurotoxin.
- **PCBs:** Often found in fish oils, and a known carcinogen.
- **Talc of Magnesium Silicate:** a filler that is very similar to asbestos with similar health ramifications.

- **Titanium Dioxide:** used as a colorant, but it causes lung inflammation among other health concerns.

19 of the Best Food-Based Supplements

Considering what toxic stuff they put in supplements, let's look at some better, food-based alternatives.

Here are 19 supplements you need to promote your brain health, energy, quality sleep, physical energy, mood, digestive health and more.

1. Magnesium

Magnesium is needed for *hundreds* of physiological processes. It helps your muscles and nerves work right, keeps your heart healthy, your bones strong, and helps to regulate your mood, sleep-cycles, and brain health.

Foods that contain magnesium in high amounts include:

- Almonds
- Cashews
- Brazil nuts
- Pecans
- Walnuts
- Tofu

simple + optimum
core routines for extraordinary living

DOWNLOAD YOUR FREE BONUS:
simpleoptimum.com/bookbonus

PLANT-BASED HEALTH: EAT CONSISTENTLY AND OPTIMIZE WITH FOOD-BASED NUTRITIONAL SUPPLEMENTS

Or you can get a high-quality, food-based magnesium supplement on Amazon or your local health food store. Try Nature's Answer or KOS Organic supplement brands.

2. Zinc

You need trace amounts of the mineral zinc for your body to do tons of things, including fight off foreign pathogens, and boost your immune system, make proteins that help create your DNA, heal wounds, and even help give you your sense of taste and smell.

Plant sources of zinc include:

- Pumpkin seeds
- Pecans
- Brazil nuts
- Almonds
- Walnuts
- Peanuts
- Lima beans
- Split peas
- Rye
- Oats

Or you can get a high-quality, food-based zinc supplement like those made by Garden of Life or other brands. You will most often find it included in a good, organic, food-based multivitamin.

3. B Vitamins (B6, B9, B12)

B Vitamins are important for the health of your blood cells, providing you with energy, formulating your DNA, and more.

Plant sources of B Vitamins include:

- Nori (seaweed)
- Shitake mushrooms
- Beans
- Peas
- Nuts
- Legumes
- Seeds
- Spinach
- Leafy greens

Or you can get a high-quality, food-based B-complex supplement like those made by Garden of Life or other brands. You will most often find B Vitamins included in a good, organic, food-based multivitamin.

4. Tyrosine

Tyrosine can be supplemented in the range of 500-1,000mg daily. It's often used in combination with tryptophan. Tyrosine is taken in the morning to stimulate and energize, focus, and regulate mood.

Tyrosine can be found in plant foods like:

- Sesame seeds

PLANT-BASED HEALTH

EAT CONSISTENTLY AND OPTIMIZE WITH FOOD-BASED NUTRITIONAL SUPPLEMENTS

- Pumpkin seeds
- Almonds
- Peanuts
- Lima beans
- Avocados
- Bananas

Or you can get a high-quality, food-based Tyrosine supplement online or at your local health food store.

5. Tryptophan

Tryptophan is incredibly mood-altering. It helps you feel calm and alert. It helps with PMS and can even alleviate anxiety and depression as it directly interacts with serotonin.

Tryptophan can be found in foods like:

- Spirulina
- Sea vegetables
- Chickpeas
- Almonds
- Sunflower seeds
- Pumpkin seeds

Or you can get a high-quality, food-based Tryptophan supplement online or at your local health food store.

6. Plant-Based Omega 3s

You don't have to get your Omega 3 fatty acids

from fish. They are abundant in plants in nature. Omega 3 fatty acids are vital to your health as they promote cognitive functioning, immune health, digestive health including healthy gut flora, lower blood pressure, increase heart health and more.

Plant-based sources of Omega 3 fatty acids include:

- Chia seeds
- Brussels sprouts
- Flaxseeds and flax oil
- Hempseeds and hemp oil
- Perilla oil
- Algae and algae oil

Or you can get a high-quality, plant-based Omega-3 supplement online or at your local health food store.

7. Korean Ginseng (Panax Ginseng)

Korean Ginseng is a root found throughout Asia and Europe that provides astounding health benefits. It is a potent antioxidant, boosts energy naturally, is anti-carcinogenic, boosts the immune system, may help with fertility and impotency, and more.

It is a root so you won't find it in other foods. Plant-based supplements of Panax ginseng are available online and at health food stores.

PLANT-BASED HEALTH: EAT CONSISTENTLY AND OPTIMIZE WITH FOOD-BASED NUTRITIONAL SUPPLEMENTS

8. Glutathione

Glutathione is extremely beneficial to your health as it is the "master antioxidant." It recycles other antioxidants like Vitamins C and E, alpha-lipoic acid, and coenzyme Q10 (CoQ10). When you boost glutathione levels, you also boost these other antioxidants.

It also helps to detox your body, scavenge free radicals, reduce disease, and slow aging, among other things.

You can boost your body's own glutathione production by:

- Eating foods rich in selenium
- Eat more sulfur-rich foods
- Getting more sleep
- Taking a turmeric supplement
- Increasing Vitamin C intake

You can also purchase a high-quality glutathione supplement online.

9. Choline

Our brains are developing at warp speed when we are infants and this is why choline is recommended for small children. This need continue into adult life, though.

Choline is necessary for our brain's health as it synthesizes the neurotransmitter, acetylcholine.

It is also the principal phospholipid used in our cells throughout the body. It is needed to synthesize certain proteins as well.

Plant-based sources of choline can be found in spinach, broccoli, and quinoa, or you can purchase a plant-based choline supplement.

10. Turmeric (Curcuma longa)

This single herb threatens to put Big Pharma out of business. Its incredible anti-inflammatory, anticarcinogenic properties are just the beginning of what turmeric can offer.

There are over 800 distinct health benefits associated with curcumin, the primary phytochemical in the bright orange root.

Studies show it is as effective as 14 conventional pharmaceuticals, yet the FDA has yet to give it a stamp of approval. (Even though it's been used for thousands of years throughout India and Asia, too.)

Purchase an organic turmeric supplement, and find one with piperine (black pepper) as it helps the body to absorb more of the phytonutrients in turmeric.

11. Maca (Lepidium meyenii)

Maca is a powerhouse in its own right. It helps to balance hormones, including promoting

PLANT-BASED HEALTH

EAT CONSISTENTLY AND OPTIMIZE WITH FOOD-BASED NUTRITIONAL SUPPLEMENTS

a healthy thyroid. It also supports a healthy reproductive system, boosts energy and has been used as a general health tonic by many cultures for thousands of years.

Maca can be found online as a supplement in powder or pill form, or at your local health food store.

12. Luna Natural Sleep Aid

There are a lot of sleep aids out there, but Luna Natural Sleep aid helps to balance your hormones, and gently calm the nervous system to help restore your circadian rhythms.

If you don't want to get hooked on prescription sleep medications, then Luna Natural Sleep will ease your body and mind into a restful state, without causing any of the unwanted side effects that come with pharmaceutical sleep aids.

It contains no melatonin, just extracts of Lemon Balm, Hops, Valerian, Passionflower, and Chamomile as well as L-Theanine, an amino acid that reduces anxiety.

A melatonin-free sleep aid may be needed by some people who don't want to take hormones for fear of negatively altering their endocrine system. New studies show that melatonin is only helpful to some people in some situations.

Luna Natural Sleep aid is found online.

13. Nopal Cactus

Prickly pear cactus, also known as Nopal Cactus can help regulate blood sugar levels, thus helping to prevent diseases like diabetes, obesity, insulin resistance, and more.

It is full of carotenoids, antioxidants, and fiber as well.

You can eat prickly pear cactus as they do throughout Latin America, or simply purchase a high-quality supplement.

14. ZMA

ZMA is a compound supplement meant to help support your body's mineral needs. It contains zinc, magnesium aspartate, and vitamin B6. The combination helps to boost immunity, relax tired muscles, regulate metabolism, and help you to sleep soundly.

You can purchase ZMA online or in a health food store near you.

15. Ginger (Zingiber officinale)

Ginger's greatest gift is reducing chronic inflammation, but it also helps to treat nausea, is a digestive aid, regulates cholesterol, boosts your metabolism and immunity, and even has anti-cancer properties.

PLANT-BASED HEALTH: EAT CONSISTENTLY AND OPTIMIZE WITH FOOD-BASED NUTRITIONAL SUPPLEMENTS

You can add it in its natural form to soups, curries and salads, or simply purchase a supplement to take daily.

16. Probiotics

People often overlook probiotics as a supplement to their diets, but it is one of the most important things to regularly take.

Probiotics regulate the friendly gut bacteria in your gut, helping them to balance out bad bacteria so that you get sick less frequently. They also contribute immensely to your good mood, the assimilation of nutrients for other foods you eat and keep your entire digestive system healthy.

They even help with weight loss and hunger management.

Quality probiotics should have several strains of healthy bacteria, and will often need to be refrigerated to keep the microorganisms active.

17. Digestive Enzymes

Digestive enzymes are important to take because they help your body break down food so it can use the parts it needs and get rid of the rest.

A plant-based digestive enzymes supplement can help digestion, proper vitamin absorption, and even preserve your cells.

Be Well makes a high-quality product that is also wheat, soy, dairy, and gluten free.

18. Multivitamin

A good multivitamin is like an insurance policy for your health. If you don't eat as well as you should one week, forget to take a few supplements, or just need an extra boost, a plant-based multi can fill in the nutritional gaps that you weren't able to fill in with your eating.

19. Vitamin C

Sailors could have prevented an early death from scurvy if they had just taken a Vitamin C supplement onboard their ships. This powerful antioxidant is immune boosting, lowers high blood pressure, lowers uric acid levels and the incidence of gout, heart disease and many other health concerns, including cancer. It also helps the body to absorb iron to prevent anemia.

There are many synthetic versions of Vitamin C so make sure yours is sourced from foods like Acerola berries, Camu-Camu, Artichoke leaves, wild grown blue-green algae, or other plants.[1]

Chapter 7: Follow an Intermittent Fasting Schedule Appropriate to Your Life's Flow

What is Intermittent Fasting?

Intermittent fasting is a period of hours, days, or multiple days at a time where you eat little or no food.

It is like a break for your digestive system and physiological functions.

Our bodies are not simple machines, but even if they were, they would need rest. Machines with much less complex interactions and moving parts require maintenance and down time.

The director of cardiovascular and genetic epidemiology at Utah's Intermountain Healthcare System, Benjamin Horne has published research on intermittent fasting. He states,

"There continues to be good evidence that intermittent fasting is producing weight-loss benefits, and we also have some evidence that these diets can reduce inflammation, they can reduce blood pressure and resting heart rate, and they seem to have beneficial effects on the cardiovascular system."

Horne continues,

"[Intermittent fasting] is something that is moving into practice in the medical field, and it's a reasonable approach for people who don't like daily restriction of their calories."

Intermittent Fasting for Weight Loss, Lean Muscle Mass, Immunity and More

Horne isn't the only proponent of intermittent fasting. Medical studies abound proving intermittent fasting improves weight loss, increases lean muscle mass, boosts immunity, and much more.

Here are just a few examples:

- Intermittent fasting helps burn fat and boost metabolism.
- Reduces obesity rates and promotes healthy weight in non-obese persons.
- Improves glucose circulation, reduces blood pressure, and reduces proinflammatory cytokines.
- Is cardioprotective.
- Increases lean muscle mass.
- Increases a sense of achievement, pride, and control over life.

There are many types of fasting, and though we won't detail them in depth here, you can

FOLLOW AN INTERMITTENT FASTING SCHEDULE APPROPRIATE TO YOUR LIFE'S FLOW

PLANT-BASED HEALTH

read more about them to learn which one may be right for you. Each of them provides a whole range of health benefits outlined here.

Types of Fasts

The following are common types of intermittent fasting schedules:

- **The 16/8 Method** – You eat for only 8 hours of the day and fast for the other 16. This is usually the easiest for most people to do since they are asleep for part of the 16 hours that they won't be eating.

- **The 5/2 Diet** – You eat for 5 days and fast for two, only drinking water or herbal tea on your fasting days. You can also just limit your calories drastically to about 500-600 on the 2 fasting days if you don't want to eliminate food completely.

- **Eat Stop Eat** – In this intermittent fast you eat a day, stop a day, and so on. This fast provides your body with calories intermittently.

- **Alternate Day Fasting** – this is similar to the Eat Stop Eat fast. You just alternate eating and fasting days, with calorie restriction as you desire.

- **The Warrior Diet** – In this intermittent fast you give yourself a four hour window to pound down as many calories as you can, and fast the rest of the day reminiscent of how warriors had to consume their food in times of war.

Each type of fast will be more appropriate for some and less for others. Choose one that follows your natural flow, and it won't seem as challenging to follow through with.

Try Your First Fast

It's time to put all this knowledge to action. We're going to get you ready to try your first fast.

Before you can fast, you should first get your doctor's opinion on your overall health. It is also ideal to do a general detox first so that your body can rid itself of toxins more easily when you are not eating and having to metabolize food.

Next, make sure you have plenty of clean water and herbal tea to help flush out toxins that are metabolized while you fast. Think of your fasting time like Spring cleaning. You'll want to give your body all the help it needs to flush junk out of your cells, organs, and digestive tract.

When you are fasting it is also a good time to journal, be grateful, meditate, or sit in quiet contemplation. As your body repairs and replenishes itself physically, also replenish your mind and spirit, as they are all connected.

PLANT-BASED HEALTH
15 FOODS FOR CARBOHYDRATES
Providing the body with slow-burning energy through fiber-rich foods.

Pumpkin
A sweet-flavored vegetable great for roasting and soups.

Key nutrients: vitamin A, vitamin C, vitamin E, beta-carotene

Total carbs per 100 grams: 6.5 grams
Net carbs per 100 grams: 6 grams

Green peas
Sweet, versatile, great for soups, sides, dips and salads.

Key nutrients: vitamin A, vitamin B6, vitamin C, magnesium, vitamin K, thiamin

Total carbs per 100 grams: 14 grams
Net carbs per 100 grams: 9 grams

Whole oats
Nutty, filling, perfect for sweet and savory dishes.

Key nutrients: fiber, protein, manganese, vitamin B1, iron, selenium, magnesium

Total carbs per 100 grams: 66.3 grams
Net carbs per 100 grams: 55.7 grams

Note: not all oats are processed in a gluten-free environment and are therefore not suitable for gluten-free diets.

Sweet potatoes
A sweet, filling vegetable great for roasting, baking and stuffing.

Key nutrients: vitamin B6, vitamin A, beta-carotene

Total carbs per 100 grams: 20 grams
Net carbs per 100 grams: 17 grams

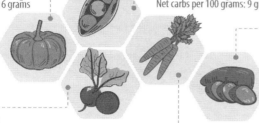

Beets
Sweet, earthy-tasting vegetable great for roasting or grating raw for salads.

Key nutrients: vitamin C, manganese, folate

Total carbs per 100 grams: 7.3 grams
Net carbs per 100 grams: 6.1 grams

Carrots
Sweet, bright, great cooked, raw, juiced, and in soups.

Key nutrients: vitamin A, vitamin K, manganese, potassium

Total carbs per 100 grams: 9.6 grams
Net carbs per 100 grams: 6.8 grams

Brown rice
Nutty, chewy, filling, great for cold salads or side dishes for curries.

Key nutrients: fiber, manganese, selenium, magnesium

Total carbs per 100 grams raw: 77 grams
Net carbs per 100 grams raw: 73.5 grams

Chickpeas
Nutty, filling, full of fiber, great for hummus, curries and salads.

Key nutrients: fiber, calcium, iron, magnesium, vitamin B6

Total carbs per 100 grams: 61 grams
Net carbs per 100 grams: 44 grams

Lentils
Excellent source of fiber, perfect for curries, soups, and cold salads.

Key nutrients: fiber, folate, manganese, iron, thiamin, vitamin B6

Total carbs per 100 grams: 20 grams
Net carbs per 100 grams: 12 grams

Buckwheat
Nutty, filling, gluten-free, rice substitute, great hot or cold.

Key nutrients: magnesium, manganese, copper, fiber

Total carbs per 100 grams raw: 71.5 grams
Net carbs per 100 grams raw: 61.5 grams

Kidney beans
Filling, full of fiber, great for dips, chili, stews and soups.

Key nutrients: dietary fiber, protein, iron, magnesium, vitamin B-6

Total carbs per 100 grams: 60 grams
Net carbs per 100 grams: 35 grams

Quinoa
Nutty, filling, ideal for warm salads, patties, and as a base for curries.

Key nutrients: protein, magnesium, folate, manganese, iron, zinc, phosphorous

Total carbs per 100 grams raw: 60 grams
Net carbs per 100 grams raw: 52 grams

Bananas
Sweet, filling, ideal for snacking and smoothies.

Key nutrients: potassium, vitamin B6, fiber, vitamin A

Total carbs per 100 grams: 23 grams
Net carbs per 100 grams: 20.4 grams

Mangos
Sweet, juicy, ideal snack food or for smoothies and cold salads.

Key nutrients: vitamin C, vitamin A, folate, vitamin B6

Total carbs per 100 grams: 15 grams
Net carbs per 100 grams: 13.4 grams

Blueberries
Seasonal, sweet, juicy, perfect for snacking, low-carb baking and desserts.

Key nutrients: vitamin K, vitamin C, manganese, fiber, antioxidants

Total carbs per 100 grams: 14 grams
Net carbs per 100 grams: 11.6 grams

simple + optimum
core routines for extraordinary living

DOWNLOAD YOUR FREE BONUS:
simpleoptimum.com/bookbonus

PLANT-BASED HEALTH — 12 FOODS FOR FATS

Help the body to absorb vital nutrients and provide fuel.

Almonds
Ideal for snacking and making nut butters.

Key nutrients: protein, vitamin E, manganese, magnesium

Total carbs per 100 grams: 22 grams
Net carbs per 100 grams: 10 grams
Total fats per 100 grams: 49 grams

Pecans
Crunchy, ideal for snacking and adding to breakfast oats.

Key nutrients: magnesium, copper, thiamin, manganese, zinc, phosphorous

Total carbs per 100 grams: 14 grams
Net carbs per 100 grams: 4 grams
Total fats per 100 grams: 72 grams

Pumpkin seeds
Oily, great for toasting or eating raw as a snack, salad sprinkle, making seed butter.

Key nutrients: calcium, magnesium, potassium, vitamin E, zinc

Total carbs per 100 grams: 54 grams
Net carbs per 100 grams: 36 grams
Total fats per 100 grams: 19 grams

Walnuts
Oily, crunchy, ideal for snacking and adding to breakfast oatmeal.

Key nutrients: antioxidants, omega-3 fat, magnesium

Total carbs per 100 grams: 14 grams
Net carbs per 100 grams: 7 grams
Total fats per 100 grams: 65 grams

Macadamia nuts
Creamy, crunchy, energy-rich, great for snacks.

Key nutrients: magnesium, iron, calcium, thiamin, copper, manganese

Total carbs per 100 grams: 14 grams
Net carbs per 100 grams: 5 grams
Total fats per 100 grams: 76 grams

Coconut oil
Mild-tasting, great for baking, grilling, roasting, coffee.

Key nutrients: medium-chain triglycerides (healthy fat)

Total carbs per 100 grams: 0 grams
Net carbs per 100 grams: 0 grams
Total fats per 100 grams: 100 grams

Olive oil
Rich, full-flavored, great for roasting, grilling, dressings, adding to smoothies.

Key nutrients: vitamin E, vitamin K, omega-6 fatty acid

Total carbs per 100 grams: 0 grams
Net carbs per 100 grams: 0 grams
Total fats per 100 grams: 100 grams

Chia seeds
Absorbent, mild-tasting, ideal for desserts and breakfast.

Key nutrients: fiber, magnesium, iron, calcium

Total carbs per 100 grams raw: 44 grams
Net carbs per 100 grams raw: 6 grams
Total fats per 100 grams raw: 31 grams

Sunflower seeds
Oily, versatile, great for toasting and snacking.

Key nutrients: vitamin E, copper, selenium, phosphorous

Total carbs per 100 grams: 20 grams
Net carbs per 100 grams: 11 grams
Total fats per 100 grams: 51 grams

Flaxseed oil
Creamy, mild, great for adding to smoothies and dressings, best uncooked.

Key nutrients: omega-3 fatty acids

Total carbs per 100 grams: 0 grams
Net carbs per 100 grams: 0 grams
Total fats per 100 grams: 100 grams

Avocados
Creamy, mild, perfect for toast, dips, salads.

Key nutrients: fiber, folate, vitamin K, riboflavin, copper

Total carbs per 100 grams: 9 grams
Net carbs per 100 grams: 2 grams
Total fats per 100 grams: 15 grams

Olives
Oily, rich, strong-flavored, ideal for snacking or adding to hot and cold dishes.

Key nutrients: fiber, vitamin E, iron, copper, calcium

Total carbs per 100 grams: 6.3 grams
Net carbs per 100 grams: 3.1 grams
Total fats per 100 grams: 10.7 grams

simple + optimum — core routines for extraordinary living

DOWNLOAD YOUR FREE BONUS: simpleoptimum.com/bookbonus

PLANT-BASED HEALTH | 12 FOODS FOR PROTEINS: SEEDS AND GRAINS

Support your body's building blocks to stay strong, stable and healthy.

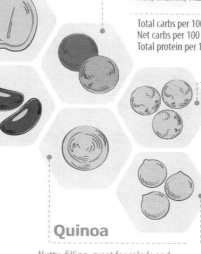

Oats

Simmer with water or plant milk to make porridge, use in plant-based baking or toast and use as a base for plant-based, sugar-free granola.

Key nutrients: fiber, manganese, selenium, antioxidants

Total carbs per 100 grams: 66.3 grams
Net carbs per 100 grams: 55.7 grams
Total protein per 100 grams: 17 grams

Note: buy only oats with "gluten-free" label as they are otherwise often contaminated by gluten. Steel-cut oats are better for effective digestion resulting in stable blood sugar/insulin balance and lower inflammation.

Kidney beans

Filling, versatile, full of protein and fiber to keep you full.

Key nutrients: dietary fiber, protein, iron, magnesium, vitamin B-6

Total carbs per 100 grams: 60 grams
Net carbs per 100 grams: 35 grams
Total protein per 100 grams: 24 grams

Pumpkin seeds

Oily, great for toasting or eating raw as a snack, salad sprinkle, making seed butter.

Key nutrients: calcium, magnesium, potassium, vitamin E, zinc

Total carbs per 100 grams: 54 grams
Net carbs per 100 grams: 36 grams
Total protein per 100 grams: 5 milligrams

Sunflower seeds

Crunchy, great raw or toasted, great as a snack.

Key nutrients: vitamin E, copper, selenium, phosphorous

Total carbs per 100 grams: 20 grams
Net carbs per 100 grams: 11 grams
Total protein per 100 grams: 21 grams

Chia seeds

Absorbent, filling, great for adding fiber and fats to desserts and breakfasts.

Key nutrients: fat, magnesium, iron, calcium

Total carbs per 100 grams raw: 44 grams
Net carbs per 100 grams raw: 6 grams
Total protein per 100 grams raw: 15.7 grams

Lentils

Affordable, filling and versatile.

Key nutrients: fiber, folate, manganese, iron, thiamin, vitamin B6

Total carbs per 100 grams: 20 grams
Net carbs per 100 grams: 12 grams
Total protein per 100 grams: 26 grams

Amaranth

Simmer with plant milk to make amaranth porridge or use as a rice substitute.

Key nutrients: calcium, iron, vitamin C, magnesium

Total carbs per 100 grams raw: 65 grams
Net carbs per 100 grams raw: 58 grams
Total protein per 100 grams: 14 grams

Quinoa

Nutty, filling, great for salads and as a substitute for white rice.

Key nutrients: protein, magnesium, folate, manganese, iron, zinc, phosphorous

Total carbs per 100 grams raw: 60 grams
Net carbs per 100 grams raw: 52 grams
Total protein per 100 grams: 16 grams

Chickpeas

Nutty, soft, great for making dips, salads and curries.

Key nutrients: fiber, calcium, iron, magnesium, vitamin B6

Total carbs per 100 grams: 61 grams
Net carbs per 100 grams: 44 grams
Total protein per 100 grams: 19 grams

Sesame seeds

Use to create homemade tahini or toast and add to salads or plant-based sushi rolls.

Key nutrients: fiber, copper, omega-6 fatty acids, sesamin

Total carbs per 100 grams: 23 grams
Net carbs per 100 grams: 11 grams
Total protein per 100 grams: 18 grams

Hemp seeds

Add to smoothies and sprinkle over fresh fruit.

Key nutrients: omega-3 fatty acids, fiber, vitamin E

Total carbs per 100 grams: 8.7 grams
Net carbs per 100 grams: 4.7 grams
Total protein per 100 grams: 32 grams

Flax seeds

Grind and add to smoothies, homemade granola, plant-based baking and salads.

Key nutrients: lignans, omega-3 fatty acids, fiber

Total carbs per 100 grams: 28.9 grams
Net carbs per 100 grams: 1.6 grams
Total protein per 100 grams: 18 grams

simple + optimum
core routines for extraordinary living

DOWNLOAD YOUR FREE BONUS:
simpleoptimum.com/bookbonus

PLANT-BASED HEALTH
9 FOODS FOR PROTEINS: DIPS AND VEGETABLES
Support your body's building blocks to stay strong, stable and healthy.

Peanut butter
Add to smoothies, spread onto celery sticks, use as a binding agent and fat-booster for plant-based baked goods.

Key nutrients: Vitamin E, manganese, antioxidants

Total carbs per 100 grams: 20 grams
Net carbs per 100 grams: 14 grams
Total protein per 100 grams: 25 grams

Tahini
Add to hummus or use as a butter substitute for a nutty flavor.

Key nutrients: iron, copper, heart-loving sesamolin, vitamin E

Total carbs per 100 grams: 21 grams
Net carbs per 100 grams: 12 grams
Total protein per 100 grams: 17 grams

Spinach
Nutrient-dense, wilts easily, light, affordable, versatile, add to salads, curries, smoothies.

Key nutrients: fiber, vitamin A, vitamin C, iron, folic acid, calcium

Total carbs per 100 grams: 3.6 grams
Net carbs per 100 grams: 1.4 grams
Total protein per 100 grams: 2.9 grams

Potatoes
Excellent source of energy and potassium. Eat boiled, fried or smashed, serve as a side-dish or make potato salad.

Key nutrients: potassium, vitamin C, vitamin B6, fiber, iron

Total carbs per 100 grams: 17 grams
Net carbs per 100 grams: 14.8 grams
Total protein per 100 grams: 2 grams

Broccoli
Crunchy, affordable, versatile.

Key nutrients: vitamin C, vitamin A, fiber, folate, vitamin K1

Total carbs per 100 grams: 7 grams
Net carbs per 100 grams: 4.4 grams
Total protein per 100 grams: 2.8 grams

Alfalfa sprouts
Light, earthy, ideal for salads and sandwiches.

Key nutrients: vitamin C, iron, vitamin K, folate, manganese

Total carbs per 100 grams: 2.1 grams
Net carbs per 100 grams: 0.2 grams
Total protein per 100 grams: 4 grams

Green peas
Sweet, affordable, versatile.

Key nutrients: vitamin A, vitamin B6, vitamin C, magnesium, vitamin K, thiamin

Total carbs per 100 grams: 14 grams
Net carbs per 100 grams: 9 grams
Total protein per 100 grams: 5 grams

Asparagus
Unique flavor, wonderful steamed or roasted.

Key nutrients: vitamin E, vitamin A, vitamin K, folate

Total carbs per 100 grams: 3.9 grams
Net carbs per 100 grams: 1.8 grams
Total protein per 100 grams: 2.2 grams

Brussels sprouts
Unique, wonderful when pan-fried in olive oil and garlic.

Key nutrients: vitamin C, vitamin K, vitamin A, folate, antioxidants

Total carbs per 100 grams: 9 grams
Net carbs per 100 grams: 5.2 grams
Total protein per 100 grams: 3.4 grams

simple + optimum
core routines for extraordinary living

DOWNLOAD YOUR FREE BONUS:
simpleoptimum.com/bookbonus

PLANT-BASED HEALTH

8 FOODS FOR PROTEINS: NUTS
Support your body's building blocks to stay strong, stable and healthy.

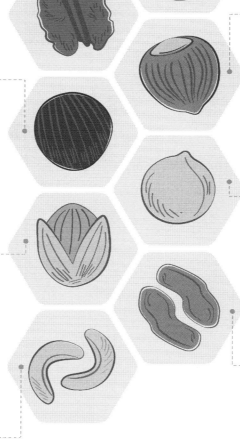

Pecans
Use to make nut butter or simply nibble as a protein-rich snack.

Key nutrients: zinc, antioxidants, vitamin E, copper, manganese

Total carbs per 100 grams: 14 grams
Net carbs per 100 grams: 4 grams
Total protein per 100 grams: 9.2 grams

Black walnuts
Add to salads, eat alone as a snack or add to nut butter recipes.

Key nutrients: selenium, omega-9 (oleic acid), manganese, omega-3 fatty acids

Total carbs per 100 grams: 10 grams
Net carbs per 100 grams: 3 grams
Total protein per 100 grams: 24 grams

Pistachios
Add to plant-based baked goods, use to boost nut mixes for a protein-rich, fat-dense snack.

Key nutrients: omega-3 fatty acids, phosphorus, vitamin B6

Total carbs per 100 grams: 28 grams
Net carbs per 100 grams: 18 grams
Total protein per 100 grams: 20 grams

Cashews
Use to create creamy nut butter, toast with a touch of sea salt for a protein-dense snack.

Key nutrients: selenium, antioxidants, fiber, omega-7 (palmitoleic acid), omega-9 (oleic acid)

Total carbs per 100 grams: 30 grams
Net carbs per 100 grams: 26.7 grams
Total protein per 100 grams: 18 grams

Almonds
Smooth, crunchy, great for making nut butters, snacks.

Key nutrients: protein, vitamin E, manganese, magnesium

Total carbs per 100 grams: 22 grams
Net carbs per 100 grams: 10 grams
Total protein per 100 grams: 21 grams

Hazelnuts
Toast and add to salads and plant-based desserts, add to nut butter recipes.

Key nutrients: vitamin E, antioxidants, manganese, omega-9 (oleic acid)

Total carbs per 100 grams: 17 grams
Net carbs per 100 grams: 7 grams
Total protein per 100 grams: 15 grams

Macadamia nuts
Add to nut butter recipes, sprinkle with sea salt and eat as a protein and fat-rich snack.

Key nutrients: omega-7 (palmitoleic acid), omega-9 (oleic acid), fiber

Total carbs per 100 grams: 14 grams
Net carbs per 100 grams: 5 grams
Total protein per 100 grams: 8 grams

Peanuts
Make peanut butter, sprinkle with sea salt or eat as a crunchy protein snack.

Key nutrients: omega-6, manganese, vitamin E, thiamin, copper, phosphorus, magnesium

Total carbs per 100 grams: 16.1 grams
Net carbs per 100 grams: 7.6 grams
Total protein per 100 grams: 25.8 grams

simple + optimum — core routines for extraordinary living

DOWNLOAD YOUR FREE BONUS: simpleoptimum.com/bookbonus

PLANT-BASED HEALTH — 13 FOODS FOR FIBER

Support blood sugar levels and help the digestive process.

Apples
Sweet, crisp, great raw, poached, as a snack or in salads.

Key nutrients: vitamin C, potassium, catechin (an antioxidant)

Total carbs per 100 grams: 14 grams
Net carbs per 100 grams: 11.6 grams
Total fiber per 100 grams: 2.4 grams

Avocados
Creamy, soft, great for dips, salads, spreads.

Key nutrients: fiber, folate, vitamin K, riboflavin, copper

Total carbs per 100 grams: 9 grams
Net carbs per 100 grams: 2 grams
Total fiber per 100 grams: 7 grams

Chickpeas
Nutty, versatile, great for roasting, dips or adding to salads.

Key nutrients: fiber, calcium, iron, magnesium, vitamin B6

Total carbs per 100 grams: 61 grams
Net carbs per 100 grams: 44 grams
Total fiber per 100 grams: 17 grams

Lentils
Affordable, easy to prepare, filling, carry flavors well.

Key nutrients: fiber, folate, manganese, iron, thiamin, vitamin B6

Total carbs per 100 grams: 20 grams
Net carbs per 100 grams: 12 grams
Total fiber per 100 grams: 8 grams

Sweet potatoes
Great for roasting, baking and mashing.

Key nutrients: vitamin A, vitamin B6, beta carotene, manganese

Total carbs per 100 grams: 20 grams
Net carbs per 100 grams: 17 grams
Total fiber per 100 grams: 3 grams

Black beans
Affordable, versatile, great for vegetarian chili and dips.

Key nutrients: fiber, iron, magnesium, copper, manganese, protein, vitamin B1

Total carbs per 100 grams: 63 grams
Net carbs per 100 grams: 47 grams
Total fiber per 100 grams: 16 grams

Brussels sprouts
Great roasted or pan-fried with garlic.

Key nutrients: vitamin C, vitamin K, vitamin A, folate, antioxidants

Total carbs per 100 grams: 9 grams
Net carbs per 100 grams: 5.2 grams
Total fiber per 100 grams: 3.8 grams

Chia seeds
Ideal for fiber-filled breakfasts, adding to smoothies and gluten-free pudding.

Key nutrients: fat, magnesium, iron, calcium

Total carbs per 100 grams raw: 44 grams
Net carbs per 100 grams raw: 6 grams
Total fiber per 100 grams: 38 grams

Pears
Sweet, crunchy, perfect snack, great poached or added to salads.

Key nutrients: vitamin C, vitamin K, potassium

Total carbs per 100 grams: 15 grams
Net carbs per 100 grams: 11.9 grams
Total fiber per 100 grams: 3.1 grams

Figs
Sweet, soft, unique, ideal as snacks and desserts.

Key nutrients: potassium, manganese, vitamin K, vitamin B6

Total carbs per 100 grams: 19 grams
Net carbs per 100 grams: 16 grams
Total fiber per 100 grams: 3 grams

Kidney beans
Mild-tasting, affordable, great for chili, dips, salads and curries.

Key nutrients: dietary fiber, protein, iron, magnesium, vitamin B-6

Total carbs per 100 grams: 60 grams
Net carbs per 100 grams: 35 grams
Total fiber per 100 grams: 25 grams

Green peas
Sweet, affordable, great for salads, sides, curries, dips.

Key nutrients: vitamin A, vitamin B6, vitamin C, magnesium, vitamin K, thiamin

Total carbs per 100 grams: 14 grams
Net carbs per 100 grams: 9 grams
Total fiber per 100 grams: 5 grams

Broccoli
Affordable, great raw or cooked.

Key nutrients: vitamin C, vitamin A, fiber, folate, vitamin K1

Total carbs per 100 grams: 7 grams
Net carbs per 100 grams: 4.4 grams
Total fiber per 100 grams: 3.4 grams

---

simple + optimum — core routines for extraordinary living

DOWNLOAD YOUR FREE BONUS: simpleoptimum.com/bookbonus

PLANT-BASED HEALTH
10 FOODS FOR VITAMIN C
Ensuring your body is supported with crucial vitamins for proper function.

Kiwi

Tart, sweet, perfect with breakfast meals, juices, snacks.

Key nutrients: fiber, folate, potassium

Total carbs per 100 grams: 15 grams
Net carbs per 100 grams: 12 grams
Total vitamin C per 100 grams: 65 milligrams

Lemons

Tart, fragrant, great for dressings, drinks and desserts.

Key nutrients: folate, potassium

Total carbs per 100 grams without peel: 9.3 grams
Net carbs per 100 grams without peel: 6.5 grams
Total vitamin C per 100 grams without peel: 53 milligrams

Papaya

Juicy, sweet, great for Summer snacks.

Key nutrients: fiber, folate, vitamin A

Total carbs per 100 grams: 11 grams
Net carbs per 100 grams: 9.3 grams
Total vitamin C per 100 grams: 60.9 milligrams

Oranges

Sweet, tart, juicy, great raw or juiced.

Key nutrients: fiber, thiamin, folate, potassium

Total carbs per 100 grams: 9.5 grams
Net carbs per 100 grams: 7.4 grams
Total vitamin C per 100 grams: 50 milligrams

Brussels sprouts

Versatile, great roasted or pan-fried.

Key nutrients: vitamin C, vitamin K, vitamin A, folate, antioxidants

Total carbs per 100 grams: 9 grams
Net carbs per 100 grams: 5.2 grams
Total vitamin C per 100 grams: 85 milligrams

Strawberries

Sweet, juicy, seasonal.

Key nutrients: fiber, antioxidants, manganese, potassium

Total carbs per 100 grams: 8 grams
Net carbs per 100 grams: 6 grams
Total vitamin C per 100 grams: 58.8 milligrams

Bell peppers

Sweet, crunchy, great raw or cooked.

Key nutrients: vitamin A, vitamin B6, vitamin A, folate

Total carbs per 100 grams: 6.7 grams
Net carbs per 100 grams: 5.5 grams
Total vitamin C per 100 grams: approx. 100 milligrams

Broccoli

Crunchy, affordable, great steamed, roasted, pan-fried or raw.

Key nutrients: vitamin C, vitamin A, fiber, folate, vitamin K1

Total carbs per 100 grams: 7 grams
Net carbs per 100 grams: 4.4 grams
Total vitamin C per 100 grams: 114 milligrams

Green chili peppers

Spicy, great for flavoring hot dishes.

Key nutrients: vitamin B6, vitamin A, vitamin K

Total carbs per 100 grams: 9.5 grams
Net carbs per 100 grams: 8 grams
Total vitamin C per 100 grams: 242.5 milligrams

Kale

Leafy, chewy, great raw or cooked.

Key nutrients: vitamin A, vitamin K, folate, fiber, calcium

Total carbs per 100 grams: 8.8 grams
Net carbs per 100 grams: 5.2 grams
Total vitamin C per 100 grams: 120 milligrams

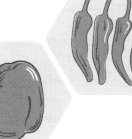

DOWNLOAD YOUR FREE BONUS:
simpleoptimum.com/bookbonus

PLANT-BASED HEALTH — 13 FOODS FOR IRON

Keeping your blood healthy and your body energized.

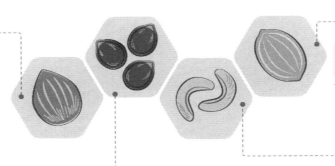

Almonds
Crunchy, great raw or toasted, great for nut butter.

Key nutrients: protein, vitamin E, manganese, magnesium

Total carbs per 100 grams: 22 grams
Net carbs per 100 grams: 10 grams
Total iron per 100 grams: 3.7 milligrams

Pumpkin seeds
Great toasted, crunchy, great as a snack.

Key nutrients: calcium, magnesium, potassium, vitamin E, zinc

Total carbs per 100 grams: 54 grams
Net carbs per 100 grams: 36 grams
Total iron per 100 grams: 3.3 milligrams

Flax seeds
Affordable, must be ground or crushed to maximize nutrients.

Key nutrients: omega-3 and omega-6 fatty acids, protein, copper

Total carbs per 100 grams: 28.9 grams
Net carbs per 100 grams: 1.6 grams
Total iron per 100 grams: 5.7 milligrams

White mushrooms
Soft, earthy, mild, great for soups, raw or cooked.

Key nutrients: antioxidants, potassium, fiber, folate, thiamin

Total carbs per 100 grams: 3.3 grams
Net carbs per 100 grams: 2.3 grams
Total iron per 100 grams: 0.5 milligrams

Cashew nuts
Crunchy, creamy, great raw or toasted, ideal for salads and nut butter.

Key nutrients: magnesium, copper, phosphorous, good fats

Total carbs per 100 grams: 30 grams
Net carbs per 100 grams: 26.7 grams
Total iron per 100 grams: 6.7 milligrams

Lentils
Filling, great for curries, salads, dips.

Key nutrients: fiber, folate, manganese, iron, thiamin, vitamin B6

Total carbs per 100 grams: 20 grams
Net carbs per 100 grams: 12 grams
Total iron per 100 grams: 7.5 milligrams

Quinoa
Filling, nutty, versatile, great rice replacement and base for veggie patties and salads.

Key nutrients: protein, magnesium, folate, manganese, iron, zinc, phosphorous

Total carbs per 100 grams raw: 60 grams
Net carbs per 100 grams raw: 52 grams
Total iron per 100 grams: 4.57 milligrams

Spinach
Affordable, great for salads, soups, curries, sandwiches.

Key nutrients: fiber, vitamin A, vitamin C, iron, folic acid, calcium

Total carbs per 100 grams: 3.6 grams
Net carbs per 100 grams: 1.4 grams
Total ion per 100 grams: 2.71 milligrams

Chickpeas
Filling, great for dips, salads, and snacks.

Key nutrients: fiber, calcium, iron, magnesium, vitamin B6

Total carbs per 100 grams: 61 grams
Net carbs per 100 grams: 44 grams
Total iron per 100 grams: approximately 2 grams

Kale
Earthy, robust, ideal for salads, soups and roasting as chips.

Key nutrients: vitamin A, vitamin K, folate, fiber, calcium

Total carbs per 100 grams: 8.8 grams
Net carbs per 100 grams: 5.2 grams
Total iron per 100 grams: 1.5 milligrams

Amaranth
Nutty, earthy, filling, ideal for salads and as a rice replacement.

Key nutrients: protein, manganese, magnesium, selenium, phosphorous, copper, antioxidants

Total carbs per 100 grams cooked: 19 grams
Net carbs per 100 grams cooked: 16.9 grams
Total iron per 100 grams cooked: 2.1 milligrams

Black beans
Affordable, versatile, great for vegetarian chili.

Key nutrients: fiber, iron, magnesium, copper, manganese, protein, vitamin B1

Total carbs per 100 grams: 63 grams
Net carbs per 100 grams: 47 grams
Total iron per 100 grams: 8.7 milligrams

Kidney beans
Affordable, filling, soft, soaks up flavor well.

Key nutrients: dietary fiber, protein, iron, magnesium, vitamin B-6

Total carbs per 100 grams: 60 grams
Net carbs per 100 grams: 35 grams
Total iron per 100 grams: 8.2 milligrams

simple + optimum — core routines for extraordinary living

DOWNLOAD YOUR FREE BONUS: simpleoptimum.com/bookbonus

PLANT-BASED HEALTH
9 FOODS FOR BONE HEALTH

Supporting your frame and keeping you strong and upright as you age. Calcium and vitamin D are key nutrients for the bones.

Collard geens
Leafy greens with a high calcium content, low carbs, and lots of vitamin A.

Key nutrients: calcium, vitamin C, vitamin A, vitamin B6

Total carbs per 100 grams: 5 grams
Net carbs per 100 grams: 1 gram

Broccoli
An affordable veggie with lots of calcium and vitamin K for the bones.

Key nutrients: calcium, vitamin C, vitamin A, fiber, folate, vitamin K1

Total carbs per 100 grams: 7 grams
Net carbs per 100 grams: 4.4 grams

Mustard greens
Full of vitamin K and calcium for bone health.

Key nutrients: vitamin K, calcium, vitamin A, vitamin, C, iron, magnesium, vitamin B6

Total carbs per 100 grams: 4.7 grams
Net carbs per 100 grams: 1.5 grams

Kale
A superfood with lots of vitamin K for strong bones.

Key nutrients: vitamin A, vitamin K, folate, fiber, calcium

Total carbs per 100 grams: 8.8 grams
Net carbs per 100 grams: 5.2 grams

Cabbage
One of the most affordable, versatile veggies packed with calcium and magnesium to fortify the bones.

Key nutrients: vitamin C, calcium, magnesium, vitamin B6, potassium

Total carbs per 100 grams: 6 grams
Net carbs per 100 grams: 3.5 grams

Almonds
Perfect snacks to support bones with lots of calcium.

Key nutrients: protein, vitamin E, manganese, magnesium

Total carbs per 100 grams: 22 grams
Net carbs per 100 grams: 10 grams

Sesame seeds
These flavor-rich seeds are absolutely packed with calcium to support the bones. Use to make seed butter, toast and add to salads, or use to coat vegetarian sushi rolls.

Key nutrients: calcium, potassium magnesium, iron, vitamin B6

Total carbs per 100 grams: 23 grams
Net carbs per 100 grams: 11 grams

Oranges
A sweet, juicy fruit with lots of vitamin C to support collagen, crucial for strong bones and skin.

Key nutrients: fiber, thiamin, folate, potassium

Total carbs per 100 grams: 9.5 grams
Net carbs per 100 grams: 7.4 grams

Black beans
Protein-packed beans to fill you up and strengthen the bones.

Key nutrients: fiber, iron, magnesium, copper, manganese, protein, vitamin B1

Total carbs per 100 grams: 63 grams
Net carbs per 100 grams: 47 grams

simple + optimum
core routines for extraordinary living

DOWNLOAD YOUR FREE BONUS:
simpleoptimum.com/bookbonus

PLANT-BASED HEALTH
10 FOODS FOR PREGNANCY HEALTH

Supporting the body as it creates a new life. These foods are full of folate.

Sweet potatoes

Perfect for roasting, steaming, and mashing. Full of plant-based vitamin A which is important for pregnant women, as animal-sourced vitamin A can be harmful.

Key nutrients: vitamin A, vitamin B6, beta carotene, manganese

Total carbs per 100 grams: 20 grams
Net carbs per 100 grams: 17 grams

Blueberries

Sweet, juicy berries, perfect for snacks and smoothies. Full of nutrients for a healthy pregnancy, and for helping with sweet cravings.

Key nutrients: vitamin K, vitamin C, manganese, fiber, antioxidants

Total carbs per 100 grams: 14 grams
Net carbs per 100 grams: 11.6 grams

Bananas

A sweet, filling fruit with lots of potassium and vitamins for general pregnancy health.

Key nutrients: potassium, vitamin B6, fiber, vitamin A

Total carbs per 100 grams: 23 grams
Net carbs per 100 grams: 20.4 grams

Avocados

A creamy, buttery fruit, ideal for salads, dips, and smoothies. Great for helping with cravings for rich, fatty foods during pregnancy.

Key nutrients: fiber, folate, vitamin K, riboflavin, copper

Total carbs per 100 grams: 9 grams
Net carbs per 100 grams: 2 grams

Spinach

Leafy, potent, great raw or cooked, full of folic acid, calcium, and vitamin C for pregnancy support.

Key nutrients: fiber, vitamin A, vitamin C, iron, folic acid, calcium

Total carbs per 100 grams: 3.6 grams
Net carbs per 100 grams: 1.4 grams

Oranges

Sweet, juicy, and a great source of folic acid, very important for pregnant women.

Key nutrients: fiber, thiamin, folate, potassium

Total carbs per 100 grams: 9.5 grams
Net carbs per 100 grams: 7.4 grams

Asparagus

A unique green vegetable with lots of folic acid and vitamin A for supporting a healthy pregnancy.

Key nutrients: vitamin E, vitamin A, vitamin K, folate, folic acid

Total carbs per 100 grams: 3.9 grams
Net carbs per 100 grams: 1.8 grams

Broccoli

Affordable, crunchy, and full of fiber to keep you regular during pregnancy, and vitamins to support a healthy baby.

Key nutrients: vitamin C, vitamin A, fiber, folate, vitamin K1

Total carbs per 100 grams: 7 grams
Net carbs per 100 grams: 4.4 grams

Almonds

A great source of magnesium for pregnancy support and healthy sleep patterns.

Key nutrients: protein, vitamin E, manganese, magnesium

Total carbs per 100 grams: 22 grams
Net carbs per 100 grams: 10 grams

Kidney beans

Full of protein which is crucial for pregnant women, very filling, affordable, and great for comforting dishes such as chili.

Key nutrients: dietary fiber, protein, iron, magnesium, vitamin B-6

Total carbs per 100 grams: 60 grams
Net carbs per 100 grams: 35 grams

simple + optimum
core routines for extraordinary living

DOWNLOAD YOUR FREE BONUS:
simpleoptimum.com/bookbonus

PLANT-BASED HEALTH — 10 FOODS FOR GUT HEALTH

Keeping the gut healthy, regular and inhabited with all the right bacteria and fiber. Fermented foods, and foods high in fiber are wonderful for the gut.

Apple cider vinegar

Perfect for mixing with water in the morning, to balance stomach acid and ease digestion.

Key nutrients: prebiotics, acetic acid

Total carbs per 100 grams: 0.9 grams
Net carbs per 100 grams: 0.9 grams

Apples

Perhaps the most popular fruit, tangy, sweet, crunchy, and packed with fiber, including pectin which helps to cleanse the body and digestive tract.

Key nutrients: fiber, vitamin C, potassium, catechin (an antioxidant)

Total carbs per 100 grams: 14 grams
Net carbs per 100 grams: 11.6 grams

Turmeric

A bright golden-orange root with anti-inflammatory properties. Helps to promote healthy gut acids, soothes inflammation, and eases tummy aches.

Key nutrients: curcumin, vitamin C, iron, copper, zinc

Total carbs per 100 grams: 65 grams
Net carbs per 100 grams: 44 grams

Ginger (raw, fresh)

A sweet, spicy, warming root great for easing sore tummies. Helps to support proper digestion and digestive tract health.

Key nutrients: gingerol (anti-inflammatory), magnesium, phosphorous

Total carbs per 100 grams: 17.9 grams
Net carbs per 100 grams: 14.3 grams

Garlic

A potent bulb used for savory flavors, it is a prebiotic which means it supports and feeds the healthy bacteria in the gut.

Key nutrients: prebiotics, vitamin C, vitamin B6, calcium, manganese, selenium

Total carbs per 100 grams: 33.1 grams
Net carbs per 100 grams: 31 grams

Seaweed/kelp

Great dried, flaked, in soups, or as a supplement.

Key nutrients: calcium, magnesium, fiber, iodine

Total carbs per 100 grams: 10 grams
Net carbs per 100 grams: 8.7 grams

Artichokes

A fiber-filled vegetable to keep digestion healthy and regular, supports healthy gut bacteria.

Key nutrients: vitamin C, magnesium, fiber (inulin)

Total carbs per 100 grams: 11 grams
Net carbs per 100 grams: 6 grams

Sauerkraut

A tangy, sour, fermented product which is full of probiotics to fortify the gut.

Key nutrients: probiotics, vitamin C, vitamin K, iron, manganese, vitamin B6

Total carbs per 100 grams: 3.2 grams
Net carbs per 100 grams: 1.2 grams

Brown rice

Nutty, filling, and full of healthy fiber for regularity, helps to keep gut bacteria healthy.

Key nutrients: fiber, manganese, selenium

Total carbs per 100 grams: 23 grams
Net carbs per 100 grams: 21.2 grams

Flax seeds

Small, shiny seeds which are great ground or crushed, full of soluble fiber and healthy oils to help the digestive process.

Key nutrients: fiber, omega-3 and omega-6 fatty acids, protein, copper

Total carbs per 100 grams: 28.9 grams
Net carbs per 100 grams: 1.6 grams

---

simple + optimum
core routines for extraordinary living

DOWNLOAD YOUR FREE BONUS:
simpleoptimum.com/bookbonus

PLANT-BASED HEALTH — 10 FOODS FOR IMMUNITY

Supporting your body during sickness and winter. These foods are full of key vitamins and minerals to protect the body against sickness.

Garlic

A powerful little bulb with immunity-boosting, flu-fighting, antiseptic abilities.

Key nutrients: prebiotics, vitamin C, vitamin B6, calcium, manganese, selenium

Total carbs per 100 grams: 33.1 grams
Net carbs per 100 grams: 31 grams

Ginger (raw, fresh)

A strong-tasting root with antibacterial and virus-fighting properties.

Key nutrients: gingerol (anti-inflammatory), magnesium, phosphorus

Total carbs per 100 grams: 17.9 grams
Net carbs per 100 grams: 14.3 grams

Red bell peppers

Crunchy, sweet, juicy vegetables, filled with vitamin C for immunity.

Key nutrients: vitamin C, water, vitamin A, vitamin B6, vitamin A, folate

Total carbs per 100 grams: 6.7 grams
Net carbs per 100 grams: 5.5 grams

Turmeric

An earthy root with lots of vitamin C and anti-inflammatory properties to support immunity.

Key nutrients: curcumin, vitamin C, iron, copper, zinc

Total carbs per 100 grams: 65 grams
Net carbs per 100 grams: 44 grams

Lemons

Sour, refreshing citrus fruit with lots of vitamin C for the immune system, as well as antiviral properties.

Key nutrients: vitamin C, folate, potassium

Total carbs per 100 grams without peel: 9.3 grams
Net carbs per 100 grams without peel: 6.5 grams

Oranges

Juicy, tangy, sweet, great for juicing, eating whole as snacks and natural sweet treats. Packed with vitamin C and vitamin A, both immune-supporting power nutrients.

Key nutrients: vitamin C, vitamin A, fiber, thiamin, folate, potassium

Total carbs per 100 grams: 9.5 grams
Net carbs per 100 grams: 7.4 grams

Strawberries

Sweet, juicy, and full of vitamin C to fortify the immune system.

Key nutrients: vitamin C, fiber, manganese, folate

Total carbs per 100 grams: 8 grams
Net carbs per 100 grams: 6 grams

Kiwi

A tart, sweet fruit with soft flesh and major amounts of vitamin C for immunity.

Key nutrients: vitamin C, fiber, folate, potassium

Total carbs per 100 grams: 15 grams
Net carbs per 100 grams: 12 grams

Green tea

A refreshing 0-carb, 0-calorie tea packed with antioxidants.

Key nutrients: catechins (a type of antioxidant which may kill viruses), folate, magnesium

Total carbs per 100 grams: 0 grams
Net carbs per 100 grams: 0 grams

Spirulina powder

An earthy, deep-green powder made from an algae. Extremely high in many nutrients which support the immune system and overall wellness.

Key nutrients: protein, thiamin, iron, magnesium, vitamin C, copper

Total carbs per 100 grams: 24 grams
Net carbs per 100 grams: 20.4 grams

simple + optimum — core routines for extraordinary living

DOWNLOAD YOUR FREE BONUS: simpleoptimum.com/bookbonus

PLANT-BASED HEALTH
9 FOODS FOR MENSTRUAL SUPPORT
Helping the body and mind to cope during menstruation.

Chamomile tea

Soothing, calming tea which can help with easing period pains and cramps. It also helps to relax you in preparation for sleep.

Key nutrients: small traces of vitamin A, folate, calcium, potassium, magnesium

Total carbs per 100 grams: 0 grams
Net carbs per 100 grams: 0 grams

Peppermint tea

A refreshing tea which helps the muscles to relax during menstrual cramps.

Key nutrients: vitamin A, vitamin C, folate

Total carbs per 100 grams: 0 grams
Net carbs per 100 grams: 0 grams

Ginger (raw, fresh)

Ginger tea made with fresh ginger is great for easing menstrual cramps and discomfort.

Key nutrients: gingerol (anti-inflammatory) magnesium, phosphorous

Total carbs per 100 grams: 17.9 grams
Net carbs per 100 grams: 14.3 grams

Turmeric

A golden root which can help with easing mood swings during menstruation.

Key nutrients: curcumin, vitamin C, iron, copper, zinc

Total carbs per 100 grams: 65 grams
Net carbs per 100 grams: 44 grams

Kale

The popular leafy green is high in magnesium which relaxes you and helps with sleep, ideal for when cramps and period-related stress makes you a little more restless.

Key nutrients: magnesium, vitamin A, vitamin K, folate, fiber, calcium

Total carbs per 100 grams: 8.8 grams
Net carbs per 100 grams: 5.2 grams

Bananas

The sweet, soft fruit is great for relieving bloating during the time of the month.

Key nutrients: potassium, vitamin B6, fiber, vitamin A

Total carbs per 100 grams: 23 grams
Net carbs per 100 grams: 20.4 grams

Peanut butter

Creamy, salty, rich. Great for easing cravings for fatty, salty food.

Key nutrients: protein, magnesium, vitamin B6, vitamin E

Total carbs per 100 grams: 20 grams
Net carbs per 100 grams: 14 grams

Fennel seed

A minty, strong-tasting seed which helps to reduce and ease bloating during menstruation.

Key nutrients: vitamin C, copper, magnesium, calcium, protein, selenium

Total carbs per 100 grams: 7 grams
Net carbs per 100 grams: 3.9 grams

Brazil nuts

Crunchy, rich, oily nuts full of magnesium to ease cramps.

Key nutrients: selenium, magnesium, good fats, vitamin E, zinc

Total carbs per 100 grams: 12 grams
Net carbs per 100 grams: 4 grams

simple + optimum
core routines for extraordinary living

DOWNLOAD YOUR FREE BONUS:
simpleoptimum.com/bookbonus

PLANT-BASED HEALTH | 12 FOODS FOR MENTAL HEALTH SUPPORT
Supporting healthy mental function and emotional balance.

Broccoli
An all-around superfood for the whole body and mind, easing inflammation which can contribute to mental disorders.

Key nutrients: vitamin C, vitamin A, fiber, folate, vitamin K1

Total carbs per 100 grams: 7 grams
Net carbs per 100 grams: 4.4 grams

Sauerkraut
Probiotics nourish the gut, which has been named "the second brain". Gut health can directly affect mental health.

Key nutrients: probiotics, vitamin C, vitamin K, iron, manganese, vitamin B6

Total carbs per 100 grams: 3.2 grams
Net carbs per 100 grams: 1.2 grams

Spinach
A leafy green high in folate, a powerful supporter of mental function and mood.

Key nutrients: folate, fiber, vitamin A, vitamin C, iron, folic acid, calcium

Total carbs per 100 grams: 3.6 grams
Net carbs per 100 grams: 1.4 grams

Walnuts
Crunchy, oily snacks, full of omega-3 fats.

Key nutrients: antioxidants, omega-3 fat, magnesium

Total carbs per 100 grams: 14 grams
Net carbs per 100 grams: 7 grams

Carrots
Sweet, affordable, bright root vegetables with lots of beta-carotene, an antioxidant which supports mental function.

Key nutrients: vitamin A, vitamin K, manganese, potassium

Total carbs per 100 grams: 9.6 grams
Net carbs per 100 grams: 6.8 grams

Blueberries
A juicy super berry with vitamins, minerals, and antioxidants.

Key nutrients: vitamin K, vitamin C, manganese, fiber, antioxidants

Total carbs per 100 grams: 14 grams
Net carbs per 100 grams: 11.6 grams

Brazil nuts
Selenium and magnesium are great supporters of mental function.

Key nutrients: selenium, magnesium, good fats, vitamin E, zinc

Total carbs per 100 grams: 12 grams
Net carbs per 100 grams: 4 grams

Mushrooms
Soft, earthy, light vegetables with lots of brain-loving B vitamins.

Key nutrients: fiber, folate, vitamin B6

Total carbs per 100 grams: 3.3 grams
Net carbs per 100 grams: 2.3 grams

Grapefruit
Sweet, tangy, bitter citrus fruit full of vitamin C which helps to keep mental function sharp and moods stable.

Key nutrients: vitamin C, vitamin A, vitamin B6

Total carbs per 100 grams: 11 grams
Net carbs per 100 grams: 9.4 grams

Sesame seeds
Tiny seeds with lots of zinc for supporting mood.

Key nutrients: zinc, calcium, potassium, magnesium, iron, vitamin B6

Total carbs per 100 grams: 23 grams
Net carbs per 100 grams: 11 grams

Flaxseed oil
Omega-3 fatty acids support mental function and mood.

Key nutrients: omega-3 fatty acids

Total carbs per 100 grams: 0 grams
Net carbs per 100 grams: 0 grams

Bananas
Soft, sweet, versatile fruits packed with mood and brain-supporting nutrients.

Key nutrients: potassium, vitamin B6, fiber, vitamin A

Total carbs per 100 grams: 23 grams
Net carbs per 100 grams: 20.4 grams

PLANT-BASED HEALTH
9 FOODS FOR HYPOTHYROIDISM
Supporting your body's most important gland.

Hemp seeds
Nutrient-dense seeds great for thyroid support.

Key nutrients: protein, iron, omega-6 and omega-3 fatty acids

Total carbs per 100 grams: 8.7 grams
Net carbs per 100 grams: 4.7 grams

Pumpkin seeds
A rich source of zinc, important for hypothyroidism.

Key nutrients: zinc, calcium, magnesium, potassium, vitamin E

Total carbs per 100 grams: 54 grams
Net carbs per 100 grams: 36 grams

Brazil nuts
These crunchy nuts contain lots of selenium, an important nutrient for hypothyroidism.

Key nutrients: selenium, magnesium, good fats, vitamin E, zinc

Total carbs per 100 grams: 12 grams
Net carbs per 100 grams: 4 grams

Brown rice
Full of selenium, and filling fiber.

Key nutrients: fiber, manganese, selenium

Total carbs per 100 grams: 23 grams
Net carbs per 100 grams: 21.2 grams

Hazelnuts
Tasty nuts packed with vitamins and minerals.

Key nutrients: vitamin E, folate, calcium, magnesium, vitamin B6, oleic acid

Total carbs per 100 grams: 17 grams
Net carbs per 100 grams: 7 grams

Chickpeas
These soft, versatile beans contain lots of zinc which is important for hypothyroidism.

Key nutrients: fiber, calcium, iron, magnesium, vitamin B6

Total carbs per 100 grams: 61 grams
Net carbs per 100 grams: 44 grams

Kidney beans
Lots of fiber for helping with digestion issues related to hypothyroidism.

Key nutrients: dietary fiber, protein, iron, magnesium, vitamin B-6

Total carbs per 100 grams: 60 grams
Net carbs per 100 grams: 35 grams

Prunes
A good source of iodine for vegans.

Key nutrients: iodine, fiber, vitamin A

Total carbs per 100 grams: 64 grams
Net carbs per 100 grams: 57 grams

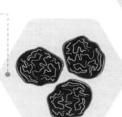

Wakame seaweed
A great source of iodine for thyroid health, great iodine source for vegans.

Key nutrients: sodium, folate, riboflavin, manganes

Total carbs per 100 grams: 9.1 grams
Net carbs per 100 grams: 8.6 grams

simple + optimum
core routines for extraordinary living

DOWNLOAD YOUR FREE BONUS:
simpleoptimum.com/bookbonus

PLANT-BASED HEALTH | 10 FOODS FOR HEART HEALTH
Keeping the heart strong and healthy.

Raspberries
Tart, sweet, juicy berries full of heart-loving vitamin C.

Key nutrients: vitamin C, vitamin K, folate

Total carbs per 100 grams: 12 grams
Net carbs per 100 grams: 5 grams

Carrots
Sweet, crunchy, and full of antioxidants which the heart loves.

Key nutrients: vitamin A, vitamin K, manganese, potassium, beta-carotene

Total carbs per 100 grams: 9.6 grams
Net carbs per 100 grams: 6.8 grams

Tomatoes
A versatile fruit with antioxidants which support a healthy heart.

Key nutrients: lycopene, water, vitamin A, vitamin C, fiber

Total carbs per 100 grams: 4 grams
Net carbs per 100 grams: 3 grams

Oats
Affordable, filling, full of minerals and vitamins to promote heart health.

Key nutrients: fiber, protein, manganese, vitamin B1, iron, selenium, magnesium

Total carbs per 100 grams: 66.3 grams
Net carbs per 100 grams: 55.7 grams

Note: buy only oats with "gluten-free" label as they are otherwise often contaminated by gluten. Steel-cut oats are better for effective digestion resulting in stable blood sugar/insulin balance and lower inflammation.

Spinach
One of the best vegetables for overall wellness and support, including heart health.

Key nutrients: folate, fiber, vitamin A, vitamin C, iron, folic acid, calcium

Total carbs per 100 grams: 3.6 grams
Net carbs per 100 grams: 1.4 grams

Blueberries
Sweet morsels, full of antioxidants.

Key nutrients: vitamin K, vitamin C, manganese, fiber, antioxidants

Total carbs per 100 grams: 14 grams
Net carbs per 100 grams: 11.6 grams

Bell peppers
Sweet, hydrating, and contain lots of vitamins which are great for the heart.

Key nutrients: vitamin C, water, vitamin A, vitamin B6, vitamin A, folate

Total carbs per 100 grams: 6.7 grams
Net carbs per 100 grams: 5.5 grams

Flax seeds
Great source of omega fatty acids which are crucial for heart health.

Key nutrients: omega-3 and omega-6 fatty acids, protein, copper

Total carbs per 100 grams: 28.9 grams
Net carbs per 100 grams: 1.6 grams

Broccoli
A green veggie favorite, with anti-inflammatory properties.

Key nutrients: vitamin C, vitamin A, fiber, folate, vitamin K1

Total carbs per 100 grams: 7 grams
Net carbs per 100 grams: 4.4 grams

Asparagus
A fiber-rich vegetable which helps to reduce the risk of heart disease.

Key nutrients: amino acids, fiber, vitamin E, vitamin A, vitamin K, folate, folic acid

Total carbs per 100 grams: 3.9 grams
Net carbs per 100 grams: 1.8 grams

PLANT-BASED HEALTH | 10 FOODS FOR LIVER SUPPORT
Supporting your body's faithful filter.

Coffee
Black coffee can help to support the liver and prevent liver disease.

Key nutrients: riboflavin, vitamin B5, manganese

Total carbs per 100 grams: 0 grams
Net carbs per 100 grams: 0 grams

Green tea
A carb-free drink with lots of antioxidants for liver health.

Key nutrients: catechins (a type of antioxidant which may kill viruses), folate, magnesium

Total carbs per 100 grams: 0 grams
Net carbs per 100 grams: 0 grams

Broccoli
An all-around organ-loving green veggie, great for supporting a healthy liver.

Key nutrients: vitamin C, vitamin A, fiber, folate, vitamin K1

Total carbs per 100 grams: 7 grams
Net carbs per 100 grams: 4.4 grams

Beets
Rich, deep-colored veggies which are rich in vitamin C and other nutrients.

Key nutrients: vitamin C, manganese, folate

Total carbs per 100 grams: 7.3 grams
Net carbs per 100 grams: 6.1 grams

Brussels sprouts
Small, green cruciferous veggies with liver-cleansing properties.

Key nutrients: vitamin C, vitamin K, vitamin A, folate, antioxidants

Total carbs per 100 grams: 9 grams
Net carbs per 100 grams: 5.2 grams

Garlic
A cooking staple which helps to cleanse the liver and get rid of toxins.

Key nutrients: prebiotics, vitamin C, vitamin B6, calcium, manganese, selenium

Total carbs per 100 grams: 33.1 grams
Net carbs per 100 grams: 31 grams

Grapefruit
A bitter citrus fruit with high levels of vitamin C for liver function.

Key nutrients: vitamin C, vitamin A, vitamin B6

Total carbs per 100 grams: 11 grams
Net carbs per 100 grams: 9.4 grams

Cranberries
A tart berry full of vitamins, and liver-loving properties.

Key nutrients: vitamin C, vitamin K, vitamin E, fiber

Total carbs per 100 grams: 12 grams
Net carbs per 100 grams: 8 grams

Olive oil
A superfood oil with liver-protecting properties.

Key nutrients: vitamin E, vitamin K, omega-6 fatty acid

Total carbs per 100 grams: 0 grams
Net carbs per 100 grams: 0 grams

Almonds
Nutrient-dense nuts with liver-loving properties.

Key nutrients: protein, vitamin E, manganese, magnesium

Total carbs per 100 grams: 22 grams
Net carbs per 100 grams: 10 grams

simple + optimum — core routines for extraordinary living

DOWNLOAD YOUR FREE BONUS:
simpleoptimum.com/bookbonus

PLANT-BASED HEALTH: 10 FOODS FOR SLEEP SUPPORT

Helping the body and mind to wind down and sleep deeply each night.

Almonds

A popular nut which contains melatonin, the sleep hormone.

Key nutrients: melatonin, protein, vitamin E, manganese, magnesium

Total carbs per 100 grams: 22 grams
Net carbs per 100 grams: 10 grams

Bananas

These sweet fruits contain relaxing nutrients magnesium and potassium.

Key nutrients: potassium, magnesium, vitamin B6, fiber, vitamin A

Total carbs per 100 grams: 23 grams
Net carbs per 100 grams: 20.4 grams

Watermelon

A hydrating fruit with lots of magnesium for supporting healthy sleep.

Key nutrients: magnesium, water, vitamin A, vitamin C, lycopene (anti-inflammatory)

Total carbs per 100 grams: 8 grams
Net carbs per 100 grams: 7.6 grams

Chamomile tea

A soothing tea for relaxing before bed.

Key nutrients: small traces of vitamin A, folate, calcium, potassium, magnesium

Total carbs per 100 grams: 0 grams
Net carbs per 100 grams: 0 grams

Tart cherry juice

A nutrient-dense juice with the sleep hormone, melatonin.

Key nutrients: melatonin, potassium, vitamin C, vitamin A

Total carbs per 100 grams: 13.7 grams
Net carbs per 100 grams: 13.7 grams

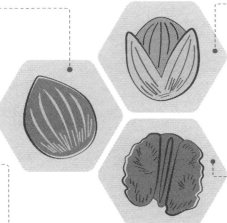

Pistachio

These green nuts have lots of vitamin B6, which helps the body to produce serotonin which helps to keep sleep cycles under control.

Key nutrients: vitamin B6, magnesium, copper, protein, fiber

Total carbs per 100 grams: 28 grams
Net carbs per 100 grams: 18 grams

Walnuts

These oily nuts create the amino acid tryptophan which helps with sleep.

Key nutrients: tryptophan amino acid, antioxidants, omega-3 fat, magnesium

Total carbs per 100 grams: 14 grams
Net carbs per 100 grams: 7 grams

Kiwi

Tangy, tart fruits with a high level of serotonin.

Key nutrients: serotonin, vitamin C, fiber, folate, potassium

Total carbs per 100 grams: 15 grams
Net carbs per 100 grams: 12 grams

Figs

Vitamin-rich, and a great source of potassium.

Key nutrients: potassium, manganese, vitamin K, vitamin B6

Total carbs per 100 grams: 19 grams
Net carbs per 100 grams: 16 grams

Oats

A breakfast favorite with magnesium and serotonin, both of which contribute to proper sleep.

Key nutrients: fiber, protein, manganese, vitamin B1, iron, selenium, magnesium

Total carbs per 100 grams: 66.3 grams
Net carbs per 100 grams: 55.7 grams

Note: not all oats are processed in a gluten-free environment and are therefore not suitable for gluten-free diets

simple + optimum
core routines for extraordinary living

DOWNLOAD YOUR FREE BONUS:
simpleoptimum.com/bookbonus

PLANT-BASED HEALTH
11 SUPERFOODS' HALL OF FAME
The best superfoods worthy of your time and taste buds.

Almonds
A long-time superfood with healthy fats and vitamin E for nourishing the skin.

Key nutrients: protein, vitamin E, manganese, magnesium

Total carbs per 100 grams: 22 grams
Net carbs per 100 grams: 10 grams

Turmeric
A deep, golden root which can help to soothe sore tummies and offers a strong anti-inflammatory effect.

Key nutrients: curcumin, vitamin C, iron, copper, zinc

Total carbs per 100 grams: 65 grams
Net carbs per 100 grams: 44 grams

Garlic
An unassuming bulb packed with nutrients for all-over wellness support. Especially great for digestion and immunity.

Key nutrients: prebiotics, vitamin C, vitamin B6, calcium, manganese, selenium

Total carbs per 100 grams: 33.1 grams
Net carbs per 100 grams: 31 grams

Ginger
A powerful root which can soothe nausea and boost immunity.

Key nutrients: gingerol (anti-inflammatory), magnesium, phosphorous

Total carbs per 100 grams: 17.9 grams
Net carbs per 100 grams: 14.3 grams

Broccoli
An affordable, potent green veggie packed with nutrients such as Vitamin C and fiber.

Key nutrients: vitamin C, vitamin A, fiber, folate, vitamin K1

Total carbs per 100 grams: 7 grams
Net carbs per 100 grams: 4.4 grams

Walnuts
A powerful nut with cancer-preventing properties.

Key nutrients: tryptophan amino acid, antioxidants, omega-3 fat, magnesium

Total carbs per 100 grams: 14 grams
Net carbs per 100 grams: 7 grams

Blueberries
A superfood stalwart full of antioxidants, vitamin C, and heart-loving properties.

Key nutrients: vitamin C, vitamin K, vitamin A, folate, antioxidants

Total carbs per 100 grams: 14 grams
Net carbs per 100 grams: 11.6 grams

Green tea
A wildly popular tea which can help with weight loss and overall wellness.

Key nutrients: catechins (a type of antioxidant which may kill viruses), folate, magnesium

Total carbs per 100 grams: 0 grams
Net carbs per 100 grams: 0 grams

Kale
One of the most nutrient-dense leafy greens, a source of many nutrients, including iron.

Key nutrients: magnesium, vitamin A, vitamin K, folate, fiber, calcium

Total carbs per 100 grams: 8.8 grams
Net carbs per 100 grams: 5.2 grams

Olive oil
An ever-popular oil with healthy fats and vitamin E. A powerful supporter of heart health, and healthy skin.

Key nutrients: vitamin E, vitamin K, omega-6 fatty acid

Total carbs per 100 grams: 0 grams
Net carbs per 100 grams: 0 grams

Flaxseed oil
A rich source of omega-3 fatty acids, crucial for a healthy heart and glowing skin.

Key nutrients: omega-3 fatty acids

Total carbs per 100 grams: 0 grams

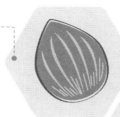

simple + optimum — core routines for extraordinary living

DOWNLOAD YOUR FREE BONUS:
simpleoptimum.com/bookbonus

PLANT-BASED HEALTH | 10 FOODS FOR HAIR, SKIN AND NAILS

Infuse your diet with foods to achieve strong nails, clear skin, and glossy hair. These foods have lots of vitamin E, vitamin C, calcium, and omega fatty acids.

Seaweed

A sea-foraged green vegetable with lots of powerful nutrients to support healthy skin.

Key nutrients: calcium, magnesium, fiber, iodine

Total carbs per 100 grams: 10 grams
Net carbs per 100 grams: 8.7 grams

Sweet potatoes

A sweet, starchy veggie with lots of Vitamin C and vitamin A, both of which are great supporters of healthy skin.

Key nutrients: vitamin B6, vitamin A, beta-carotene, vitamin C

Total carbs per 100 grams: 20 grams
Net carbs per 100 grams: 17 grams

Avocados

A creamy fruit with high amounts of healthy fats for glowing skin and hair.

Key nutrients: healthy fats, vitamin C, vitamin E, fiber, folate, vitamin K, riboflavin, copper

Total carbs per 100 grams: 9 grams
Net carbs per 100 grams: 2 grams

Flax seeds

Tiny, shiny seeds with lots of fatty acids for plump, hydrated skin, and shiny hair.

Key nutrients: omega-3 and omega-6 fatty acids, protein, copper

Total carbs per 100 grams: 28.9 grams
Net carbs per 100 grams: 1.6 grams

Oats

A filling, versatile plant food with anti-inflammatory properties for calm, moisturized skin.

Key nutrients: vitamin K, vitamin C, manganese, fiber, antioxidants

Total carbs per 100 grams: 14 grams
Net carbs per 100 grams: 11.6 grams

Note: buy only oats with "gluten-free" label as they are otherwise often contaminated by gluten. Steel-cut oats are better for effective digestion resulting in stable blood sugar/insulin balance and lower inflammation.

Blueberries

Deep-blue berries with lots of antioxidants and vitamins for youthful, healthy skin.

Key nutrients: vitamin E, vitamin A, vitamin K, vitamin C, manganese, fiber, antioxidants

Total carbs per 100 grams: 14 grams
Net carbs per 100 grams: 11.6 grams

Spinach

An all-over leafy green super vegetable with vitamin C, vitamin A, and antioxidants for clear skin.

Key nutrients: fiber, vitamin A, vitamin C, iron, folic acid, calcium

Total carbs per 100 grams: 3.6 grams
Net carbs per 100 grams: 1.4 grams

Pumpkin seeds

A healthy snacking seed with lots of skin and hair-loving nutrients such as vitamin E and healthy fats.

Key nutrients: healthy fats, calcium, magnesium, potassium, vitamin E, zinc

Total carbs per 100 grams: 54 grams
Net carbs per 100 grams: 36 grams

Walnuts

Rich in omega-3 fatty acids, walnuts have anti-inflammatory properties, and help to keep skin moisturized.

Key nutrients: antioxidants, omega-3 fatty acids, magnesium, vitamin B6

Total carbs per 100 grams: 14 grams
Net carbs per 100 grams: 7 grams

Almonds

Crunchy, oily nuts with lots of fatty acids for healthy skin.

Key nutrients: omegas 3 and 6, protein, vitamin E, manganese, magnesium

Total carbs per 100 grams: 22 grams
Net carbs per 100 grams: 10 grams

simple + optimum
core routines for extraordinary living

DOWNLOAD YOUR FREE BONUS:
simpleoptimum.com/bookbonus

PLANT-BASED HEALTH: 10 FOODS FOR HEALTHY EYES AND VISION

Keep your eyes sharp and moisturized with brightly-colored veggies, whole grains, seeds, and oils.

Bell peppers

Warm-colored bell peppers contain lots of carotenoids which are extremely supportive of vision and eye health.

Key nutrients: carotenoids, vitamin A, vitamin B6, vitamin A, folate

Total carbs per 100 grams: 6.7 grams
Net carbs per 100 grams: 5.5 grams

Brown rice

This filling grain contains lots of zinc, excellent for supporting eye and vision health.

Key nutrients: zinc, fiber, manganese, selenium, magnesium

Total carbs per 100 grams raw: 77 grams
Net carbs per 100 grams raw: 73.5 grams

Pine nuts

Strong source of lutein, a strong supporter of the eyes.

Key nutrients: lutein, iron, magnesium, vitamin E, vitamin K

Total carbs per 100 grams: 13 grams
Net carbs per 100 grams: 9.3 grams

Black currant seed oil

A powerful oil with healthy fats to help the eyes to stay lubricated and comfortable.

Key nutrients: omega-3 fatty acid, omega-6 fatty acid

Total carbs per 100 grams: 0 grams
Net carbs per 100 grams: 0 grams

Flaxseed oil

Due to the high amounts of omega-3 fatty acids, flaxseed oil keeps the eyes moist, and can help to prevent dry eye.

Key nutrients: omega-3 fatty acids

Total carbs per 100 grams: 0 grams
Net carbs per 100 grams: 0 grams

Carrots

Well-known for supporting eye health and keeping vision sharp.

Key nutrients: beta-carotene, vitamin A, vitamin K, manganese, potassium

Total carbs per 100 grams: 9.6 grams
Net carbs per 100 grams: 6.8 grams

Kale

Great source of lutein which helps to prevent degenerative eye conditions.

Key nutrients: lutein, vitamin A, vitamin K, folate, fiber, calcium

Total carbs per 100 grams: 8.8 grams
Net carbs per 100 grams: 5.2 grams

Quinoa

A great source of eye-loving zinc.

Key nutrients: protein, magnesium, folate, manganese, iron, zinc, phosphorous

Total carbs per 100 grams raw: 60 grams
Net carbs per 100 grams raw: 52 grams

Sunflower seeds

Healthy, crunchy seeds with lots of zinc, an eye-loving nutrient.

Key nutrients: zinc, vitamin E, copper, selenium, phosphorous

Total carbs per 100 grams: 20 grams
Net carbs per 100 grams: 11 grams

Oranges

Juicy, sweet citrus with lots of flavonoids known to prevent failing eyesight and eye-related health issues.

Key nutrients: flavonoids, fiber, thiamin, folate, potassium

Total carbs per 100 grams: 9.5 grams
Net carbs per 100 grams: 7.4 grams

simple + optimum — core routines for extraordinary living

DOWNLOAD YOUR FREE BONUS: simpleoptimum.com/bookbonus

PLANT-BASED HEALTH
9 FOODS FOR PRE AND POST-WORKOUT MEALS
Feed your muscles and replace salts, fluid and energy after a hard gym session.

Peanut butter
Lots of good fat and protein to help the muscles to grow, and replace some of your hard-spent energy. It also gives you a burst of energy before you get going.

Total carbs per 100 grams: 20 grams
Net carbs per 100 grams: 14 grams

Chia seeds
Lots of healthy carbs and fats to replenish your energy stores and feed recovering muscles. Magnesium for helping muscles to relax as they repair.

Total carbs per 100 grams raw: 44 grams
Net carbs per 100 grams raw: 6 grams

Almonds
Great little snacks for nibbling on straight after a workout. Gives you a bit of energy to feed the muscles until your next meal.

Total carbs per 100 grams: 22 grams
Net carbs per 100 grams: 10 grams

Beans
Healthy carbs and protein to feed the muscles as they recover. A great dinner ingredient after a particularly strenuous afternoon gym session.

Total carbs per 100 grams: 60 grams (kidney beans)
Net carbs per 100 grams: 35 grams (kidney beans)

Total carbs per 100 grams: 63 grams (black beans)
Net carbs per 100 grams: 47 grams (black beans)

Bananas
Healthy carbs for replacing energy and helping the muscles to recover. Potassium supports muscles as they recover.

Total carbs per 100 grams: 23 grams
Net carbs per 100 grams: 20.4 grams

Avocado
Avocado has good carbs and lots of healthy fat to fuel your tank before hitting the gym.

Total carbs per 100 grams: 9 grams
Net carbs per 100 grams: 2 grams

Oranges
Pack yourself with hydration and vitamin C from oranges after a tough sweat.

Total carbs per 100 grams: 9.5 grams
Net carbs per 100 grams: 7.4 grams

Leafy greens
Choose greens such as broccoli, green beans, kale and spinach to pack your body with antioxidants to help deal with any inflammation from the workout.

Total carbs per 100 grams: 7 grams (broccoli)
Net carbs per 100 grams: 4.4 grams (broccoli)

Total carbs per 100 grams: 8.8 grams (kale)
Net carbs per 100 grams: 5.2 grams (kale)

Whole grains such as oats
Whole grains are nutrient-dense and offer healthy carbs for sustaining intense workouts. For a pre-workout breakfast, opt for oats.

Total carbs per 100 grams: 66.3 grams (oats)
Net carbs per 100 grams: 55.7 grams (oats)

Note: not all oats are processed in a gluten-free environment and are therefore not suitable for gluten-free diets.

simple + optimum
core routines for extraordinary living

DOWNLOAD YOUR FREE BONUS:
simpleoptimum.com/bookbonus

PLANT-BASED HEALTH — 10 FOODS FOR ECZEMA

Helping to calm and reduce eczema flare-ups. Probiotic foods and foods with anti-inflammatory properties feature highly on this list. Foods with beta-carotene, omega-3 fatty acids, and flavonoids are great for soothing eczema. Note that for some people, greens such as broccoli and kale can trigger eczema.

Green beans
Lovely source of vitamin C.

Total carbs per 100 grams: 7 grams
Net carbs per 100 grams: 3.6 grams

Olive oil
Nourishes the skin with Omega-3 fatty acids.

Total carbs per 100 grams: 0 grams
Net carbs per 100 grams: 0 grams

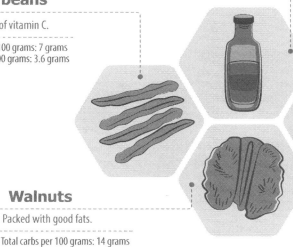

Walnuts
Packed with good fats.

Total carbs per 100 grams: 14 grams
Net carbs per 100 grams: 7 grams

Flaxseed oil
Another fantastic source of Omega-3 fatty acids.

Total carbs per 100 grams: 0 grams
Net carbs per 100 grams: 0 grams

Apples
Contains flavanols which help to ease itching.

Total carbs per 100 grams: 14 grams
Net carbs per 100 grams: 11.6 grams

Blueberries
Rich in anti-oxidants and bioflavonoids.

Total carbs per 100 grams: 14 grams
Net carbs per 100 grams: 11.6 grams

Turmeric
A powerful anti-inflammatory.

Total carbs per 100 grams: 65 grams
Net carbs per 100 grams: 44 grams

Celery
A hydrating choice to get your dose of greens.

Total carbs per 100 grams: 3.8 grams
Net carbs per 100 grams: 2 grams

Sauerkraut
Anti-inflammatory and probiotic powerhouse.

Total carbs per 100 grams: 3.2 grams
Net carbs per 100 grams: 1.2 grams

Red cabbage
Contains skin-protecting properties and vitamin C.

Total carbs per 100 grams: 7 grams
Net carbs per 100 grams: 4.9 grams

simple + optimum — core routines for extraordinary living

DOWNLOAD YOUR FREE BONUS: simpleoptimum.com/bookbonus

PLANT-BASED HEALTH — 17 FOODS FOR INFLAMMATION

Soothe inflammation in the body with a plant-based diet. Berries, nuts, oils, greens, and green tea are all are all wonderful choices for reducing inflammation in the body.

BERRIES
Full of antioxidants to fight inflammation.

Raspberries
Total carbs per 100 grams: 12 grams
Net carbs per 100 grams: 5 grams

Blueberries
Total carbs per 100 grams: 14 grams
Net carbs per 100 grams: 11.6 grams

Almonds
Total carbs per 100 grams: 22 grams
Net carbs per 100 grams: 10 grams

Pecans
Total carbs per 100 grams: 14 grams
Net carbs per 100 grams: 4 grams

NUTS
Great source of Omega-3 fatty acids which our body uses to fight inflammation.

Walnuts
Total carbs per 100 grams: 14 grams
Net carbs per 100 grams: 7 grams

GOOD OILS
Healthy oils contain zero carbohydrates, and nourish our body from the inside out, soothing inflammation with their high dosage of Omega-3 and Omega-6 fatty acids. These some of the best and most available healthy oils.

Olive oil
Nutritional information: all you need to remember is that oils contain zero carbs and are 100% fat.

Coconut oil

Avocado oil

Flaxseed oil

Pineapple
Total carbs per 100 grams: 13 grams
Net carbs per 100 grams: 11.6 grams

Apples
Total carbs per 100 grams: 14 grams
Net carbs per 100 grams: 11.6 grams

Tomatoes
Total carbs per 100 grams: 4 grams
Net carbs per 100 grams: 3 grams

Avocado
Total carbs per 100 grams: 9 grams
Net carbs per 100 grams: 2 grams

FRUITS
Certain fruits contain special antioxidants and enzymes which get to work in our bodies to fight and soothe inflammation. Pineapple contains an enzyme called bromelain which helps to fight inflammation among other benefits. Tomatoes have lots of lycopene, a great anti-inflammatory antioxidant. Apples contain lots of polyphenols, and avocados are a tasty source of healthy fats.

GREEN VEGGIES
The healthiest foods we can eat, green vegetables, are fantastic at reducing inflammation in the body. Try to eat as many different varieties as you can each day.

Broccoli
Total carbs per 100 grams: 7 grams
Net carbs per 100 grams: 4.4 grams

Kale
Total carbs per 100 grams: 8.8 grams
Net carbs per 100 grams: 5.2 grams

Spinach
Total carbs per 100 grams: 3.6 grams
Net carbs per 100 grams: 1.4 grams

Green tea
Total carbs per 100 grams: 0 grams
Net carbs per 100 grams: 0 grams

GREEN TEA
Known for its high content of antioxidants (especially catechins) which help to soothe and prevent inflammation.

DOWNLOAD YOUR FREE BONUS:
simpleoptimum.com/bookbonus

PLANT-BASED HEALTH: 10 FOODS FOR HIGH BLOOD PRESSURE

Help to lower blood pressure with powerful plants. These plant-based foods are full of nutrients such as potassium and magnesium. High-fiber foods are also fantastic for lowering blood pressure.

Flax seeds

High in fiber.

Total carbs per 100 grams: 28.9 grams
Net carbs per 100 grams: 1.6 grams

Pistachios

Studies have shown that pistachios may be a great fighter of high blood pressure.

Total carbs per 100 grams: 28 grams
Net carbs per 100 grams: 18 grams

Leafy greens

Leafy greens: high in potassium and fiber.

Total carbs per 100 grams: 3.6 grams (spinach)
Net carbs per 100 grams: 1.4 grams (spinach)
Total carbs per 100 grams: 3.7 grams (Swiss chard/silverbeet)
Net carbs per 100 grams: 2.1 grams (Swiss chard/silverbeet)

Beets

Contains nitrates which help to lower blood pressure.

Total carbs per 100 grams: 7.3 grams
Net carbs per 100 grams: 6.1 grams

Cocoa

Lots of flavanols.

Total carbs per 100 grams: 58 grams
Net carbs per 100 grams: 25 grams

Olive oil

High in omega-3 fatty acid, proven to lower blood pressure.

Total carbs per 100 grams: 0 grams
Net carbs per 100 grams: 0 grams

Oats

A powerful anti-inflammatory.

Total carbs per 100 grams: 65 grams
Net carbs per 100 grams: 44 grams

Note: buy only oats with "gluten-free" label as they are otherwise often contaminated by gluten. Steel-cut oats are better for effective digestion resulting in stable blood sugar/insulin balance and lower inflammation.

Pomegranates

Anti-inflammatory, anti-oxidant, and proven to have a positive effect on high blood pressure.

Total carbs per 100 grams: 19 grams
Net carbs per 100 grams: 15 grams

Berries

Lots of flavonoids.

Total carbs per 100 grams: 10 grams (blackberries)
Net carbs per 100 grams: 5 grams (blackberries)

Total carbs per 100 grams: 12 grams (raspberries)
Net carbs per 100 grams: 5 grams (raspberries)

Bananas

Full of potassium and fiber.

Total carbs per 100 grams: 23 grams
Net carbs per 100 grams: 20.4 grams

simple + optimum — core routines for extraordinary living

DOWNLOAD YOUR FREE BONUS: simpleoptimum.com/bookbonus

PLANT-BASED HEALTH | 10 FOODS FOR ARTHRITIS

Help soothe arthritic pain and stiffness with plant-based foods high in anti-inflammatory properties. Foods high in vitamin C help the body to produce collagen, which supports the joints and cartilage.

Strawberries

Proven to reduce the risk of arthritis by reducing inflammation.

Total carbs per 100 grams: 8 grams
Net carbs per 100 grams: 6 grams

Kiwifruit

Vitamin C powerhouse.

Total carbs per 100 grams: 15 grams
Net carbs per 100 grams: 12 grams

Cherries

Studies show that cherries can help with gout symptoms.

Total carbs per 100 grams: 12 grams
Net carbs per 100 grams: 10.4 grams

Citrus fruits

The high vitamin C levels help the body to make collagen, therefore supporting bones, joints, and cartilage.

Total carbs per 100 grams: 9.5 grams (oranges)
Net carbs per 100 grams: 7.4 grams (oranges)

Walnut oil

Great source of fatty acids.

Total carbs per 100 grams: 0 grams
Net carbs per 100 grams: 0 grams

Brussels sprouts

Also a member of the cruciferous family.

Total carbs per 100 grams: 9 grams
Net carbs per 100 grams: 5.2 grams

Cabbage

A part of the cruciferous family which are good for reducing inflammation.

Total carbs per 100 grams: 6 grams
Net carbs per 100 grams: 3.5 grams

Turmeric

One of the best-known anti-inflammatory foods.

Total carbs per 100 grams: 65 grams
Net carbs per 100 grams: 44 grams

Garlic

Helps to protect cartilage.

Total carbs per 100 grams: 33.1 grams
Net carbs per 100 grams: 31 grams

Oats

Helps to lower CRP, thus reducing inflammation and risk of arthritis.

Total carbs per 100 grams: 14 grams
Net carbs per 100 grams: 11.6 grams

Note: not all oats are processed in a gluten-free environment and are therefore not suitable for gluten-free diets.

PLANT-BASED HEALTH | 12 FOODS FOR STRESS MANAGEMENT

Support the body and mind during times of stress.

Blueberries
Full of antioxidants and vitamin C which both protect the body during hard, stressful phases.

Total carbs per 100 grams: 14 grams
Net carbs per 100 grams: 11.6 grams

Raspberries
Full of vitamin C to protect your body during hard, stressful times.

Total carbs per 100 grams: 12 grams
Net carbs per 100 grams: 5 grams

Herbal tea
Relaxes the body and mind, and gives you a chance to sit quietly and relax.

Total carbs per 100 grams: 7 grams
Net carbs per 100 grams: 6.7 grams

Cocoa
Helps to lower blood pressure and lift mood.

Total carbs per 100 grams: 58 grams (cocoa powder)
Net carbs per 100 grams: 25 grams (cocoa powder)

Broccoli
Great source of magnesium which supports sleep and relaxation during stressful times.

Total carbs per 100 grams: 7 grams
Net carbs per 100 grams: 4.4 grams

Cashews
Good source of magnesium and vitamin B6, both of which help with relaxation and serotonin production.

Total carbs per 100 grams: 30 grams
Net carbs per 100 grams: 26.7 grams

Pistachio nuts
Full of potassium which supports the heart during stressful times.

Total carbs per 100 grams: 28 grams
Net carbs per 100 grams: 18 grams

Spinach
Great source of magnesium which supports sleep and relaxation during stressful times.

Total carbs per 100 grams: 3.6 grams
Net carbs per 100 grams: 1.4 grams

Lettuce
Great source of magnesium which supports sleep and relaxation during stressful times.

Total carbs per 100 grams: 2.9 grams
Net carbs per 100 grams: 1.6 grams

Sunflower seeds
Contains omega fatty acids and an amino acid called trytophan which supports serotonin production.

Total carbs per 100 grams: 20 grams
Net carbs per 100 grams: 11 grams

Oats
Keeps your blood sugar and energy levels stable, and even helps with serotonin production.

Total carbs per 100 grams: 66.3 grams
Net carbs per 100 grams: 55.7 grams

Note: buy only oats with "gluten-free" label as they are otherwise often contaminated by gluten. Steel-cut oats are better for effective digestion resulting in stable blood sugar/insulin balance and lower inflammation.

Red bell peppers
Full of vitamin C which helps the body to process raised cortisol levels when stress arises.

Total carbs per 100 grams: 6.7 grams
Net carbs per 100 grams: 5.5 grams

DOWNLOAD YOUR FREE BONUS:
simpleoptimum.com/bookbonus

PLANT-BASED HEALTH
15 FOODS FOR PROSTATE HEALTH

Foods for optimum male health. Foods rich with selenium, phytonutrients, zinc, and healthy fats are all wonderful for keeping the prostate healthy, and for reducing the risk of prostate cancer.

CHILI PEPPERS
Contains capsaicin, which has been positively studied for its cancer-fighting abilities.

Green chili pepper
Total carbs per 100 grams: 9.5 grams
Net carbs per 100 grams: 8 grams

Red chili pepper
Total carbs per 100 grams: 9 grams
Net carbs per 100 grams: 7.5 grams

Tomatoes
Proven to help reduce the risk of prostate cancer because of their high lycopene (an antioxidant) content.
Total carbs per 100 grams: 4 grams
Net carbs per 100 grams: 3 grams

Avocados
Lots of healthy fats for a healthy prostate.
Total carbs per 100 grams: 9 grams
Net carbs per 100 grams: 2 grams

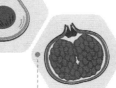

Pomegranates
Studies have shown that pomegranates can slow prostate cancer growth.
Total carbs per 100 grams: 19 grams
Net carbs per 100 grams: 15 grams

Pecans
Great source of beta-sitosterol which is important for prostate health.
Total carbs per 100 grams: 14 grams
Net carbs per 100 grams: 4 grams

Sesame seeds
They contain lots of prostate-loving zinc.
Total carbs per 100 grams: 23 grams
Net carbs per 100 grams: 11 grams

Shiitake mushrooms
Total carbs per 100 grams: 7 grams
Net carbs per 100 grams: 4.5 grams

Pumpkin seeds
Great source of zinc which is important for prostate health.
Total carbs per 100 grams: 6.5 grams
Net carbs per 100 grams: 6 grams

White mushrooms
Total carbs per 100 grams: 3.3 grams
Net carbs per 100 grams: 2.3 grams

Brazil nuts
High in selenium which is important for prostate health.
Total carbs per 100 grams: 12 grams
Net carbs per 100 grams: 4 grams

Brussels sprouts
Total carbs per 100 grams: 9 grams
Net carbs per 100 grams: 5.2 grams

MUSHROOMS
Mushrooms (especially shiitake) have been studied for their positive results on cancer reduction.

Green tea
Contains special antioxidants which can fight against cancer and protect the cells.
Total carbs per 100 grams: 0 grams
Net carbs per 100 grams: 0 grams

Broccoli
Total carbs per 100 grams: 7 grams
Net carbs per 100 grams: 4.4 grams

CRUCIFEROUS VEGGIES
Fantastic sources of cancer-fighting phytonutrients.

Cabbage
Total carbs per 100 grams: 6 grams
Net carbs per 100 grams: 3.5 grams

simple + optimum
core routines for extraordinary living

DOWNLOAD YOUR FREE BONUS:
simpleoptimum.com/bookbonus

PLANT-BASED HEALTH | 13 FOODS FOR BUDGET-FRIENDLY SHOPPING

These plant-based foods are affordable all year round, or when in season. Make them a part of your weekly list and harness their powerful nutritional values. Eating a healthy, plant-based diet can be done on a tight budget!

Chickpeas

Affordable and versatile. Use to make hummus, falafels, vegetarian burger patties, or simply add to curries, stews and salads for fiber and texture.

Total carbs per 100 grams: 61 grams
Net carbs per 100 grams: 44 grams

Lentils

Dried lentils from the bulk bins are extremely affordable and can be tossed into soups, stews, and curries, or made into patties or cold salads. They are full of filling fiber and folate.

Total carbs per 100 grams: 20 grams
Net carbs per 100 grams: 12 grams

Brown rice

Super affordable, great source of fiber and nutrients, and a healthy way to add carbohydrates and energy to busy days.

Total carbs per 100 grams raw: 77 grams
Net carbs per 100 grams raw: 73.5 grams

Beans

Black beans and kidney beans are a superfood worthy of any pantry, and they are very affordable too. Stock up on beans and use them in chilis, soups, dips, salads, and any dish which needs a hit of extra fiber and protein.

Total carbs per 100 grams: 60 grams (kidney beans)
Net carbs per 100 grams: 35 grams (kidney beans)
Total carbs per 100 grams: 63 grams (black beans)
Net carbs per 100 grams: 47 grams (black beans)

Snap-frozen green beans

An affordable back-up to have in the freezer for tight times. Blanch and drizzle with olive oil, or add to vegetable curries for a fresh pop of color and crunch.

Total carbs per 100 grams: 7 grams
Net carbs per 100 grams: 3.6 grams

Apples

Sweet, crunchy, affordable, and a wonderful source of fiber and energy. Eat fresh, crisp apples raw, and poach or bake soft, overripe apples.

Total carbs per 100 grams: 14 grams
Net carbs per 100 grams: 11.6 grams

Bananas

You can cut and freeze fresh bananas for smoothies to save them from going brown, or eat them as a fresh, sweet snack. The best source of potassium.

Total carbs per 100 grams: 23 grams
Net carbs per 100 grams: 20.4 grams

Oats

Affordable way to start the morning with slow-burning energy and fiber. Also a great anti-inflammatory.

Total carbs per 100 grams: 66.3 grams
Net carbs per 100 grams: 55.7 grams

Note: buy only oats with "gluten-free" label as they are otherwise often contaminated by gluten. Steel-cut oats are better for effective digestion resulting in stable blood sugar/insulin balance and lower inflammation.

Flax seeds

A cheap source of fatty acids to support the body in a wide range of ways. Grind them and add them to smoothies, or sprinkle over your oatmeal or fruit salad.

Total carbs per 100 grams: 28.9 grams
Net carbs per 100 grams: 1.6 grams

Tip: shop seasonally, make the most of bulk bins for dried legumes, seeds and nuts

Citrus fruits

Affordable when in season, and a tasty source of vitamin C. Eat whole and raw, or juice for a powerful morning drink.

Total carbs per 100 grams without peel: 9.3 grams (lemons)
Net carbs per 100 grams without peel: 6.5 grams (lemons)
Total carbs per 100 grams: 9.5 grams (oranges)
Net carbs per 100 grams: 7.4 grams (oranges)

Spices

Long-lasting, and a little bit goes a long way to completely change the flavor profile of vegetable dishes. Cumin, paprika, chili, coriander, cinnamon, pepper, cloves, ginger and cardamom are all wonderful spices to keep in the pantry.

Net carbs: per tablespoon of dried spices, there is generally no more than 3 grams of net carbs, and some with a far lower carb count than that. Therefore, a small pinch of spice per serving won't add any extra carbs to worry about.

Dried herbs

They last a long time in the pantry, and can adjust the flavor of any dish. Dried parsley, mint, thyme, oregano, rosemary, basil and sage are all great herbs to start your herb collection.

Net carbs: per tablespoon of dried herbs, there is generally no more than 2 grams of net carbs. So a pinch of herbs in your dish will barely affect your carb intake at all.

Carrots

Great for eye health and overall nutrition. Grate or slice for cold salads. Roast or add to soups for Winter dishes.

Total carbs per 100 grams: 9.6 grams
Net carbs per 100 grams: 6.8 grams

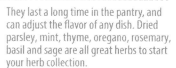

PLANT-BASED HEALTH
11 FOODS FOR POWERFUL BREAKFASTS

These foods are easy to prepare in the morning, or the night before. They're packed with slow-burning energy so you can start the day with a burst, while still feeling full and energized until your next meal.

Berries
Full of vitamin C, fiber, and healthy carbs to get the day going.

Total carbs per 100 grams: 14 grams (blueberries)
Net carbs per 100 grams: 11.6 grams (blueberries)
Total carbs per 100 grams: 12 grams (raspberries)
Net carbs per 100 grams: 5 grams (raspberries)

Chia seeds
Filling, full of fiber, and ideal for remaining full through till lunch.

Total carbs per 100 grams raw: 44 grams
Net carbs per 100 grams raw: 6 grams

Bananas
Sweet, filling, and versatile. Eat plain or add to porridge or smoothies.

Total carbs per 100 grams: 23 grams
Net carbs per 100 grams: 20.4 grams

Walnuts
A great source of healthy fats to start the day.

Total carbs per 100 grams: 14 grams
Net carbs per 100 grams: 7 grams

Almonds
Chopped and sprinkled over porridge, or simply snacked on, the protein content keeps you full.

Total carbs per 100 grams: 22 grams
Net carbs per 100 grams: 10 grams

Lemon juice
Lemon juice and warm water first thing in the morning boosts the digestive process.

Total carbs per 100 grams: 7 grams
Net carbs per 100 grams: 6.7 grams

Avocados
Sprinkle with sea salt and lemon juice and eat straight from the skin, or add to smoothies.

Total carbs per 100 grams: 9 grams
Net carbs per 100 grams: 2 grams

Peanut butter
Spread on apples or added smoothies, a great source of fat and energy.

Total carbs per 100 grams: 20 grams
Net carbs per 100 grams: 14 grams

LSA
A mixture of ground linseed (i.e. flaxseed), sunflower seed, and almonds for fats and energy.

Total and net carbs per 100 grams can vary between brands. Check the nutrition label for an accurate reading.

Oats
Make hot porridge in the morning, or prepare overnight oats to eat cold.

Total carbs per 100 grams: 66.3 grams
Net carbs per 100 grams: 55.7 grams

Note: buy only oats with "gluten-free" label as they are otherwise often contaminated by gluten. Steel-cut oats are better for effective digestion resulting in stable blood sugar/insulin balance and lower inflammation.

Quinoa
A great option for savory breakfast bowls.

Total carbs per 100 grams raw: 60 grams
Net carbs per 100 grams raw: 52 grams

simple + optimum
core routines for extraordinary living

DOWNLOAD YOUR FREE BONUS:
simpleoptimum.com/bookbonus

PLANT-BASED HEALTH

11 SLOW-COOKED DINNER INGREDIENTS FOR COLD WINTERS

These veggies, pulses, and legumes are perfect ingredients for the slow cooker as they offer robust flavor, texture, and natural sweetness. Warming, filling textures and flavors for cold nights during the Winter seasons. Slow cook with vegetable stock to create soups, stews, and curries.

Kidney beans

An affordable way to add fiber, protein, and energy to your slow-cooked soups, stews, curries and chili dishes. With a mild flavor, kidney beans absorb and carry any rich flavors you choose to pair them with.

Total carbs per 100 grams: 60 grams
Net carbs per 100 grams: 35 grams

Onions

Onions are savory and sweet when slow cooked with other plant-based ingredients. They add a depth of flavor to any savory dish.

Total carbs per 100 grams: 9 grams
Net carbs per 100 grams: 7.3 grams

Garlic

Garlic is full of antibacterial properties, and adds one of the most delicious background flavors to any slow-cooked savory dish. Peel and chop garlic cloves to enhance the flavor profile of your slow cooked soups and stews.

Total carbs per 100 grams: 33.1 grams
Net carbs per 100 grams: 31 grams

Black beans

Dark, filling, and full of healthy fiber, black beans are an affordable addition to any slow cooked meal in need of a hit of energy, fiber, and protein.

Total carbs per 100 grams: 63 grams
Net carbs per 100 grams: 47 grams

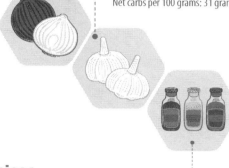

Lentils

Lentils are full of fiber and plant-based protein. When slow cooked with spices and stock, they become soft, creamy and rich. Add to soups for extra bulk, or use to make dahl and vegetarian curry.

Total carbs per 100 grams: 20 grams
Net carbs per 100 grams: 12 grams

Spices

Spices such as cumin, coriander, turmeric, paprika, chili, cloves, star anise and cardamom are all incredibly tasty when added to slow cooked meals. They provide rich and multi-dimensional flavor. Some are earthy, some are sweet, some are spicy, and some are a combination of all. Spend some time with your local spice seller and get to know the different spices available to you.

It depends on which spices you choose, but most common spices have between 50 to 60 total grams of carbohydrates.

Pumpkin

Perfect for slow-cooked soups and plant-based stews and curries. Becomes soft and creamy when slow-cooked, and provides vibrant color.

Total carbs per 100 grams: 6.5 grams
Net carbs per 100 grams: 6 grams

Sweet corn

A colorful addition to slow-cooked vegetarian chili and Mexican-inspired stews. Corn retains shape and color when slow cooked.

Total carbs per 100 grams: 19 grams
Net carbs per 100 grams: 16.3 grams

Butternut squash

A sweet, creamy vegetable which makes the ultimate soup when slow cooked with spices and vegetable stock.

Total carbs per 100 grams: 12 grams
Net carbs per 100 grams: 10 grams

Tomatoes

A low-carb, lycopene-rich ingredient perfect as a base for soups, curries, stews, chili and slow-cooked sauces.

Total carbs per 100 grams: 4 grams
Net carbs per 100 grams: 3 grams

Sweet potatoes

The comforting, nutrient-dense alternative to potatoes. They make a lovely soup, but also add sweetness and bulk to stews and curries.

Total carbs per 100 grams: 20 grams
Net carbs per 100 grams: 17 grams

simple + optimum
core routines for extraordinary living

DOWNLOAD YOUR FREE BONUS:
simpleoptimum.com/bookbonus

PLANT-BASED HEALTH

4 PLANT-COMBOS TIPS FOR SPECTACULAR SALADS

Some of the tastiest and easiest plant-based meals come served in a salad bowl. A cacophony of bright, nutrient-dense plant foods carefully combined for maximum flavor and satisfaction.

INGREDIENTS FOR A SALAD BASE
Your leafy greens and low-carb veggies as lettuce, tomato and cucumber.

Lettuce
Total carbs per 100 grams: 2.9 grams
Net carbs per 100 grams: 1.6 grams

Spinach leaves
Total carbs per 100 grams: 3.6 grams
Net carbs per 100 grams: 1.4 grams

Arugula
Total carbs per 100 grams: 3.7 grams
Net carbs per 100 grams: 2.1 grams

Cucumbers
Total carbs per 100 grams: 4 grams
Net carbs per 100 grams: 4 grams

Tomatoes
Total carbs per 100 grams: 4 grams
Net carbs per 100 grams: 3 grams

Bell peppers
Total carbs per 100 grams: 6.7 grams
Net carbs per 100 grams: 5.5 grams

TO ADD FOR FATS
Your nuts, seeds, and avocado.

Walnuts
Total carbs per 100 grams: 14 grams
Net carbs per 100 grams: 7 grams

Sunflower seeds
Total carbs per 100 grams: 20 grams
Net carbs per 100 grams: 11 grams

Avocados
Total carbs per 100 grams: 9 grams
Net carbs per 100 grams: 2 grams

Pumpkin seeds
Total carbs per 100 grams: 54 grams
Net carbs per 100 grams: 36 grams

TO ADD BULK
Your denser veggies.

Roasted pumpkin
Total carbs per 100 grams: 6.5 grams (raw)
Net carbs per 100 grams: 6 grams (raw)

Roasted sweet potatoes
Total carbs per 100 grams: 20 grams (raw)
Net carbs per 100 grams: 17 grams (raw)

Roasted portobello mushrooms
Total carbs per 100 grams: 3.3 grams (raw)
Net carbs per 100 grams: 2.3 grams (raw)

Roasted beets
Total carbs per 100 grams: 7.3 grams (raw)
Net carbs per 100 grams: 6.1 grams (raw)

TO ADD FOR COLOR AND CRUNCH
Your bright, crisp veggies prepared raw.

Grated raw zucchini
Total carbs per 100 grams: 3.1 grams
Net carbs per 100 grams: 3 grams

Grated raw carrots
Total carbs per 100 grams: 9.6 grams
Net carbs per 100 grams: 6.8 grams

Freshly sliced raw fennel
Total carbs per 100 grams: 7.3 grams
Net carbs per 100 grams: 4.2 grams

Fresh radishes
Total carbs per 100 grams: 3.4 grams
Net carbs per 100 grams: 1.8 grams

Grated raw beetroot
Total carbs per 100 grams: 7.3 grams
Net carbs per 100 grams: 6.1 grams

simple + optimum
core routines for extraordinary living

DOWNLOAD YOUR FREE BONUS:
simpleoptimum.com/bookbonus

PLANT-BASED HEALTH

4 PLANT-COMBOS TIPS FOR SPECTACULAR SALADS

Some of the tastiest and easiest plant-based meals come served in a salad bowl. A cacophony of bright, nutrient-dense plant foods carefully combined for maximum flavor and satisfaction.

TO ADD BITE AND SPICE
A little goes a long way.

Raw red onion
Total carbs per 100 grams: 35 grams
Net carbs per 100 grams: 34 grams

A sprinkling of fresh red chili pepper
Total carbs per 100 grams: 9 grams
Net carbs per 100 grams: 7.5 grams

TO ADD FOR SWEETNESS
Add a small amount of fresh, seasonal fruits.

Apples
Total carbs per 100 grams: 14 grams
Net carbs per 100 grams: 11.6 grams

Mangos
Total carbs per 100 grams: 15 grams
Net carbs per 100 grams: 13.4 grams

Strawberries
Total carbs per 100 grams: 8 grams
Net carbs per 100 grams: 6 grams

Pear
Total carbs per 100 grams: 15 grams
Net carbs per 100 grams: 11.9 grams

TO DRESS
Combine oils, vinegars, and lemon juice.

Olive oil
Total carbs per 100 grams: 0 grams
Net carbs per 100 grams: 0 grams

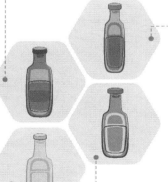

Avocado oil
Total carbs per 100 grams: 0 grams
Net carbs per 100 grams: 0 grams

Apple cider vinegar
Total carbs per 100 grams: 0.9 grams
Net carbs per 100 grams: 0.9 grams

Lemon juice
Total carbs per 100 grams: 7 grams
Net carbs per 100 grams: 6.7 grams

TO ADD FRAGRANCE
Fresh herbs add color and floral flavors.

Net carbs: a small handful (around 4 tablespoons) of fresh herbs will contain no more than 1 or 2 carbs, so you can feel free to add as much fresh herbs to your dishes as you wish, as they won't add excessive carbohydrates to your daily intake.

Fresh coriander
Fresh chives
Fresh basil
Fresh rosemary
Fresh mint
Fresh oregano
Fresh parsley
Fresh dill
Fresh lemon balm

simple + optimum
core routines for extraordinary living

DOWNLOAD YOUR FREE BONUS:
simpleoptimum.com/bookbonus

PLANT-BASED HEALTH

8 FOODS FOR LOSING WEIGHT WITHOUT HUNGER PANGS

These foods are full of key nutrients, as well as good fats for keeping you full and satisfied, without cravings or overeating. Some foods, such as cinnamon, can help to speed the metabolism to burn energy more efficiently.

Sweet potatoes

Filling, satisfying, and full of healthy energy. Sweet potato is a great food option for when you need a little dose of carbohydrates to sustain a strenuous workout, but without sabotaging your weight loss progress.

Total carbs per 100 grams: 20 grams
Net carbs per 100 grams: 17 grams

Almonds

Keeps you full between meals due to the high protein content. A great snacking food to turn to when your mind and stomach rumble with thoughts of food during a restricted calorie eating plan for weight loss.

Total carbs per 100 grams: 22 grams
Net carbs per 100 grams: 10 grams

Peanut butter

Creamy and salty, but a great source of energy and fat, especially for fueling workouts. A dose of peanut butter will help to keep you satisfied, therefore less likely to overeat or succumb to cravings.

Total carbs per 100 grams: 20 grams
Net carbs per 100 grams: 14 grams

Cinnamon

A great flavor-booster, cinnamon helps to speed the metabolism and regulate blood sugar. Add a teaspoon to your smoothies, herbal teas or even your soups and veggie-based stews to give your metabolism a boost.

Total carbs per 100 grams raw: 81 grams
Net carbs per 100 grams raw: 23 grams

Butternut squash

Low-carb but filling and great for bulking-out meals. Butternut squash provides the satisfaction of eating a starch-like vegetable without the added carbs.

Total carbs per 100 grams: 12 grams
Net carbs per 100 grams: 10 grams

Walnuts

Full of healthy fats to keep you satisfied during the day. Snack on a few walnuts to bridge the hunger gap between main meals.

Total carbs per 100 grams: 14 grams
Net carbs per 100 grams: 7 grams

Coconut oil

A healthy oil option for cooking and low-carb baking. Coconut oil has been proven to speed weight loss by boosting the metabolism, therefore burning more calories. Coconut oil is a favored ingredient by those on the ketogenic diet as it is converted to energy very quickly.

Total carbs per 100 grams: 0 grams
Net carbs per 100 grams: 0 grams

Strawberries

great for satisfying sweet cravings. Nibble on fresh strawberries for dessert if you are struggling with a nagging sweet tooth during a weight-loss regime.

Total carbs per 100 grams: 8 grams
Net carbs per 100 grams: 6 grams

simple + optimum
core routines for extraordinary living

DOWNLOAD YOUR FREE BONUS:
simpleoptimum.com/bookbonus

PLANT-BASED HEALTH

11 ALTERNATIVES FOR YOUR MOST-CRAVED COMFORT FOODS

When we crave sugar, carb, and gluten-laden foods, we don't need to completely deprive ourselves. We can choose plant-based alternatives which are both healthy and satisfying.

CRAVING CHOCOLATE
A common weakness

Cocoa/hazelnut spread (homemade)
Blend together hazelnuts and cocoa until creamy and spreadable.

Total carbs per 100 grams: 17 grams (hazelnuts)
Net carbs per 100 grams: 7 grams (hazelnuts)
Total carbs per 100 grams: 58 grams (cocoa powder)
Net carbs per 100 grams: 25 grams (cocoa powder)

Almond milk hot chocolate
Mix together hot almond milk and cocoa powder, with stevia to sweeten.

Total carbs per 100 grams: 1.5 grams (almond milk)
Net carbs per 100 grams: 1.5 grams (almond milk)
Total carbs per 100 grams: 58 grams (cocoa powder)
Net carbs per 100 grams: 25 grams (cocoa powder)

Cocoa-coated hazelnuts
Toss hazelnuts in a cocoa powder and a pinch of sea salt.

Total carbs per 100 grams: 17 grams (hazelnuts)
Net carbs per 100 grams: 7 grams (hazelnuts)
Total carbs per 100 grams: 58 grams (cocoa powder)
Net carbs per 100 grams: 25 grams (cocoa powder)

Cocoa/almond/coconut balls
Blitz in a blender with a drizzle of water, then roll into balls and refrigerate.

Total carbs per 100 grams: 15 grams (desiccated coconut)
Net carbs per 100 grams: 6 grams (desiccated coconut)
Total carbs per 100 grams: 22 grams (almonds)
Net carbs per 100 grams: 10 grams (almonds)
Total carbs per 100 grams: 58 grams (cocoa powder)
Net carbs per 100 grams: 25 grams (cocoa powder)

CRAVING FRENCH FRIES
Salty, starchy.

Sweet potato fries
Cut a sweet potato into fries or wedges and bake in the oven with a drizzle of olive oil.

Total carbs per 100 grams: 20 grams (sweet potato)
Net carbs per 100 grams: 17 grams (sweet potato)

CRAVING POTATO CHIPS
Moreish, crunchy, salty, full of bad fats

Natural popcorn
Pop corn kernels in the microwave with a pinch of sea salt

Total carbs per 100 grams: 74 grams (popcorn)
Net carbs per 100 grams: 61 grams (popcorn)

Toasted pumpkin seeds with sea salt and spices
Toss pumpkin seeds in a dry pan over a medium heat and sprinkle with sea salt, paprika, chili, and any other spice.

Total carbs per 100 grams: 54 grams (pumpkin seeds, plain)
Net carbs per 100 grams: 36 grams (pumpkin seeds, plain)

CRAVING CANDY OR SWEETS

Raspberries
Tangy, sweet, soft, and juicy. Better than any sugary candy.

Total carbs per 100 grams: 12 grams
Net carbs per 100 grams: 5 grams

Dried cranberries
A few of these sweet, chewy morsels will appease any sweet craving.

Total carbs per 100 grams: 82 grams
Net carbs per 100 grams: 76 grams

Strawberries
Juicy Summertime favorite, eat fresh and raw.

Total carbs per 100 grams: 8 grams
Net carbs per 100 grams: 6 grams

CRAVING ICE CREAM

Whipped frozen bananas
Lace frozen bananas into a powerful food processor or blender and blitz until smooth and creamy.

Total carbs per 100 grams: 23 grams (banana)
Net carbs per 100 grams: 20.4 grams (banana)

simple + optimum
core routines for extraordinary living

DOWNLOAD YOUR FREE BONUS:
simpleoptimum.com/bookbonus

PLANT-BASED HEALTH

11 FOODS CHILDREN WILL LOVE

Children respond well to food which is bright, colorful, and can be eaten with their hands. Fresh fruits such as berries and oranges are sweet, fun to eat, and pretty to look at. Crunchy, colorful veggies are fun and easy to dip into healthy dips such as hummus and nut butters. Get the kids to help you prepare the food so they feel included in the task, and become more knowledgeable about where there food comes from and how it is prepared!

SWEET, BRIGHT FRUITS

Kids love the sweetness, freshness, and color of fresh fruits. They can eat them with their hands without having to fuss with utensils.

Bananas
Total carbs per 100 grams: 23 grams
Net carbs per 100 grams: 20.4 grams

Apples
Total carbs per 100 grams: 14 grams
Net carbs per 100 grams: 11.6 grams

Blueberries
Total carbs per 100 grams: 14 grams
Net carbs per 100 grams: 11.6 grams

Oranges
Total carbs per 100 grams: 9.5 grams
Net carbs per 100 grams: 7.4 grams

Raspberries
Total carbs per 100 grams: 12 grams
Net carbs per 100 grams: 5 grams

Strawberries
Total carbs per 100 grams: 8 grams
Net carbs per 100 grams: 6 grams

Green peas
Total carbs per 100 grams: 14 grams
Net carbs per 100 grams: 9 grams

VERSATILE VEGGIES

Veggies with bright colors and mild, sweet flavors are great for kids to learn to enjoy the tasty benefits of fresh vegetables.

Sweet corn
Total carbs per 100 grams: 19 grams
Net carbs per 100 grams: 16.3 grams

Sweet potatoes
Total carbs per 100 grams: 20 grams
Net carbs per 100 grams: 17 grams

Sugar snap peas
Total carbs per 100 grams: 32 grams
Net carbs per 100 grams: 28 grams

Carrot sticks
Total carbs per 100 grams: 9.6 grams
Net carbs per 100 grams: 6.8 grams

TO DIP INTO

Hummus dip
(Made only with chickpeas, salt, and pepper.)
Total carbs per 100 grams: 61 grams
Net carbs per 100 grams: 44 grams

TO SIP ON AS A TREAT

Hot almond milk with cocoa and a drop or two of stevia
Total carbs per 100 grams: 1.5 grams (almond milk)
Net carbs per 100 grams: 1.5 grams (almond milk)
Total carbs per 100 grams: 58 grams (cocoa powder)
Net carbs per 100 grams: 25 grams (cocoa powder)

Almond butter
Total carbs per 100 grams: 19 grams
Net carbs per 100 grams: 9 grams

Peanut butter
Total carbs per 100 grams: 20 grams
Net carbs per 100 grams: 14 grams

PLANT-BASED HEALTH
11 PLANTS FOR JUICING AND BLENDING

When you have an abundance of produce and cannot manage to eat it all, juicing is a great way to harness the nutrients without wastage. For homemade mixed juices, aim for at least three veggies and one fruit to ensure the sugars are properly balanced.

FRUITS

Oranges
A vitamin C favorite.

Total carbs per 100 grams: 9.5 grams
Net carbs per 100 grams: 7.4 grams

Grapefruit
Hydrating, helps to support a healthy weight.

Total carbs per 100 grams: 11 grams
Net carbs per 100 grams: 9.4 grams

Lemons
High in vitamin C, great for cleansing the kidneys.

Total carbs per 100 grams without peel: 9.3 grams
Net carbs per 100 grams without peel: 6.5 grams

Pomegranates
Vitamin C and anti-inflammatory.

Total carbs per 100 grams: 19 grams
Net carbs per 100 grams: 15 grams

Apples
A sweet and tangy addition to vitamin-rich juices.

Total carbs per 100 grams: 14 grams
Net carbs per 100 grams: 11.6 grams

VEGGIES, ROOTS, AND GRASSES

Carrots
Great for vision.

Total carbs per 100 grams: 9.6 grams
Net carbs per 100 grams: 6.8 grams

Kale
In small portions as vast amounts of raw kale can be detrimental to health.

Total carbs per 100 grams: 8.8 grams
Net carbs per 100 grams: 5.2 grams

Spinach
Full of iron, vitamin C, and vitamin A.

Total carbs per 100 grams: 3.6 grams
Net carbs per 100 grams: 1.4 grams

Celery
Hydrating, great source of vitamin K.

Total carbs per 100 grams: 3.8 grams
Net carbs per 100 grams: 2 grams

Wheatgrass
Helps with digestion, full of vitamins and minerals.

Total carbs per 100 grams: 2 grams
Net carbs per 100 grams: 2 grams

Fresh ginger
Great for when you have a cold or a sore tummy.

Total carbs per 100 grams: 17.9 grams
Net carbs per 100 grams: 14.3 grams

simple + optimum
core routines for extraordinary living

DOWNLOAD YOUR FREE BONUS:
simpleoptimum.com/bookbonus

PLANT-BASED HEALTH — 15 FOODS FOR MEAL PREPPING

These foods are all reasonably affordable, easy to store, and will last the week once you have prepared them into tasty meals.

LONG-LASTING VEGGIES

Broccoli
Blanched or lightly steamed is the best way to make the color and crunch last.
Total carbs per 100 grams: 7 grams (raw)
Net carbs per 100 grams: 4.4 grams (raw)

Onion
Raw or roasted.
Total carbs per 100 grams: 9 grams (raw)
Net carbs per 100 grams: 7.3 grams (raw)

Zucchini
Sauté or roast to last longer.
Total carbs per 100 grams: 3.1 grams (raw)
Net carbs per 100 grams: 3 grams (raw)

Bell peppers
Raw or roasted.
Total carbs per 100 grams: 6.7 grams (raw)
Net carbs per 100 grams: 5.5 grams (raw)

LONG-LASTING FIBER SOURCES

Lentils
Great for cold salads or Winter dahl.
Total carbs per 100 grams: 20 grams
Net carbs per 100 grams: 12 grams

Quinoa
Use to make veggie patties or salads
Total carbs per 100 grams raw: 60 grams
Net carbs per 100 grams raw: 52 grams

Chickpeas
Use for hummus, veggie curry, or cold salads.
Total carbs per 100 grams: 61 grams
Net carbs per 100 grams: 44 grams

Beans
Make into vegetarian chili and either freeze or store in the fridge for the week.
Total carbs per 100 grams: 60 grams (kidney beans)
Net carbs per 100 grams: 35 grams (kidney beans)
Total carbs per 100 grams: 63 grams (black beans)
Net carbs per 100 grams: 47 grams (black beans)

LONG-LASTING HEALTHY CARBS

Buckwheat
Stir into salads or use as a rice substitute.
Total carbs per 100 grams raw: 71.5 grams
Net carbs per 100 grams raw: 61.5 grams

Brown rice
Stir a small portion into salads with raw veggies and cashews
Total carbs per 100 grams raw: 77 grams
Net carbs per 100 grams raw: 73.5 grams

LONG-LASTING FAT SOURCES

Olive oil
Use for sautéing, dressings, baking, or roasting during meal prep sessions.
Total carbs per 100 grams: 0 grams
Net carbs per 100 grams: 0 grams

Walnuts
Pack into a container and keep at your desk for a healthy snack.
Total carbs per 100 grams: 14 grams
Net carbs per 100 grams: 7 grams

Pumpkin seeds
Toast and stir into salads or use to make nut/seed butters.
Total carbs per 100 grams: 54 grams
Net carbs per 100 grams: 36 grams

Sunflower seeds
Toast and stir into salads
Total carbs per 100 grams: 20 grams
Net carbs per 100 grams: 11 grams

Flaxseed oil
Drizzle over fruit and nuts for a fat-filled prepped dessert.
Total carbs per 100 grams: 0 grams
Net carbs per 100 grams: 0 grams

DOWNLOAD YOUR FREE BONUS:
simpleoptimum.com/bookbonus

PLANT-BASED HEALTH: 5 EGG REPLACEMENTS FOR BAKING, BREAKFAST, AND BEYOND

Ground flaxseeds
For each egg required in the recipe, stir together 1 tablespoon of ground flaxseeds with 2 or 3 tablespoons of water.

Total carbs per 100 grams: 28.9 grams
Net carbs per 100 grams: 1.6 grams

Chia seeds
For each egg required in the recipe, use 1 tablespoon of chia seeds mixed with 3 tablespoons of water.

Total carbs per 100 grams raw: 44 grams
Net carbs per 100 grams raw: 6 grams

Apple sauce
For each egg required in the recipe, use a ¼ cup of apple sauce.

Total carbs per 100 grams: 17 grams
Net carbs per 100 grams: 15.8 grams

Bananas
For each egg required in the recipe, use a whole mashed small banana, or half a large mashed banana.

Total carbs per 100 grams: 23 grams
Net carbs per 100 grams: 20.4 grams

Avocados
For each egg required in the recipe, use approximately 3 tablespoons of mashed avocado.

Total carbs per 100 grams: 9 grams
Net carbs per 100 grams: 2 grams

simple + optimum — core routines for extraordinary living

DOWNLOAD YOUR FREE BONUS: simpleoptimum.com/bookbonus

PLANT-BASED HEALTH | 11 SOURCES OF ANTIOXIDANTS

These foods help to fight against cell damage as we age. Beta-carotene, vitamin C, vitamin A, and selenium are all examples of antioxidants we can source from plant foods.

Blueberries
Add to smoothies, or eat raw and fresh as snacks.

Total carbs per 100 grams: 14 grams
Net carbs per 100 grams: 11.6 grams

Blackberries
Eat raw, or smash into an inky sauce to drizzle over coconut yogurt.

Total carbs per 100 grams: 10 grams
Net carbs per 100 grams: 5 grams

Oranges
When in season, eat raw for a juicy treat.

Total carbs per 100 grams: 9.5 grams
Net carbs per 100 grams: 7.4 grams

Cherries
Eat raw and fresh, their juicy sweetness needs no enhancement.

Total carbs per 100 grams: 12 grams
Net carbs per 100 grams: 10.4 grams

Hazelnuts
Roast and eat as crunchy snacks or add to homemade granola.

Total carbs per 100 grams: 17 grams
Net carbs per 100 grams: 7 grams

Goji berries
Add to homemade granolas or energy snack mixes.

Total carbs per 100 grams: 51 grams
Net carbs per 100 grams: 30 grams

Tea
Drink liberally for a refreshing hot or cold drink or alternative to coffee.

Total carbs per 100 grams: 0.2 grams
Net carbs per 100 grams: 0 grams

Cocoa
Whisk into hot almond milk for a bitter, chocolatey drink.

Total carbs per 100 grams: 58 grams
Net carbs per 100 grams: 25 grams

Tomatoes
Endless possibilities! Eat raw, roasted, in soups, or in salads.

Total carbs per 100 grams: 4 grams
Net carbs per 100 grams: 3 grams

Coriander/cilantro
Use liberally in sauces, salads, and to garnish hot dishes.

Total carbs per 100 grams: 3.7 grams
Net carbs per 100 grams: 0.9 grams

Leeks
Saute with garlic and olive oil, or add to Winter soups and stews.

Total carbs per 100 grams: 14 grams
Net carbs per 100 grams: 12.2 grams

simple + optimum — core routines for extraordinary living

DOWNLOAD YOUR FREE BONUS: simpleoptimum.com/bookbonus

PLANT-BASED HEALTH | 9 PURPLE FOODS FOR ANTIOXIDANTS

EATING THE RAINBOW

Grapes
Nature's candy! Eat whole, fresh, and raw for a bit of sweetness.

Total carbs per 100 grams: 18 grams
Net carbs per 100 grams: 17.1 grams

Dark berries
Eat fresh when you can, but keep frozen when out of season.

Total carbs per 100 grams: 10 grams (blackberries)
Net carbs per 100 grams: 5 grams (blackberries)

Plums
Perfect snacks, or poached with herbs and rosewater.

Total carbs per 100 grams: 11.4 grams
Net carbs per 100 grams: 10 grams

Passionfruit seeds
Scoop out the sweet, tangy seeds and eat with a spoon.

Total carbs per 100 grams: 23 grams
Net carbs per 100 grams: 13 grams

Purple cauliflower
If you can find it, simply steam or sauté with garlic.

Total carbs per 100 grams: 5 grams
Net carbs per 100 grams: 3 grams

Eggplant
Drizzle with olive oil and roast, or use to make vegetarian curry.

Total carbs per 100 grams: 6 grams
Net carbs per 100 grams: 3 grams

Red cabbage
Finely slice to make a nutrient-dense slaw.

Total carbs per 100 grams: 7 grams
Net carbs per 100 grams: 4.9 grams

Lavender
Dry the purple flowers and use to make herbal tea.

Total carbs per 100 grams: 3 grams
Net carbs per 100 grams: 0 grams

Figs
Eat whole as a unique snack.

Total carbs per 100 grams: 19 grams
Net carbs per 100 grams: 16 grams

simple + optimum
core routines for extraordinary living

DOWNLOAD YOUR FREE BONUS:
simpleoptimum.com/bookbonus

PLANT-BASED HEALTH

8 ORANGE FOODS
For essential vitamins, especially vitamin A and vitamin C. Great for the eyes, the skin, and the immune system.

EATING THE RAINBOW

Oranges
Eat whole, add to salads, or turn into fresh juice.

Total carbs per 100 grams: 9.5 grams
Net carbs per 100 grams: 7.4 grams

Apricots
Fresh, raw, poached, or stewed.

Total carbs per 100 grams: 11 grams
Net carbs per 100 grams: 9 grams

Peaches
Eat as a fresh, juicy snack, or poach and dollop over coconut yogurt.

Total carbs per 100 grams: 10 grams
Net carbs per 100 grams: 8.5 grams

Nectarines
Perfect seasonal snack for sweet cravings.

Total carbs per 100 grams: 11 grams
Net carbs per 100 grams: 9.3 grams

Carrots
Eat as a snack with hummus, add to soups, or roast and add to warm salads.

Total carbs per 100 grams: 9.6 grams
Net carbs per 100 grams: 6.8 grams

Orange bell peppers
Use in hot soups, eat raw, or roast with garlic.

Total carbs per 100 grams: 6.7 grams
Net carbs per 100 grams: 5.5 grams

Pumpkin
A perfect soup veggie, or simply roasted until soft.

Total carbs per 100 grams: 6.5 grams
Net carbs per 100 grams: 6 grams

Sweet potatoes
Roast, steam, mash, or even slice and pop in the toaster.

Total carbs per 100 grams: 20 grams
Net carbs per 100 grams: 17 grams

simple + optimum
core routines for extraordinary living

DOWNLOAD YOUR FREE BONUS:
simpleoptimum.com/bookbonus

PLANT-BASED HEALTH — 7 YELLOW FOODS

For skin-loving vitamins. Yellow fruits and veggies contain beta-carotene which is converted to skin-loving vitamin A in the body.

EATING THE RAINBOW

Bananas
Add to smoothies or eat whole as a snack.

Total carbs per 100 grams: 23 grams
Net carbs per 100 grams: 20.4 grams

Lemons
Squeeze into water or mix with olive oil to create a simple salad dressing.

Total carbs per 100 grams without peel: 9.3 grams
Net carbs per 100 grams without peel: 6.5 grams

Cantaloupe
Eat as a refreshing Summer snack.

Total carbs per 100 grams: 8 grams
Net carbs per 100 grams: 7.1 grams

Mangos
Add to smoothies, or simply eat fresh and raw.

Total carbs per 100 grams: 15 grams
Net carbs per 100 grams: 13.4 grams

Yellow bell peppers
Use to dip into homemade hummus, or chargrill on a barbeque.

Total carbs per 100 grams: 6.7 grams
Net carbs per 100 grams: 5.5 grams

Sweet corn
Grill, boil, or steam for a seasonal addition to your dinner meal.

Total carbs per 100 grams: 19 grams
Net carbs per 100 grams: 16.3 grams

Turmeric
Grate fresh turmeric into hot water with lemon for a soothing drink.

Total carbs per 100 grams: 65 grams
Net carbs per 100 grams: 44 grams

simple + optimum — core routines for extraordinary living

DOWNLOAD YOUR FREE BONUS: simpleoptimum.com/bookbonus

PLANT-BASED HEALTH | 11 | RED FOODS

EATING THE RAINBOW

Red fruits and veggies are full of antioxidants such as lycopene (tomatoes and watermelon), vitamin C (strawberries) and potassium (cherries). Their bright, rich, rosy colors tell us that they are rich in nutrients for overall health, but especially heart health and disease prevention.

Tomatoes
Amazing source of lycopene (powerful antioxidant). Eat raw, cooked, in soups, in salads.

Total carbs per 100 grams: 4 grams
Net carbs per 100 grams: 3 grams

Beets
The prettiest shade of red, provides lots of folate, fiber, and vitamin C.

Total carbs per 100 grams: 7.3 grams
Net carbs per 100 grams: 6.1 grams

Red bell peppers
Sweet, crunchy source of vitamin C, folate, and potassium.

Total carbs per 100 grams: 6.7 grams
Net carbs per 100 grams: 5.5 grams

Rhubarb
Great for the bones with lots of calcium and vitamin K.

Total carbs per 100 grams: 4.5 grams
Net carbs per 100 grams: 2.7 grams

Red chili peppers
The best way to add heat and bright color to any dish. Full of vitamin C, vitamin K, and vitamin B6.

Total carbs per 100 grams: 9 grams
Net carbs per 100 grams: 7.5 grams

Radishes
A rich source of a variety of vitamins and minerals such as potassium and magnesium.

Total carbs per 100 grams: 3.4 grams
Net carbs per 100 grams: 1.8 grams

Strawberries
One of the very best, and tastiest sources of vitamin C. Make the most of these juicy berries when they're in season.

Total carbs per 100 grams: 8 grams
Net carbs per 100 grams: 6 grams

Cranberries
A rich source of B vitamins.

Total carbs per 100 grams: 12 grams
Net carbs per 100 grams: 8 grams

Apples
A fantastic source of dietary fiber. Affordable, sweet, and versatile.

Total carbs per 100 grams: 14 grams
Net carbs per 100 grams: 11.6 grams

Watermelon
Rich, juicy source of lycopene.

Total carbs per 100 grams: 8 grams
Net carbs per 100 grams: 7.6 grams

Cherries
Wonderful source of potassium and fiber.

Total carbs per 100 grams: 12 grams
Net carbs per 100 grams: 10.4 grams

PLANT-BASED HEALTH | 17 GREEN FOODS | EATING THE RAINBOW

Green fruits and veggies are the best possible foods we can choose to nourish and fuel our bodies. Green veggies are packed with the most nutrients of any food source, while offering a low-carb, high-fiber way to fill our plates and tummies. Buy seasonal greens and explore different ways to use them to keep things fresh and exciting all year round.

Spinach
A low-calorie source of fiber, iron, calcium and folic acid. Fantastic both fresh and raw.

Total carbs per 100 grams: 3.6 grams
Net carbs per 100 grams: 1.4 grams

Arugula
A low-carb green with a peppery flavor and lots of nutrients, especially iron, calcium and vitamin A

Total carbs per 100 grams: 3.7 grams
Net carbs per 100 grams: 2.1 grams

Collard greens
A low-calorie, low-carb cruciferous veggie with lots of vitamin K, fiber and antioxidants.

Total carbs per 100 grams: 2 grams
Net carbs per 100 grams: 1 grams

Green apples
A sweet, tangy and crunchy source of fiber and antioxidants. Wonderful raw or cooked.

Total carbs per 100 grams: 14 grams
Net carbs per 100 grams: 11.6 grams

Avocados
A creamy, mild-tasting source of fiber and omega-9 fatty acids (oleic acid).

Total carbs per 100 grams: 9 grams
Net carbs per 100 grams: 2 grams

Kiwi
One of the most potent sources of vitamin C and fiber, kiwifruit are a sweet and tart fruit to enjoy fresh.

Total carbs per 100 grams: 15 grams
Net carbs per 100 grams: 12 grams

Asparagus
A low-calorie veggie with lots of fiber, B vitamins, antioxidants and folate. Asparagus is a prebiotic which means it feeds the healthy bacteria in your gut.

Total carbs per 100 grams: 3.9 grams
Net carbs per 100 grams: 1.8 grams

Green beans
A low-calorie and very versatile green veggie which provides you with manganese, vitamin C, protein and fiber.

Total carbs per 100 grams: 7 grams
Net carbs per 100 grams: 3.6 grams

Zucchini
A very low-calorie, hydrating veggie with lots of vitamin C and potassium.

Total carbs per 100 grams: 3.1 grams
Net carbs per 100 grams: 3 grams

Green peas
Full of fiber and very affordable, green peas pack your diet with nutrients such as vitamin C, vitamin K and manganese.

Total carbs per 100 grams: 14 grams
Net carbs per 100 grams: 9 grams

Watercress
Extremely low in calories, but very high in antioxidants, vitamin K and vitamin C.

Total carbs per 100 grams: 1.3 grams
Net carbs per 100 grams: 0.8 grams

Chard
A low-calorie leafy green with multiple health benefits. Packed with vitamin K, vitamin A and magnesium.

Total carbs per 100 grams: 3.7 grams
Net carbs per 100 grams: 2.1 grams

Bok choy
An extremely low-calorie cruciferous veggie with cancer-fighting nutrients such as folate and various antioxidants. Bok choy is also a great source of selenium.

Total carbs per 100 grams: 2 grams
Net carbs per 100 grams: 1 grams

Broccoli
One of the best sources of vitamin C, with lots of fiber and barely any calories or carbs. A hydrating green veggie with lots of vitamin K1 and folate.

Total carbs per 100 grams: 3.6 grams
Net carbs per 100 grams: 1.4 grams

Artichokes
A wonderful source of fiber, vitamin K, vitamin C and potassium.

Total carbs per 100 grams: 11 grams
Net carbs per 100 grams: 6 grams

Iceberg lettuce
Full of vitamins such as C, A and K. A great source of folate with barely any calories or carbs. A hydrating veggie for your salad base.

Total carbs per 100 grams: 2.9 grams
Net carbs per 100 grams: 1.6 grams

Kale
Completely packed with nutrients including vitamin C, vitamin K and antioxidants such as lutein which protect the eyes.

Total carbs per 100 grams: 8.8 grams
Net carbs per 100 grams: 5.2 grams

DOWNLOAD YOUR FREE BONUS:
simpleoptimum.com/bookbonus

PLANT-BASED HEALTH 5 — BLUE FOODS

EATING THE RAINBOW

You may have noticed that there are very, very few blue plant-based foods out there. There are basically no blue vegetables...unless you count purple or reddish veggies as blue! The reasons behind this are fascinating and highly scientific, to do with the absorption of light and the dominant red, green and yellow colors of fruits and veggies. However, we can incorporate natural blue hues into our plant-based diet by adding edible flowers...and blueberries, of course! But there are a few other blue plant-based foods which are a little more exotic and harder to source, but they're interesting to learn about and look out for all the same.

Blueberries

Low-calorie and extremely delicious, blueberries are one of the very best foods for antioxidants.

Total carbs per 100 grams: 14 grams
Net carbs per 100 grams: 11.6 grams

Blue corn

Blue corn has more protein and less of a carb-hit than regular corn, plus it's a great source of anthocyanins (a powerful antioxidant).

Total carbs per 100 grams: 11.7 grams
Net carbs per 100 grams: 10.6 grams

Borage flower

A delicate and beautiful source of vitamin C. Use as a gorgeous garnish for your dishes, especially if you've got borage growing in your garden.

Total carbs per 100 grams: 3.1 grams
Net carbs per 100 grams: 3.1 grams

Indigo Milk Cap

These elusive and mysterious mushrooms are very hard to come by, and are hard to gather nutritional information about. But we can consider the nutritional value of other mushrooms to get a rough idea of what these special blue fungi contain.

Purple potatoes

Yes, they're called "purple" potatoes, but their hue is cool-toned and almost blue! A great source of antioxidants, fiber, iron and vitamin C.

Total carbs per 100 grams: 17.58 grams
Net carbs per 100 grams: 16.41 grams

simple + optimum
core routines for extraordinary living

DOWNLOAD YOUR FREE BONUS:
simpleoptimum.com/bookbonus

PLANT-BASED HEALTH

12 NON-ACIDIC VEGETABLES, LEGUMES, AND GRAINS

Too much acid in the diet can lead to complications in the body such as kidney stones, brittle bones, and stomach ulcers. Most fresh vegetables have a fairly high pH level (the higher the pH, the least acidic the food, 7 being considered neutral and 14 considered extremely alkaline or non-acidic).

Potatoes
They are high in carbs, but a little bit goes a long way to bulk out your meals. Low acid and rich in minerals.

Total carbs per 100 grams: 17 grams
Net carbs per 100 grams: 14.8 grams

Carrots
The humble carrot is sweet, low-acid, and tasty raw or cooked.

Total carbs per 100 grams: 9.6 grams
Net carbs per 100 grams: 6.8 grams

Sweet corn
Sweet and juicy, great for salads or grilling.

Total carbs per 100 grams: 19 grams
Net carbs per 100 grams: 16.3 grams

White mushrooms
Low carb, low acid, and a versatile addition to any savory dish.

Total carbs per 100 grams: 3.3 grams
Net carbs per 100 grams: 2.3 grams

Collard greens
Very low carb, low acid, and full of vitamins.

Total carbs per 100 grams: 5 grams
Net carbs per 100 grams: 1 gram

Shiitake mushrooms
Low carb, low acid, and a versatile addition to any savory dish.

Total carbs per 100 grams: 7 grams
Net carbs per 100 grams: 4.5 grams

Broccoli
Low carb, low acid, and one of the best greens ever, a real superfood.

Total carbs per 100 grams: 7 grams
Net carbs per 100 grams: 4.4 grams

Cabbage
Affordable, versatile, low-acid, and easy to prepare raw or cooked.

Total carbs per 100 grams: 6 grams
Net carbs per 100 grams: 3.5 grams

Kale
A low-acid leafy green veggie to pump your diet with nutrients, (best cooked if eating in large quantities).

Total carbs per 100 grams: 8.8 grams
Net carbs per 100 grams: 5.2 grams

Zucchini
A low-acid, water rich vegetable which can be enjoyed raw or cooked.

Total carbs per 100 grams: 3.1 grams
Net carbs per 100 grams: 3 grams

Brown rice
A fiber-rich grain great for low-acid, slow-releasing energy.

Total carbs per 100 grams: 23 grams
Net carbs per 100 grams: 21.2 grams

White beans/navy beans
A low-acid source of fiber and energy. Great for dips and soups.

Total carbs per 100 grams: 13 grams
Net carbs per 100 grams: 7 grams

simple + optimum
core routines for extraordinary living

DOWNLOAD YOUR FREE BONUS:
simpleoptimum.com/bookbonus

PLANT-BASED HEALTH

8 NON-ACIDIC FRUITS

Fruits for an alkaline diet (i.e. low-acid diet) for caring for sensitive stomachs. Watch out for citrus fruits as they are one of the higher acidity fruits. Fill your fruit bowl or fruit drawer with these fruits.

Bananas
One of the best low-acid fruits. Filling, sweet, and full of potassium.

Total carbs per 100 grams: 23 grams
Net carbs per 100 grams: 20.4 grams

Papayas
Low in acid, and high in vitamin C.

Total carbs per 100 grams: 11 grams
Net carbs per 100 grams: 9.3 grams

Strawberries
Another fruit which is full of vitamin C but low in acid, one of the tastiest fresh fruits.

Total carbs per 100 grams: 8 grams
Net carbs per 100 grams: 6 grams

Pears
A wonderful source of fiber with a low acid content.

Total carbs per 100 grams: 15 grams
Net carbs per 100 grams: 11.9 grams

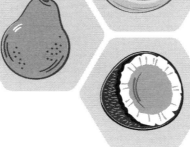

Avocados
Full of healthy fat, low in acid, great source of fiber.

Total carbs per 100 grams: 9 grams
Net carbs per 100 grams: 2 grams

Mangos
A juicy, tropical fruit with low acid and lots of vitamin C.

Total carbs per 100 grams: 15 grams
Net carbs per 100 grams: 13.4 grams

Honeydew Melons
A low-acid melon with lots of vitamin C natural sweetness.

Total carbs per 100 grams: 9 grams
Net carbs per 100 grams: 8.2 grams

Coconut flesh
Low in acid and high in fat and fiber.

Total carbs per 100 grams: 15 grams
Net carbs per 100 grams: 6 grams

simple + optimum
core routines for extraordinary living

DOWNLOAD YOUR FREE BONUS:
simpleoptimum.com/bookbonus

PLANT-BASED HEALTH

10 LOW GLYCEMIC INDEX FOODS

Foods which contain carbohydrates affect blood sugar levels. Some affect blood sugar levels greatly, causing huge spikes and crashes. These are high glycemic index foods. The foods we should be eating most of are low glycemic index foods, or "low GI" foods. They provide us with energy, but keep our blood sugar levels reasonably steady so we don't crash and feel lethargic. Starchy, sugary and processed foods are generally high GI, whereas fruits, veggies, and whole grains are generally low GI.

Yams

A low GI starchy vegetable for providing energy and bulk to meals without spiking blood sugar.

Total carbs per 100 grams: 28 grams
Net carbs per 100 grams: 23.9 grams

Carrots

One of the most affordable veggies with a low GI and lots of vitamin A.

Total carbs per 100 grams: 9.6 grams
Net carbs per 100 grams: 6.8 grams

Sweet potatoes (boiled)

A great substitute for high GI foods, consider veggies such as potatoes. (Boiled sweet potatoes have a much lower GI than baked or roasted sweet potatoes.)

Total carbs per 100 grams: 20 grams
Net carbs per 100 grams: 17 grams

Red bell peppers

A refreshing veggie with lots of vitamin C and a low GI.

Total carbs per 100 grams: 6.7 grams
Net carbs per 100 grams: 5.5 grams

Eggplants

A low GI veggie with a wide range of nutrients.

Total carbs per 100 grams: 6 grams
Net carbs per 100 grams: 3 grams

Apricots

Small, sweet stone fruits with a low GI and vitamin A.

Total carbs per 100 grams: 11 grams
Net carbs per 100 grams: 9 grams

Grapefruits

Tangy, sour citrus with a low GI and lots of antioxidants.

Total carbs per 100 grams: 11 grams
Net carbs per 100 grams: 9.4 grams

Lentils

Affordable source of fiber and low GI energy.

Total carbs per 100 grams: 20 grams
Net carbs per 100 grams: 12 grams

Green peas

A high-fiber, nutrient dense green veggie with a low GI.

Total carbs per 100 grams: 14 grams
Net carbs per 100 grams: 9 grams

Oats

One of the best whole grains to eat for energy without a blood sugar hike.

Total carbs per 100 grams: 66.3 grams
Net carbs per 100 grams: 55.7 grams

Note: buy only oats with "gluten-free" label as they are otherwise often contaminated by gluten. Steel-cut oats are better for effective digestion resulting in stable blood sugar/insulin balance and lower inflammation.

simple + optimum
core routines for extraordinary living

DOWNLOAD YOUR FREE BONUS:
simpleoptimum.com/bookbonus

PLANT-BASED HEALTH

10 FOODS FOR NOURISHING YOURSELF AFTER A STOMACH BUG

Eating food after suffering a stomach bug, virus or flu is very difficult, especially if you're still a little nauseated. But it's important to get your strength and hydration back. Plain foods with low-moderate fiber are great as they replace energy without irritating the tummy. Lots of hydration is also key as you lose vast amounts of hydration during a stomach virus.

Bananas
Soft and mild-flavored, with enough energy to give you some strength, without being too fibrous.

Total carbs per 100 grams: 23 grams
Net carbs per 100 grams: 20.4 grams

Ginger
Grate raw, fresh ginger into water and sip slowly. Ginger is known for its tummy soothing abilities.

Total carbs per 100 grams: 17.9 grams
Net carbs per 100 grams: 14.3 grams

Coconut water
Very hydrating, and full of potassium which helps with balancing electrolytes in the body which can be disrupted after a stomach flu.

Total carbs per 100 grams: 3.7 grams
Net carbs per 100 grams: 2.6 grams

Applesauce
Stew plain apples into a sauce for a gentle, easy to eat food. Cooked apples are less fibrous than raw apples.

Total carbs per 100 grams: 11 grams
Net carbs per 100 grams: 9.9 grams

Peppermint tea
Helps to calm the tummy and relieve pain after stomach bugs.

Total carbs per 100 grams: 0 grams
Net carbs per 100 grams: 0 grams

Butternut squash
A mild, soft veggie which gives energy without upsetting the gut.

Total carbs per 100 grams: 12 grams
Net carbs per 100 grams: 10 grams

Kombucha
Replaces good bacteria in the gut, and helps to hydrate.

Total carbs per 100 grams: 4.4 grams
Net carbs per 100 grams: 4.4 grams

Water
Of course, lots of water is key to rehydrating after a stomach flu. Sip slowly and constantly.

Total carbs per 100 grams: 0 grams
Net carbs per 100 grams: 0 grams

White rice
Plain, mild and starchy to settle the tummy and replace energy.

Total carbs per 100 grams: 28 grams
Net carbs per 100 grams: 27.6 grams

Fennel tea
Soothes upset, irritated tummies.

Total carbs per 100 grams: 0 grams
Net carbs per 100 grams: 0 grams

simple + optimum
core routines for extraordinary living

DOWNLOAD YOUR FREE BONUS:
simpleoptimum.com/bookbonus

PLANT-BASED HEALTH

11 FOODS WITH CANCER-FIGHTING PROPERTIES

Cancer cannot be completely prevented or cured by any diet, plant-based or other. But one of the best ways to heavily reduce your risk of certain cancers is to eat a plant-based diet. Plant-based foods are full of nutrients which help the body to fight disease and stay strong. These foods are some of the very best for helping your body to stay strong against the risk of cancer.

Blueberries
Full of antioxidants and acids such as ellagic acid which can help to stop cancer cells from growing.

Total carbs per 100 grams: 14 grams
Net carbs per 100 grams: 11.6 grams

Strawberries
Full of antioxidants and acids such as ellagic acid which can help to stop cancer cells from growing.

Total carbs per 100 grams: 8 grams
Net carbs per 100 grams: 6 grams

Oats
Contains fiber and antioxidants, both of which help to lower the risk of cancer, especially colorectal cancer.

Total carbs per 100 grams: 66.3 grams
Net carbs per 100 grams: 55.7 grams

Note: buy only oats with "gluten-free" label as they are otherwise often contaminated by gluten. Steel-cut oats are better for effective digestion resulting in stable blood sugar/insulin balance and lower inflammation.

Broccoli
Contains a special substance called sulforaphane which has been proven to help fight and kill cancer cells.

Total carbs per 100 grams: 7 grams
Net carbs per 100 grams: 4.4 grams

Olive oil
Studies have shown olive oil can help prevent breast and bowel cancer, thanks to the many nutrients such as antioxidants and healthy fats.

Total carbs per 100 grams: 0 grams
Net carbs per 100 grams: 0 grams

Green tea
Contains catechins, an antioxidant which helps to fight cancer.

Total carbs per 100 grams: 0 grams
Net carbs per 100 grams: 0 grams

Rapsberries
Full of antioxidants and acids such as ellagic acid which can help to stop cancer cells from growing.

Total carbs per 100 grams: 12 grams
Net carbs per 100 grams: 5 grams

Walnuts
High in healthy fats, and have been proven to help fight against prostate cancer.

Total carbs per 100 grams: 14 grams
Net carbs per 100 grams: 7 grams

Garlic
Studies have shown that garlic can kill cancer cells in animals. Great for strengthening the immune system and providing antibacterial help to the body.

Total carbs per 100 grams: 33.1 grams
Net carbs per 100 grams: 31 grams

Tomatoes
Contains high amounts of antioxidant lycopene, a powerful cancer fighter.

Total carbs per 100 grams: 4 grams
Net carbs per 100 grams: 3 grams

Beans
Extremely high in fiber, they're known to help reduce the risk of colorectal cancer.

Total carbs per 100 grams: 60 grams (kidney beans)
Net carbs per 100 grams: 35 grams (kidney beans)
Total carbs per 100 grams: 63 grams (black beans)
Net carbs per 100 grams: 47 grams (black beans)

DOWNLOAD YOUR FREE BONUS:
simpleoptimum.com/bookbonus

PLANT-BASED HEALTH

8 FOODS FOR SENSITIVE DIGESTIVE SYSTEMS

Foods with low acid, and gentle fiber are great for sensitive tummies. Of course, if you have a particular ailment or stomach condition, follow your doctor's nutrition advice. But for IBS or general sensitivity, try eating these foods to see if they help to ease the discomfort. Foods with low-moderate fiber are gentle on sensitive tummies. It's best to cook fruits and veggies, as it makes them easier to digest.

Bananas
Easy to digest and known to ease diarrhea by adding bulk.

Total carbs per 100 grams: 23 grams
Net carbs per 100 grams: 20.4 grams

Potatoes
A plain, starchy veggie to provide energy without irritation.

Total carbs per 100 grams: 17 grams
Net carbs per 100 grams: 14.8 grams

Ginger
Helps to ease nausea and soothe inflamed tummies.

Total carbs per 100 grams: 17.9 grams
Net carbs per 100 grams: 14.3 grams

Applesauce
Known to help both diarrhea and constipation. Easy to make and good to have on hand during times when your stomach is more sensitive than usual.

Total carbs per 100 grams: 11 grams
Net carbs per 100 grams: 9.9 grams

Oats
Mild, bland, but very nutritious and filling when cooked as oatmeal. Contain gentle fiber to encourage digestion

Total carbs per 100 grams: 66.3 grams
Net carbs per 100 grams: 55.7 grams

Note: buy only oats with "gluten-free" label as they are otherwise often contaminated by gluten. Steel-cut oats are better for effective digestion resulting in stable blood sugar/insulin balance and lower inflammation.

Peppermint tea
Great for soothing irritation and pain, and helping to ease gas and bloating.

Total carbs per 100 grams: 0 grams
Net carbs per 100 grams: 0 grams

Apple cider vinegar
Contains probiotics and helpful enzymes. Diluted in water, it can help to ease digestion and reduce symptoms such as gas and bloating.

Total carbs per 100 grams: 0.9 grams
Net carbs per 100 grams: 0.9 grams

Brown rice
Provides energy and sustenance, with enough fiber to help digestion to flow, but not as fiber-rich as beans and lentils which can be hard on sensitive tummies (however, not the best for diarrhea or a stomach bug as the fiber may be too hard to digest).

Total carbs per 100 grams raw: 77 grams
Net carbs per 100 grams raw: 73.5 grams

PLANT-BASED HEALTH — 11 FOODS FOR RUNNERS

These foods provide powerful, long-lasting energy for runners to fuel-up on before a run. They're also great for after a long or intense run as they replace energy and help the body to repair.

Bananas

An easy to digest source of energy which can help to settle stomachs which are prone to becoming upset after or during a tough run.

Total carbs per 100 grams: 23 grams
Net carbs per 100 grams: 20.4 grams

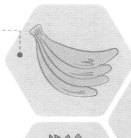

Strawberries

Great for keeping you full and energized during a run. Full of vitamin C to help fight oxidative stress, and potassium to help prevent cramped, sore muscles.

Total carbs per 100 grams: 8 grams
Net carbs per 100 grams: 6 grams

Oranges

A great source of vitamin C which is important for runners as long-term strenuous exercise can cause oxidative damage which vitamin C helps to repair

Total carbs per 100 grams: 9.5 grams
Net carbs per 100 grams: 7.4 grams

Blueberries

Great for keeping you full and energized during a run. Full of vitamin C to help fight oxidative stress, and potassium to help prevent cramped, sore muscles.

Total carbs per 100 grams: 14 grams
Net carbs per 100 grams: 11.6 grams

Raspberries

Great for keeping you full and energized during a run. Full of vitamin C to help fight oxidative stress, and potassium to help prevent cramped, sore muscles.

Totalcarbs per 100 grams: 12 grams
Net carbs per 100 grams: 5 grams

Peanut butter

An energy-dense snack for an extra blast of fuel before a run.

Total carbs per 100 grams: 20 grams
Net carbs per 100 grams: 14 grams

Almonds

Lots of protein and healthy fats, making them a great snack for before a run, and after a run when the muscles are repairing.

Total carbs per 100 grams: 22 grams
Net carbs per 100 grams: 10 grams

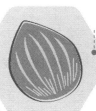

Coffee

Known to give endurance and running performance a boost.

Total carbs per 100 grams: 0 grams (black coffee)
Net carbs per 100 grams: 0 grams (black coffee)

Sweet potatoes

A healthy source of energy for runners to fuel-up on before a long run, and to replace energy afterward.

Total carbs per 100 grams: 20 grams
Net carbs per 100 grams: 17 grams

Black beans

Slow-burning energy to fuel your run, fiber to keep you full, and nutrients such as potassium to help the muscles repair and recover.

Total carbs per 100 grams: 63 grams
Net carbs per 100 grams: 47 grams

Coconut water

Deeply hydrating and great for replacing electrolytes lost due to sweating and exertion.

Total carbs per 100 grams: 3.7 grams
Net carbs per 100 grams: 2.6 grams

simple + optimum — core routines for extraordinary living

DOWNLOAD YOUR FREE BONUS: simpleoptimum.com/bookbonus

PLANT-BASED HEALTH
12 FOODS FOR MEAT CRAVINGS

Sometimes it can be hard for previous meat-eaters to transition to a plant-based diet. If you are craving meat, try these ingredients which may help to satisfy you. Plants with chewier textures and the ability to soak up savory flavors are great for dealing with meat cravings.

Almonds
Chopped or ground nuts can add chewiness and satiating fats to vegetarian dishes which have been adjusted to replace meat.

Total carbs per 100 grams: 22 grams
Net carbs per 100 grams: 10 grams

Pecans
Chopped or ground nuts can add chewiness and satiating fats to vegetarian dishes which have been adjusted to replace meat.

Total carbs per 100 grams: 14 grams
Net carbs per 100 grams: 4 grams

Walnuts
Chopped or ground nuts can add chewiness and satiating fats to vegetarian dishes which have been adjusted to replace meat.

Total carbs per 100 grams: 14 grams
Net carbs per 100 grams: 7 grams

Pumpkin
Can replace meat in dishes such as curries, burger patties, and risottos.

Total carbs per 100 grams: 6.5 grams
Net carbs per 100 grams: 6 grams

Spices
Spices at a wide range of layered flavors to vegetables and legumes, creating a rounded dish without the need for meat.

It depends on which spices you choose, but most common spices have between 50 to 60 total grams of carbohydrates per 100 grams of spice

Eggplant
An absorbent vegetable which can soak up flavor. A soft, meaty texture.

Total carbs per 100 grams: 6 grams
Net carbs per 100 grams: 3 grams

Portobello mushrooms
A meaty texture with an earthy, savory flavor. Great for replacing meat in patties and burgers. Great for adding to stews and pastas.

Total carbs per 100 grams: 3.3 grams
Net carbs per 100 grams: 2.3 grams

Sweet potatoes
A starchy, nutrient-dense vegetable which can be added to any traditional meat dish for a vegetarian alternative.

Total carbs per 100 grams: 20 grams
Net carbs per 100 grams: 17 grams

Garlic
Adds depth of flavor to vegetarian dishes, often satiating the craving for meat.

Total carbs per 100 grams: 33.1 grams
Net carbs per 100 grams: 31 grams

Onions
The savory flavor of onions can often satisfy meat cravings in dishes such as stews and curries.

Total carbs per 100 grams: 9 grams (white onions)
Net carbs per 100 grams: 7.3 grams (white onions)

Black beans
Beans provide a substantial texture to replace the bulk of meat. They absorb flavors really well, so can be seasoned to create satisfying savory vegetarian dishes.

Total carbs per 100 grams: 63 grams
Net carbs per 100 grams: 47 grams

Chickpeas
Great for using as the basis for patties and rissoles, replacing ground meats.

Total carbs per 100 grams: 61 grams
Net carbs per 100 grams: 44 grams

PLANT-BASED HEALTH
7 FOODS FOR BUTTERS AND SPREADS

Nut and seed butters are a wonderful alternative to animal-derived butters and spreads. Make them yourself by grinding in a powerful blender with a pinch of sea salt.

Peanuts
The classic nut butter, full of energy in small doses.

Total carbs per 100 grams: 16.1 grams
Net carbs per 100 grams: 7.6 grams

Almonds
Lots of healthy fats and protein, great for spreading on fruit slices.

Total carbs per 100 grams: 22 grams
Net carbs per 100 grams: 10 grams

Hazelnuts
Combine with cocoa to create a healthy homemade chocolate-nut spread.

Total carbs per 100 grams: 17 grams
Net carbs per 100 grams: 7 grams

Cashew nuts
Tasty way to up your vitamin E intake.

Total carbs per 100 grams: 30 grams
Net carbs per 100 grams: 26.7 grams

Brazil nuts
A lesser-known nut butter, but very tasty and great for providing magnesium.

Total carbs per 100 grams: 12 grams
Net carbs per 100 grams: 4 grams

Pumpkin seeds
Provides lots of Omega-3 fatty acids to care for your skin and heart.

Total carbs per 100 grams: 6.5 grams
Net carbs per 100 grams: 6 grams

Sesame seeds
Slow-roasted sesame seeds create a seed butter rich in healthy fats.

Total carbs per 100 grams: 23 grams
Net carbs per 100 grams: 11 grams

PLANT-BASED HEALTH
6 SPICES: BENEFITS, FLAVOR AND USES
Benefits, flavors and uses of some of the most popular and delicious spices to add to your cooking arsenal.

Net carbs: per tablespoon of dried spices, there is generally no more than 3 grams of net carbs, and some with a far lower carb count than that. Therefore, a small pinch of spice per serving won't add any extra carbs to worry about.

Cinnamon
Benefits: helps to lower blood sugar, lower the risk of heart disease, offers anti-inflammatory properties, and antioxidants.

Flavor: warming, earthy, slightly sweet, slightly spicy.

Uses: add to oatmeal, plant-based baking, or add a cinnamon quill to herbal teas and hot citrus drinks. Can also be added to spice mixes for curries.

Cumin
Benefits: fantastic for encouraging good digestion, can help to soothe IBS symptoms. A good source of iron.

Flavor: a very warm, earthy flavor, but does not hold any spice. Some describe it as very slightly lemony, and very fragrant.

Uses: add to Mexican seasoning mixes, curries, and rubs for roasted veggies. Use as whole seeds, or as a ground powder.

Chili
Benefits: great for supporting immunity and fighting inflammation.

Flavor: characteristically hot and spicy.

Uses: adds spice to any savory dish or spice mix. Add to Mexican dishes, vegetarian chili, or to add heat anywhere needed. Can also be added to non-dairy hot chocolate to add a unique hit of heat

Turmeric
Benefits: a powerful anti-inflammatory, as well as being an effective antioxidant.

Flavor: distinctively bitter, with a vibrant golden color.

Uses: commonly used in curries and spice mixes, grated fresh turmeric can be added to teas or plant milk to create a turmeric latte (can use powdered turmeric too).

Coriander seeds
Benefits: the antiseptic nature of coriander seeds helps to soothe certain skin issues such as eczema. Helps to regulate healthy blood sugar levels. Helps to encourage proper digestion.

Flavor: warm, fragrant, nutty, and slightly citrusy to the palate.

Uses: a staple in curry spice mixes, Mexican seasonings, relishes and chutneys, and as a rub for vegetables. Also used for medicinal purposes especially related to digestion and upset stomachs.

Paprika
Benefits: provides a lot of antioxidants and supports heart health.

Flavor: sweet or smoky, adds a unique, rounded flavor to savory dishes.

Uses: add to vegetarian chili, roasted veggies, vegetarian stews and soups.

PLANT-BASED HEALTH 9

LEAFY GREENS: BENEFITS AND USES

We all know that leafy green vegetables are among the very best foods we can eat on a daily basis. But it pays to know what nutrients and benefits each leafy green can provide us, as well as a few tips on how to utilize them.

Spinach

Benefits: spinach provides the body with fiber which is great for keeping the bowels regular and healthy, as well as regulating healthy cholesterol levels. Famously, spinach is a great vegetarian source of iron, as well as a wide variety of vitamins such as vitamin A.

Uses: add to smoothies, salads, curries, stews, and gluten free pasta dishes (i.e. zucchini noodles).

Total carbs per 100 grams: 3.6 grams
Net carbs per 100 grams: 1.4 grams

Lettuce

(Specifically iceberg lettuce but all lettuces have high nutritional value.)

Benefits: a hydrating veggie thanks to the high water content. It provides you with vitamin C, protein, folate, vitamin A, and potassium. Thanks to these nutrients, lettuce is great to add to your diet for immunity, skin health, muscle repair, healthy blood pressure, and eye health.

Uses: a favorite, leafy base for salads. Add to sandwiches and rolls. Use in place of tortillas and rice paper for tacos and fresh spring rolls. Use in place of burger buns for low-carb veggie burgers.

Total carbs per 100 grams: 2.9 grams
Net carbs per 100 grams: 1.6 grams

Watercress

Benefits: supports healthy bones with a high content of vitamin K, reducing the risk of osteoporosis. Full of antioxidants which support your body at cell level, helping to fight illnesses such as cancer. Contains cancer-fighting compounds called isothiocyanates. Supports the immune system with a generous dose of vitamin C.

Uses: add raw to salads for a peppery hit. Sauté with other leafy greens and olive oil for a healthy side dish. Add to sandwich fillings.

Total carbs per 100 grams: 1.3 grams
Net carbs per 100 grams: 0.8 grams

Broccoli

Benefits: contains sulforaphane which has been proven to help fight and kill cancer cells. Strengthens the immune system with plenty of vitamin C. Aids digestion with plenty of healthy fiber, which is also great for healthy cholesterol. Provides lots of antioxidants to protect the body at cell level. Vitamin K and calcium are great for keeping the bones healthy and strong.

Uses: use raw in salads or with veggie dips. Sauté in stir-fries. Add to roasted veggie salads. Use to make broccoli soup, or add to curries. Simply steam and serve as a side to any dish.

Total carbs per 100 grams: 7 grams
Net carbs per 100 grams: 4.4 grams

Kale

Benefits: kale contains lutein which is great for supporting eye health. It provides you with protein, fiber, folate, and vitamin C (as well as many other vitamins). These nutrients make kale a great supporter of the immune system, the bones, and overall wellness.

Uses: make kale chips with sea salt, add small amounts to smoothies, sauté, add to soups, salads, and stews. (Only use small portions of raw kale as it studies show it can be detrimental to your thyroid. You'd have to eat an awful lot of raw kale to experience this, but it pays to be careful).

Total carbs per 100 grams: 8.8 grams
Net carbs per 100 grams: 5.2 grams

Collard greens

Benefits: high levels of vitamin A protect your eyes and skin. Vitamin K and folate both work to keep your bones dense and strong. Like most green veggies, collard greens are a great source of vitamin C.

Uses: chop and add to soups, stews, rissottos, or vegetarian lasagnas. You can add them to any cooked veggie side dish for a nutrient boost.

Total carbs per 100 grams: 5 grams
Net carbs per 100 grams: 1 gram

Cabbage

Benefits: contains sulforaphane which helps to lower risk of cancer. High levels of vitamin K which support the bones, and also help to slow and prevent blood clots.

Uses: finely shred and use to make coleslaw. Add raw cabbage to salads and sandwich fillings. Lightly sauté with garlic and olive oil as a side dish.

Total carbs per 100 grams: 6 grams
Net carbs per 100 grams: 3.5 grams

Swiss chard

Benefits: packed with bone-loving vitamin K which also prevents risk of blood clots. Vitamin A supports skin and eyes. Low-carb, low-calorie, and nutrient-dense.

Uses: finely slice and sauté as a side dish. Add to rissottos, stews, and soups.

Total carbs per 100 grams: 3.7 grams
Net carbs per 100 grams: 2.1 grams

Bok choy

Benefits: provides lots of vitamin C for supporting the immune system. Vitamin K and calcium for the bones, and vitamin A for the eyes and vital organs.

Uses: sauté with sesame oil, steam and serve with Asian-inspired veggie dishes.

Total carbs per 100 grams: 2 grams
Net carbs per 100 grams: 1 gram

DOWNLOAD YOUR FREE BONUS:
simpleoptimum.com/bookbonus

PLANT-BASED HEALTH 9 — PLANT MILKS: FLAVOR AND USES

Following a plant-based diet means swapping dairy milk for plant-based alternatives. Small nuts, rice, and coconut provide delicious, nutritious milks. Add plant-based milks to your coffee, tea, hot chocolate, smoothies, or simply as a cold drink.

Almond milk
Flavor: mild, slightly floral.

Uses: add to smoothies and baking, or pour over cereal. You may find it curdles when added to hot coffee.

Total carbs per 1 cup/250mls: 8 grams
Net carbs per 1 cup/250mls: 7 grams

Coconut milk
Flavor: creamy, tropical, coconutty.

Uses: great added to black coffee or to make lattes. Add to smoothies, baking, and even curries and soups.

Total carbs per 1 cup/250mls: 12.5 grams
Net carbs per 1 cup/250mls: 12 grams

Rice milk
Flavor: mild, watery, a little sweet.

Uses: add to smoothies and baking, pour over cereal.

Total carbs per 1 cup/250mls: 22 grams
Net carbs per 1 cup/250mls: 21.3 grams

Oat milk
Flavor: mild, watery flavor.

Uses: add to smoothies and baking. It may curdle when added to hot coffee. A high-carb plant-based milk best for morning meals when you need extra energy.

Total carbs per 1 cup/250mls: 28.8 grams
Net carbs per 1 cup/250mls: 25 grams

Cashew milk
Flavor: creamy, nutty.

Uses: pour over cereal, add to smoothies, use to make lattes.

Total carbs per 1 cup/250mls: 1 gram
Net carbs per 1 cup/250mls: 1 gram

Hemp milk
(Nutrition may differ from brand to brand.)

Flavor: nutty and light.

Uses: add to cereal, smoothies, coffee, baking.

Total carbs per 1 cup/250mls: 0 grams
Net carbs per 1 cup/250mls: 0 grams

PLANT-BASED HEALTH — 8 POPULAR SEEDS

Seeds are like tiny little powerhouses of nutrition. They contain healthy fats (omega-3 fatty acids), fiber, and a wide range of other nutrients. Great as snacks on their own or with fruit. Great for making seed butters or toasting and adding to salads and various vegetarian dishes.

Chia seeds

Absorbent, gelatinous, and full of fiber. Mix with nut milk to create chia pudding. Add to homemade granola, plant-based baked goods and smoothies.

Total carbs per 100 grams raw: 44 grams
Net carbs per 100 grams raw: 6 grams

Pumpkin seeds

Full of healthy fats. Toast and add to salads or eat as a snack. Grind to make pumpkin seed butter. Add to homemade cereals.

Total carbs per 100 grams: 54 grams
Net carbs per 100 grams: 36 grams

Sunflower seeds

Amazing source of vitamin E. Eat alone as a snack. Add to salads, breakfast dishes such as granola, and vegetarian patties.

Total carbs per 100 grams: 20 grams
Net carbs per 100 grams: 11 grams

Poppy seeds

Great source of fiber, omega-6 fatty acids, copper and iron. Add to salad dressings, baking, and dry veggie curries.

Total carbs per 100 grams raw: 28 grams
Net carbs per 100 grams raw: 8 grams

Sesame seeds

Wonderful source of protein, copper and selenium. Toast and add to baking, salads, or grind to make sesame butter.

Total carbs per 100 grams: 23 grams
Net carbs per 100 grams: 11 grams

Quinoa

A rich source of protein, fiber, magnesium, and folate. Rinse before you cook, to remove the bitter coating. Boil and mix with veggies to make a warm salad, or use as a base for patties.

Total carbs per 100 grams raw: 60 grams
Net carbs per 100 grams raw: 52 grams

Hemp seeds

Great plant-based source of protein and omega fatty acids (3 and 6).

Total carbs per 100 grams raw: 6.7 grams
Net carbs per 100 grams raw: 3.4 grams

Flax seeds

Affordable, plant-based source of fiber and omega-3 fatty acids. Grind them up and use in baking, or sprinkle into your smoothies or over your chia seed pudding.

Total carbs per 100 grams: 28.9 grams
Net carbs per 100 grams: 1.6 grams

PLANT-BASED HEALTH
9 POPULAR NUTS

Nuts are a tasty, crunchy source of many nutrients such as healthy fats and vitamins. Keep a jar of nuts in the pantry to grab when you need a healthy snack. You can even toast them with a pinch of sea salt, or toss them with cinnamon and honey for a sweet treat.

Almonds
Total carbs per 100 grams: 22 grams
Net carbs per 100 grams: 10 grams

Walnuts
Total carbs per 100 grams: 14 grams
Net carbs per 100 grams: 7 grams

Pecans
Total carbs per 100 grams: 14 grams
Net carbs per 100 grams: 4 grams

Macadamia nuts
Total carbs per 100 grams: 14 grams
Net carbs per 100 grams: 5 grams

Pistachio nuts
Total carbs per 100 grams: 28 grams
Net carbs per 100 grams: 18 grams

Hazelnuts
Total carbs per 100 grams: 17 grams
Net carbs per 100 grams: 7 grams

Peanuts
Total carbs per 100 grams: 16.1 grams
Net carbs per 100 grams: 7.6 grams

Brazil nuts
Total carbs per 100 grams: 12 grams
Net carbs per 100 grams: 4 grams

Chestnuts
Total carbs per 100 grams: 28 grams
Net carbs per 100 grams: 23 grams

DOWNLOAD YOUR FREE BONUS:
simpleoptimum.com/bookbonus

PLANT-BASED HEALTH — 17 TASTY SNACKS

Easy foods to eat with your hands, no cooking required. Most of these foods can be stored in the pantry and will last a while, so there's no risk of wastage. Eat veggies as raw snacks when they're at their freshest point, and add to soups, stews, and roast when they get a little past their peak freshness.

NUTS

A great source of energy and filling fats. Rich in nutrients such as selenium.

Almonds
Total carbs per 100 grams: 22 grams
Net carbs per 100 grams: 10 grams

Walnuts
Total carbs per 100 grams: 14 grams
Net carbs per 100 grams: 7 grams

Pistachio nuts
Total carbs per 100 grams: 28 grams
Net carbs per 100 grams: 18 grams

Macadamia nuts
Total carbs per 100 grams: 14 grams
Net carbs per 100 grams: 5 grams

Pecans
Total carbs per 100 grams: 14 grams
Net carbs per 100 grams: 4 grams

Popcorn
A low-calorie snack when air popped, with only a pinch of sea salt added. Great source of fiber.
Total carbs per 100 grams: 74 grams
Net carbs per 100 grams: 61 grams

BUTTER

Peanut butter
Salty, satisfying, and a little goes a long way. Make yourself by blending roasted peanuts until creamy.
Total carbs per 100 grams: 20 grams
Net carbs per 100 grams: 14 grams

Almond butter
A creamy alternative to peanut butter. A tasty source of vitamin E and protein. Spread onto apple slices or plant-based, gluten-free crackers.
Total carbs per 100 grams: 19 grams
Net carbs per 100 grams: 9 grams

SEEDS

Great for adding to nuts and dried fruits to make raw, plant-based snack bags. Seeds top up your intake of healthy fats and fiber.

Pumpkin seeds
Total carbs per 100 grams: 54 grams
Net carbs per 100 grams: 36 grams

Sunflower seeds
Total carbs per 100 grams: 20 grams
Net carbs per 100 grams: 11 grams

VEGGIE STICKS

Celery, carrot, cucumber, and bell pepper are all wonderful snacks when sliced raw and eaten alone or dipped into homemade hummus and bean dips.

Dates
Sticky, sweet morsels, great for satisfying a major sweet craving.
Total carbs per 100 grams: 75 grams
Net carbs per 100 grams: 67 grams

Bell peppers
Total carbs per 100 grams: 6.7 grams
Net carbs per 100 grams: 5.5 grams

Carrots
Total carbs per 100 grams: 9.6 grams
Net carbs per 100 grams: 6.8 grams

Cucumbers
Total carbs per 100 grams: 4 grams
Net carbs per 100 grams: 4 grams

Celery
Total carbs per 100 grams: 3.8 grams
Net carbs per 100 grams: 2 grams

DRIED

Dried seaweed/nori
A tasty, crunchy alternative to potato chips.
Total carbs per 100 grams: 5 grams
Net carbs per 100 grams: 4.7 grams

Dried chickpeas
When roasted in the oven, chickpeas dry out and become crispy. Coat in sea salt and spices for a moreish snack.
Total carbs per 100 grams: 61 grams
Net carbs per 100 grams: 44 grams

simple + optimum — core routines for extraordinary living

DOWNLOAD YOUR FREE BONUS:
simpleoptimum.com/bookbonus

PLANT-BASED HEALTH

11 SWEET TREATS

Cravings for sweet foods can be difficult to satisfy. Luckily, there are many plant-based goodies which are sweet on their own, or create a delectable sweet treat when paired with other plant-based foods. Plant-based foods which are very sweet are often high in carbohydrates and natural sugars. For this reason, they're best enjoyed in small doses.

BERRIES
Nature's candy. Eat fresh and raw for a nutrient-dense sweet, tangy treat.

COCOA
Combine with honey and nut milk for a decadent, plant-based hot chocolate.

Rapsberries
Total carbs per 100 grams: 12 grams
Net carbs per 100 grams: 5 grams

Strawberries
Total carbs per 100 grams: 8 grams
Net carbs per 100 grams: 6 grams

Blueberries
Total carbs per 100 grams: 14 grams
Net carbs per 100 grams: 11.6 grams

Boysenberries
Total carbs per 100 grams: 22 grams
Net carbs per 100 grams: 19.4 grams

Cocoa
Total carbs per 100 grams: 58 grams
Net carbs per 100 grams: 25 grams

DATES
Sticky, chewy, and extremely sweet. High in carbs, so one or two should suffice.

Figs
Total carbs per 100 grams: 19 grams
Net carbs per 100 grams: 16 grams

FIGS AND HONEY
Two sweet foods combined, perfect for a breakfast or dessert treat.

Dates
Total carbs per 100 grams: 75 grams
Net carbs per 100 grams: 67 grams

Prunes
Total carbs per 100 grams: 64 grams
Net carbs per 100 grams: 57 grams

Honey
Total carbs per 100 grams: 82 grams
Net carbs per 100 grams: 81.8 grams

APPLE AND ALMOND BUTTER
A sweet, tangy treat with added protein and vitamin E.

PRUNES
Sweet, easy to eat, and great for adding extra fiber.

Apples
Total carbs per 100 grams: 14 grams
Net carbs per 100 grams: 11.6 grams

Almond butter
Total carbs per 100 grams: 19 grams
Net carbs per 100 grams: 9 grams

simple + optimum
core routines for extraordinary living

DOWNLOAD YOUR FREE BONUS:
simpleoptimum.com/bookbonus

PLANT-BASED HEALTH 4

FAQ ABOUT TURMERIC

The golden root with many uses and an impressive variety of health benefits. You can use fresh turmeric, dried and powdered turmeric, or both.

WHAT IS TURMERIC?

- A root similar to ginger...in fact they're in the same family!
- The turmeric plant has a straight, long stem and stiff, green leaves
- The turmeric we eat is called a "rhizome", which grows underground a root
- The main ingredient in cumin is a compound called "curcumin" which holds the medicinal properties
- Turmeric likes to grow in warm climates with decent rain
- Its original birthplace is thought to be Southeast Asia and India
- Turmeric rhizomes are used fresh, or dried to create pastes, powder mixes, and medicines
- Turmeric has been used for thousands of years to make dye, medicines, and in certain religious ceremonies
- You can buy dried turmeric powder in the spice section of your supermarket
- Good supermarkets, Asian stores, and specialty produce stores will have fresh turmeric rhizomes

Turmeric

Nutritional value per 100 grams (fresh turmeric root):
Calories: 354
Fat: 9.88 grams
Protein: 7.83 grams
Total carbs: 64.9 grams
Net carbs: 43.9 grams

HOW DOES IT HELP THE BODY?

- Turmeric has strong anti-inflammatory abilities
- Chronic inflammation contributes to many diseases, so anti-inflammatory foods and medicines are very important for health and longevity
- A powerful antioxidant to fight against aging and disease
- Turmeric can help to support people suffering from depression
- Turmeric helps to keep brain function strong, and reduces risk of Alzheimer's
- Turmeric supports the heart and reduces risk of heart disease
- Turmeric (thanks to curcumin) can help to reduce risk of cancer
- Due to the anti-inflammatory properties, turmeric can ease arthritis symptoms

DRIED OR FRESH?

- Use both if you can!
- Fresh turmeric does retain more nutrients and oils, but dried turmeric is handy to have on hand as it lasts longer and is easy to use
- When choosing a fresh turmeric rhizome, find nice and firm ones as they're fresher and better quality
- You can freeze fresh turmeric rhizomes to make them last longer
- To use fresh turmeric, grate it, cut into slices, and boil or add straight to dishes and drinks

Add to plant milk, juice or tea

Add to salads

HOW TO USE TURMERIC?

- Use dried turmeric to make your own curry pastes and powder mixes, it will give a rich golden shade
- Add grated fresh turmeric to curries, stews, and soups for color and flavor
- Add powdered turmeric to plant milk to make a turmeric latte
- Boil fresh turmeric with plant milk and spices to make a fresh turmeric drink
- Add a chunk of fresh turmeric to your juicer or smoothie for a nutrient-dense addition
- Simmer fresh turmeric with water and other spices such as ginger, cinnamon, and cloves to make a warming turmeric tea
- Grate fresh turmeric and add to salads, vegetarian patties, and any other dish where you want a rich color and earthy flavor
- Mix together turmeric and honey and use as an anti-bacterial face mask to treat acne and make the skin glow (do a test patch first, to ensure you're not allergic, and beware you might look a little golden for a moment!)

simple + optimum
core routines for extraordinary living

DOWNLOAD YOUR FREE BONUS:
simpleoptimum.com/bookbonus

PLANT-BASED HEALTH 3

FAQ ABOUT APPLE CIDER VINEGAR
An affordable, fermented liquid with many uses and great benefits to health.

WHAT IS APPLE CIDER VINEGAR, HOW IS IT MADE?

- Apple cider vinegar is a very sharp vinegar made from apples with a two-step fermentation process
- The juice of apples is mixed with yeast and bacteria
- The fermentation process begins and the sugars in the apple juice turn into alcohol
- The next fermentation process is begun by adding another kind of bacteria which turns the alcohol into acetic acid (vinegar!)
- Some apple cider vinegars have a cloudy appearance as opposed to clear, this is because they still have the cultures and bacteria which were added to begin the fermentation processes

Apple cider vinegar

Nutritional value per 100 grams:
Calories: 22
Fat: 0 grams
Protein: 0 grams
Total carbs: 0.9 grams
Net carbs: 0.9 grams

HOW DOES IT HELP THE BODY?

- Apple cider vinegar helps to keep blood sugar levels at a healthy place, and improves insulin sensitivity. This makes it a great ingredient for sufferers of type 2 diabetes to use
- Apple cider vinegar can help to keep you full and reduces the risk of overeating
- It can help you to reach your weight loss goals by keeping your appetite at bay
- Apple cider vinegar can support your heart and reduce the risk of heart disease, as it helps to regulate healthy cholesterol levels
- Applying apple cider vinegar topically to the hair can restore proper pH levels, leaving the hair strong, clean, and lustrous
- Apple cider vinegar helps digestion by helping to break down foods more efficiently
- Some people find that drinking apple cider vinegar helps to reduce bloating and keeps their digestion regular and comfortable

Add to salad dressings

Always dilute with water!

HOW TO USE APPLE CIDER VINEGAR?

- Never drink undiluted apple cider vinegar, it will not taste or feel good! Always dilute with water
- Add a dash to your morning water and sip slowly (drinking all in one go on an empty stomach can make you feel sick)
- Start off with small amounts if you're new to drinking apple cider vinegar, then you can slowly increase the dosage from 1 teaspoon to 1 tablespoon
- Since vinegar kills bacteria, you can use it to make homemade cleaning spray for disinfecting household surfaces
- Add to salad dressings

PLANT-BASED HEALTH

STEVIA: SWEETENER WITHOUT THE NASTIES

Sweeten your tea, coffee, desserts and sweet treats without using blood sugar spiking sugar.

WHAT IS STEVIA?

- Stevia is a plant belonging to the chrysanthemum family
- Stevia leaves contain a sweet component called rebaudioside A which is extracted from the leaves and used as a powder or a liquid
- There have been some studies which suggest that large amounts of stevia may have an adverse effect on health, but this is not a worry to you if you only use small amounts
- Stevia is said to be 200 times sweeter than sugar!

200 times sweeter than sugar!
For every cup of sugar, add 1 teaspoon of liquid or powder stevia.

White powder

Liquid

Green powder

Stevia
Nutritional value per teaspoon:
(may vary slightly between brands)
Calories: 0
Fat: 0 grams
Protein: 0 grams
Total carbs: 3 grams
Net carbs: 3 grams

Add to tea or coffee

HOW TO USE STEVIA:

- Look for pure, organic stevia products without any other added ingredients
- Use in modest amounts, a little pinch into your tea or coffee to add sweetness should suffice
- Since stevia is so much sweeter than sugar, use it sparingly in baking. Start off with a small amount, taste, and add more if need be
- A good general rule to follow is for every cup of sugar, add 1 teaspoon of liquid or powder stevia

simple + optimum
core routines for extraordinary living

DOWNLOAD YOUR FREE BONUS:
simpleoptimum.com/bookbonus

PLANT-BASED HEALTH 3: FAQ ABOUT GARLIC

Garlic is a small bulb with a huge amount of flavor. It is a favorite ingredient for giving savory dishes depth of flavor. It also has some pretty amazing nutritional benefits, which we will explore below.

WHAT IS GARLIC?

- Garlic is a bulb which is part of the onion family. Its siblings are onions, shallots, leeks and chives
- Garlic comprises of little cloves, each wrapped in skin, making them easy to separate from the bulb and use in small or large amounts
- The history of garlic being used as a medicinal plant dates far, far back, as far as ancient Egypt and ancient Greece
- Interestingly, garlic was given to sportsmen and laborers in ancient societies because it was known to boost endurance and performance

Garlic

Nutritional value per 100 grams:
Calories: 149
Fat: 1 gram
Protein: 6 grams
Total carbs: 33 grams
Net carbs: 31 grams

WHAT ARE THE BENEFITS?

- Garlic supports the immune system, making it a great ingredient to use during cold and flu seasons
- Garlic is a great source of antioxidants to help the body to repair at cell level. This is good news for reducing signs of aging
- Garlic can help to reduce levels of cholesterol, therefore protecting the heart and reducing risk of heart disease
- Garlic can help to reduce the risk of Alzheimer's disease
- When garlic is consumed in high doses, it can help to reduce high blood pressure
- Garlic has antiviral and antibacterial properties, which can be harnessed by using garlic topically on acne and skin infections
- Garlic is an anti-inflammatory which helps to reduce risk of chronic diseases

Add to hummus and dips

Add to warm veggie salads

HOW TO USE GARLIC?

- Finely chop and add to savory dishes such as curries, soups, stews, veggie patties and falafels
- Roast in the oven to create a soft texture and add to warm veggie salads
- Use as a topical treatment for skin issues such as acne (check with your doctor first, and do a spot test)
- Use to add strong flavor to any savory dish, raw or cooked
- Add to hummus and dips

PLANT-BASED HEALTH 3: FAQ ABOUT GINGER: THE MIRACLE ROOT, THE TOP BENEFITS AND HOW TO HARNESS THEM

WHAT IS GINGER?

- Ginger is a flowering plant which has a "rhizome" anchoring it to the soil. A rhizome is a root which grows beneath the earth, and it's the part of the ginger plant that we eat. It has an outer skin which is removed to reveal the fleshy, moist, somewhat tough and stringy interior.

- Ginger has been harvested and used for thousands of years, for culinary and medicinal purposes. Indian and Chinese cultures were the first to harness the powerful properties of ginger, but it eventually made its way across the world and is now a popular staple in international kitchens.

- Ginger can be dried and powdered, pickled, or simply grated or sliced and used raw.

Ginger

Nutritional value per 100 grams:
(raw ginger rhizome)
Calories: 80
Fat: 0.8 grams
Protein: 1.8 grams
Total carbs: 18 grams
Net carbs: 16 grams

WHAT ARE THE TOP BENEFITS?

- Anti-inflammatory (which helps to stave off diseases)
- A great source of antioxidants
- Helps to soothe joint and muscular aches and pains
- Soothes bloated tummies
- Helps to ease nausea and stomach aches, especially after overindulging
- Helps to keep insulin levels steady and stable
- It is antimicrobial and antifungal which is why we consume ginger when we have a cold or flu

Add to smoothies, hot chocolate or tea

HOW TO USE GINGER?

- Grate fresh, raw ginger and combine with spices to make curry pastes
- Add finely grated fresh ginger to dressings and sauces
- Add an inch of fresh ginger to your smoothies or whole juices
- Mix fresh ginger with boiling water and lemon juice for a tummy-soothing tea
- Chew on fresh ginger as a fast remedy for a tummy ache
- Use dried ginger to add warmth and depth to natural hot chocolates or chai teas

PLANT-BASED HEALTH
4 FABULOUS FUNGHI – GUIDE TO MUSHROOMS AND HOW TO USE THEM

WHAT ARE MUSHROOMS? WHERE AND HOW DO THEY GROW?

Mushrooms are the spongy, earthy, soft veggies we find growing in damp, dark areas such as forests and woods. Technically, mushrooms are a fungus; they grow above the earth from a network of mold beneath the soil. Mushrooms are different from other familiar plant foods such as leafy greens, as they don't gather energy from sunlight. Instead, they gather everything they need from the organic matter in the soil they're growing in. Another interesting fact to remember is that unlike other plants, mushrooms aren't born from seeds, they're born from spores.

Mushrooms absolutely love damp, dark environments with temperatures ranging from 60 to 90 degrees Fahrenheit depending on the kind of mushroom. This is why we often find mushrooms growing at the base of trees, as there's enough shade, organic matter, and lots of moisture for the mushrooms to thrive.

TYPES OF MUSHROOMS
and their nutritional values per 100 grams (raw):

Portabella

Calories: 149
Fat: 1 gram
Protein: 6 grams
Total carbs: 33 grams
Net carbs: 31 grams

Button (white)

Calories: 149
Fat: 1 gram
Protein: 6 grams
Total carbs: 33 grams
Net carbs: 31 grams

Shiitake
Calories: 149
Fat: 1 gram
Protein: 6 grams
Total carbs: 33 grams
Net carbs: 31 grams

Porcini
Calories: 149
Fat: 1 gram
Protein: 6 grams
Total carbs: 33 grams
Net carbs: 31 grams

NUTRITIONAL BENEFITS OF MUSHROOMS:

- They contain lots of B vitamins such as riboflavin and niacin
- Button mushrooms are a source of vitamin D
- They have a high water content which makes them a great veggie for hydration
- They have lots of potassium (especially portabella mushrooms)
- Packed with antioxidants to fight free-radicals
- Great source of fiber
- They can help our bodies to fight against cancer
- They protect the heart by lowering cholesterol
- Mushrooms are low-carb and low calorie, but very tasty and filling

HOW TO USE MUSHROOMS:

- Interestingly, cooking your mushrooms (as opposed to eating raw) actually raises the antioxidant levels
- Mushrooms are best used right away, as they can tend to get a little hard if left in the fridge for too long
- Use a variety of mushroom types to make a rich, earthy, mushroom soup with vegetable stock and fresh thyme
- Slice and saute mushrooms with olive oil and garlic and serve over wholegrain toast for an energy-rich breakfast
- Grill portabella mushrooms with olive oil and fresh rosemary and serve in place of meat steaks or beef burger patties
- Add mushrooms to curries, risottos, and veggie stews

DOWNLOAD YOUR FREE BONUS:
simpleoptimum.com/bookbonus

11 PRETTY FOODS: GUIDE TO EDIBLE FLOWERS

PLANT-BASED HEALTH

BEST EDIBLE FLOWERS:

- Cornflower
- Viola
- Pansy
- Borage
- Rosemary flower
- Sage flowers
- Hollyhock
- Rose
- Calendula
- Marigold
- Nasturtium

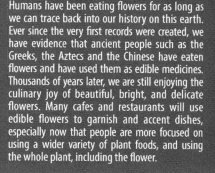

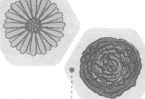

Humans have been eating flowers for as long as we can trace back into our history on this earth. Ever since the very first records were created, we have evidence that ancient people such as the Greeks, the Aztecs and the Chinese have eaten flowers and have used them as edible medicines. Thousands of years later, we are still enjoying the culinary joy of beautiful, bright, and delicate flowers. Many cafes and restaurants will use edible flowers to garnish and accent dishes, especially now that people are more focused on using a wider variety of plant foods, and using the whole plant, including the flower.

WHY EAT FLOWERS?

Flowers are not only gorgeous, but many of them are very nutritious. Generally, plants which have rich and vibrant colors are full of antioxidants and powerful nutrients. Many edible flowers are great sources of minerals such as iron, calcium, and potassium. Edible flowers are also rich in antioxidants, protecting our bodies from free radicals and inflammation. Eating edible flowers is a great way to utilize more of what the earth has to offer us by way of plant-based foods. Plus, they make your meals look amazing.

HOW TO KNOW WHICH ONES ARE SAFE TO EAT

Utilize the internet, gardening books, magazines, and the professionals at your local garden center to learn which flowers are the safest to eat. Don't eat any flower unless you have identified it as a safe plant to eat. You can do this by matching its image and characteristics to a reliable source. You can also buy packets of seeds especially for edible flowers. Look for "edible flower garden" seed mixes, and plant yourself a pretty garden to nibble from.

PLANT-BASED HEALTH
9 REASONS WHY TO CHOOSE PLANT-BASED DIET – WHAT CAN IT DO FOR YOUR BODY AND MIND?

Protects the heart
Your heart is one of your most precious organs. Eating a diet full of meat, animal fats, sugars and processed carbohydrates will put your heart under stress. Eating a diet full of veggies, fruits, grains and legumes will help to keep your cholesterol and blood pressure at a healthy level. Plants love your heart!

Protects the bones
Eating too much meat can actually raise your chances of experiencing osteoporosis. A diet rich in leafy greens and nuts will feed your bones with calcium, vitamin K, folic acid and potassium. Keep your bones dense and strong with a wide variety of plant-based foods!

Protects the eyes
Eating lots of orange-colored veggies such as carrots, and dark leafy greens such as kale provides lots of carotenoids such as lutein. Carotenoids love your retinas, and help to keep them healthy and functional.

Supports healthy digestion
Sugars, processed carbs and gluten-rich grains can be very hard for the body to process and they can irritate the gut. Many people experience bloating, digestive issues and pain due to food choices. A great remedy is a plant-based diet. Lots of dietary fiber found in plants helps your digestive system to run smoothly and regularly. Give it a try! If you still experience digestive discomfort, ask your doctor or nutritionist how to cater a plant-based diet to suit you and your health needs.

Boosts energy levels
Leaving processed carbs and sugars behind, and replacing them with veggies, fruits, nuts, seeds, grains and legumes will do wonders for your energy. Without carbs and sugars, your blood sugar will be more stable and you won't experience energy highs and lows. Most plant foods offer slow-release energy and keep you going steady all day.

Supports a healthy weight
Plant-based foods are full of nutrition and contain very few empty calories. By cutting out fatty meats, sugary treats, starchy breads and baked goods from your diet, you are removing thousands of empty calories. By replacing those foods with plant-based, whole, fresh foods you are filling yourself with ample nutrition and energy without overloading on calories.

Supports healthy sleep habits
A plant-based diet boosts your body with vitamin B6, selenium and magnesium, all of which help to lull you into sound sleep. Removing meat and dairy from your diet gives your digestive system a welcome break. A struggling, overworked digestive system can disrupt your sleep, resulting in tiredness and irritability. Remember that your sleep is your body's time to replenish and repair!

Supports glowing skin
Sugars and processed carbs can cause inflammation, which causes some people to experience skin issues such as redness and acne. Eating lots of healthy fat found in foods such as nuts, seeds, olive oil and avocado nourishes the skin from the inside. This boost moisture and gives you a healthy glow. Some plant-based foods even provide antibacterial properties, and most are great sources of hydration which your skin needs and loves.

Encourages a relationship with nature
When you start to source all of your food from natural, plant-based sources, your relationship with nature grows. You will begin to learn more about where your food comes from, which will foster a growing respect and appreciation for nature. You may even feel compelled to grow your own plant-based foods, drawing you closer to your own part of the world. You will feel more connected to your food, your earth, and ultimately yourself, by sourcing all of your sustenance from the plant world around you.

simple + optimum
core routines for extraordinary living

DOWNLOAD YOUR FREE BONUS:
simpleoptimum.com/bookbonus

PLANT-BASED HEALTH
18 FOODS FOR A HOME-GROWN EDIBLE GARDEN: HERBS, VEGGIES AND BERRIES

The easiest fruits, herbs and veggies to grow at home: these plants are great to start with, as they're fairy low maintenance. Of course, your climate will dictate what you can and can't grow, but most of these are fairly happy in most climates!

One of the most rewarding things we can do in life is grow and harvest our own fresh, plant-based foods. There's something incredibly joyful and grounding about watching a crop grow and flourish into a nutritious food source, helped by your own initiative and care. Growing your own fruits, veggies and herbs is an affordable way to make the most of seasonal fresh produce. It's also a great way to get out into the garden and enjoy the fresh air, quiet and beauty that nature has to offer us. Go to your local garden center and find seedlings to plant in a garden plot, planter box or even small pots.

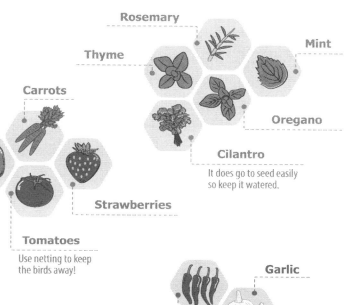

- Radishes
- Zucchini
- Squash
- Spinach
- Lettuce
- Swiss chard
- Bok choy
- Bell peppers
- Carrots
- Tomatoes — Use netting to keep the birds away!
- Strawberries
- Rosemary
- Thyme
- Mint
- Oregano
- Cilantro — It does go to seed easily so keep it watered.
- Chili peppers
- Garlic

TIPS FOR GROWING YOUR OWN FRESH, PLANT-BASED FOODS AT HOME:

- Study your local climate and the most compatible plants. There are so many free gardening resources online to guide you, as well as books and knowledge from the keen gardeners in your life
- Get yourself a local gardening calendar, it will tell you what to do each month (i.e. sowing, harvesting, pruning)
- Make sure you're aware of how much space to give each plant, some can grow huge and take up lots of garden space (i.e. zucchini plants)
- Prepare your soil first. Ask your local garden center for the best natural products to enrich and fortify the soil before planting
- Buy some netting for plants such as strawberries and tomatoes, the birds love them!
- Plant some flowers among your veggies, as they can help to repel bugs. Marigolds are especially effective!
- Start off slowly by choosing a few select plants and grow your garden from there
- Be patient, have fun and make sure you take the time to enjoy each little process, from the first flower to the first ripe fruit

FOR SMALL APARTMENTS OR TINY GARDENS:

- Make use of your patio or small balcony by planting herbs in pots
- Make or buy a planter box and tuck it into a sunny spot, fill with soil and plant a small selection of seasonal veggies you will use the most. Veggies such as spinach and kale are great because you can pick leaves as you require them then leave them to continue growing
- Make use of vertical space with climbing walls and plant tomatoes or beans
- Hang planters out of your kitchen window and plant herbs, ready to be freshly picked while you cook

simple + optimum — core routines for extraordinary living

DOWNLOAD YOUR FREE BONUS: simpleoptimum.com/bookbonus

PLANT-BASED HEALTH
10 GLUTEN-FREE WHOLE GRAINS

Grains are a fantastic way to add bulk and energy to your meals while still maintaining a gluten-free and low-GI plant-based diet. Whole grains offer lots of dietary fiber, minerals and vitamins, as well as adding nutty flavor to dishes.

Oats
Cook with water and almond milk and serve with fresh berries for a fiber-filled breakfast packed with minerals. Add to smoothies and homemade granola.

Total carbs per 100 grams: 66.3 grams
Net carbs per 100 grams: 55.7 grams

Note: buy only oats with "gluten-free" label as they are otherwise often contaminated by gluten. Steel-cut oats are better for effective digestion resulting in stable blood sugar/insulin balance and lower inflammation.

Amaranth
Full of protein, iron and manganese, amaranth is a very smart whole grain to add to your plant-based diet. Boil amaranth in water or vegetable stock (use 3 times more liquid than amaranth) until cooked. Stir into salads, or even combine with grated apples, cinnamon and nut milk for an amaranth oatmeal-style breakfast.

Total carbs per 100 grams: 65 grams
Net carbs per 100 grams: 58 grams

Wild rice
Wild rice is actually a seed which comes from freshwater grasses. It provides lots of manganese and zinc. Soak your wild rice overnight, rinse and cook as you would with brown rice. Mix with salads for a nutty taste.

Total carbs per 100 grams: 75 grams
Net carbs per 100 grams: 69 grams

Teff
An ancient grain popular in African countries, teff is a tiny grain with a very high calcium content. It's a wonderful source of dietary fiber which promotes healthy blood sugar levels. Use the whole grains to make teff porridge, or grind to make teff flour for gluten-free breads and baked goods.

Total carbs per 100 grams: 65 grams
Net carbs per 100 grams: 57 grams

Whole grain cornmeal
Wholegrain cornmeal contains all parts of the corn kernel and is ground to various sizes (i.e. coarse or fine). Cornmeal is a gluten-free wholegrain food with high amounts of Vitamin A. Cornmeal can be cooked in a variety of ways.

Total carbs per 100 grams: 76.9 grams
Net carbs per 100 grams: 69.6 grams

Quinoa
A great source of fiber and protein, quinoa keeps you full and satisfied. Rinse the bitter coating off, boil in water or vegetable stock and serve with fresh salad greens and seeds for a filling lunch.

Total carbs per 100 grams raw: 60 grams
Net carbs per 100 grams raw: 52 grams

Buckwheat
A gluten-free whole grain with lots of protein, fiber and magnesium. Boil dried buckwheat with water (2 cups of water per 1 cup of dried buckwheat) until soft. Add to salads, use as a rice substitute, or add to soups and stews for extra energy and fiber.

Total carbs per 100 grams raw: 71.5 grams
Net carbs per 100 grams raw: 61.5 grams

Brown rice
Brown rice is extra nutritious because it has the bran, the germ and the endosperm, making it a whole grain. It's a high-fiber grain which keeps you full without adding too many calories. It's a low GI food so it will give you energy slowly and steadily without a spike in blood sugar. Rinse and boil brown rice and add to any dish or salad which requires a little extra energy and fiber.

Total carbs per 100 grams raw: 77 grams
Net carbs per 100 grams raw: 73.5 grams

Sorghum
An ancient grain with a rich history in Africa and India. Wholegrain sorghum is a great source of antioxidants and studies are being developed which suggest it may help to prevent melanoma. Full of calcium and fiber, sorghum is great when boiled and served in salads or as a rice alternative. Sorghum can be ground and used as a gluten-free flour.

Total carbs per 100 grams raw: 72 grams
Net carbs per 100 grams raw: 65.3 grams

Millet
Millet is a little seed which has been used for centuries. It is a great source of B vitamins, magnesium and fiber. A wonderful gluten-free grain to use as a rice substitute. You can use millet to make a hearty porridge, mix into salads, stuff root veggies or make patties.

Total carbs per 100 grams raw: 73 grams
Net carbs per 100 grams raw: 64 grams

PLANT-BASED HEALTH
5 MEAL IDEAS FOR MEAT-EATING GUESTS

Cooking for meat-eaters when trying to maintain your own plant-based diet may seem tricky, but it's really not! Once your meat-eating friends and family see the delicious meals you have prepared, they'll forget all about meat and will be won over by the versatility and depth of flavor of plant-based food.

Mushroom Bolognese:

Mushrooms have a meaty, savory flavor and texture. They're particularly delicious when finely diced and slowly cooked with chopped tomatoes and herbs. Serve with quinoa spaghetti, a shaving of vegan parmesan and fresh basil leaves. Your guests will be begging for the recipe.

Brown rice and avocado sushi rolls:

The joy of sushi rolls is all in the chewiness of the rice, the unique flavor of the nori (seaweed) and the creaminess of the fresh avocado. Add any other veggies you like such as carrot and cucumber. Roll in toasted sesame seeds and serve with coconut aminos as a soy-free substitute for soy sauce. Fresh, filling, varied in texture and completely plant-based.

Eggplant curry with coconut wild rice:

The best part about curry is the aroma and depth of flavor from the curry paste. Eggplant has an amazing ability to carry flavors while providing a delicious texture. Make a Thai green, red, yellow or Massaman curry paste from scratch using fresh herbs, ginger, chilies and spices. There are plenty of authentic recipes online to choose from. Serve with fresh, hot wild or brown rice cooked in water and coconut milk. Garnish with fresh cilantro and cashew nuts. Not even the most avid meat eater could resist a dish like that.

Creamy polenta with garlic and herb roasted veggies:

Boil fine cornmeal with water, salt and olive oil until creamy and soft. Serve with roasted vegetables such as parsnip, carrot, pumpkin and eggplant. Add plenty of whole garlic cloves and dried herbs to the veggies and you'll have a well-rounded, filling and satisfying meat-free meal.

Chickpea and quinoa cakes with homemade pesto dipping sauce:

Make patties with mashed chickpeas, cooked quinoa and fresh herbs. Mashed chickpeas create a thick consistency which glues together the cakes, ready to pan-fry in olive oil. Pesto made with olive oil, sea salt, pine nuts and fresh basil is a perfect drizzle or dipping sauce to give flavor, freshness and color.

Classic meat dishes such as Bolognese, shepherd's pie, tacos and chili are even better when made entirely with plant-based ingredients. You just have to balance your textures, flavors and seasonings to ensure all of the crucial culinary elements are there. Make sure there's a starchier component such as lentils or beans to bulk the meal out and ensure your guests are satiated. Use herbs, spices, oils and vinegars to add different layers of flavor.

Make use of the rainbow of color provided by plant-based foods and create dishes which are appealing to the eye. People often respond to a dish visually, before they've even tasted it! Along with your main dish, try to add a couple of side dishes to further showcase the beauty and deliciousness of plant-based foods.

PLANT-BASED HEALTH | 6 MEAL IDEAS FOR MEAT-EATING GUESTS

Cooking for meat-eaters when trying to maintain your own plant-based diet may seem tricky, but it's really not! Once your meat-eating friends and family see the delicious meals you have prepared, they'll forget all about meat and will be won over by the versatility and depth of flavor of plant-based food.

Spiced butternut and coconut soup:

Soup is the perfect light meal and butternut squash is one of the very best vegetables to use. Coconut cream gives smoothness, creaminess and a touch of extra flavor. You can add red chilis for a touch of spice if you wish. Serve with gluten-free toast and a drizzle of olive oil.

Bean and lentil shepherd's pie with fluffy potato topping:

A hot, savory pie is one of the most universally-delicious food items, especially during cold seasons. Shepherd's pie doesn't need meat to be warming, filling, nourishing and flavorsome. Lentils and beans mimic meat in the sense that they become thick and stew-like when cooked with tomatoes and spices. They have a similar mouthfeel and texture, and carry added flavors exceptionally well. Mash boiled potatoes with salt, pepper and a dash of nut milk and spread over the top of the pie.

Cauliflower, mango and peanut rice paper rolls with coconut peanut sauce:

This is a perfect idea for a plant-based snack, starter, or light lunch. Cauliflower has a great texture when sautéed, and is great for filling rice paper rolls in place of fish or meat. Stir together sautéed cauliflower, fresh mango, peanuts, fresh mint, a dash of lime and use it to fill hydrated rice paper sheets. Melt together coconut cream, organic peanut butter, salt and lime juice and you've got a moreish, plant-based dipping sauce.

Plant-based pizzas with gluten-free crust

You can create an incredible pizza crust with gluten free flours, and top it with vegetables and vegan mozzarella. Ingredients such as sundried tomatoes and olives are great replacements for cured meats as they supply the chewiness and saltiness. Make your own tomato sauce base and find a plant-based cheese, or simply go cheese-free! Scatter with fresh arugula and sea salt.

Sweet potato nachos with corn, cilantro, avocado and vegan crema:

Sweet potatoes cut into wedges and roasted in the oven with olive oil and sea salt can be treated like nachos. Serve them with vegan crema, guacamole, fresh limes, cilantro, fresh salsa and a side of homemade refried black beans. No one will be searching for the meat, I assure you!

Slow-cooked bean chili with garlic and onions:

Chili is a comfort food, hands down. But it doesn't need meat, not at all. In fact, black beans and kidney beans make the best, most nutritious chili. Soften onions and lots of garlic with spices before adding beans and tomatoes. Simmer until thick and deeply flavored. Serve with corn tortillas, vegan crema, avocado and cilantro.

DOWNLOAD YOUR FREE BONUS:
simpleoptimum.com/bookbonus

PLANT-BASED HEALTH
5 TIPS FOR HOW TO USE HERBS, NUTS, VINEGARS AND OILS TO CREATE DRESSINGS AND DIPPING SAUCES

Dressings and sauces can make the difference between a good meal and a great meal. They add different levels of tastes to layer the flavor profile of your dish. They are a great way to balance your meals with any flavors which might be missing. You can add an acidic hit to mild food, an oily softness to sharp foods, and freshness to rich foods.

FIND A VESSEL:
Cold dipping sauces and dressings can be made very simply. Either use a bowl and a whisk, a small food processor or blender, or a cocktail shaker.

START WITH YOUR OIL:
Oil is the best base for a dressing because it easily coats fresh vegetables and grains when poured over and tossed. Oils such as olive oil and avocado oil give your dishes a soft, glossy appearance and a subtle but present flavor. They're also a great way to incorporate more healthy fats into your diet.

Great oils for dressings and cold sauces:
Pour a little oil into your vessel and go from there. You can always add more later.

- Extra virgin olive oil
- Grapeseed oil
- Avocado oil
- Sesame oil — Use sparingly as it has a strong flavor.
- Flaxseed oil

CHOOSE YOUR ACID:
A good dressing or dipping sauce needs an acidic component to it. It cuts through the oil and any fattiness or richness in your dish. A dressing or sauce is a great opportunity to satisfy the sour part of your palate to balance any saltiness, sweetness or bitterness in your dish.

Use acids such as...
Add a dash of your acid to your oil.

- Apple cider vinegar
- Lime juice
- Lemon juice
- Balsamic vinegar
- Red wine vinegar
- White wine vinegar

PICK YOUR FRESHNESS:
A simple salad dressing can end at oil, vinegar, and seasoning. But if you're creating a comprehensive dipping sauce or dressing to really add flavor, color and freshness to your dish, you need fresh herbs. Herbs such as parsley, mint, cilantro and basil add vibrant color and fresh flavor to any dressing or sauce. When blitzed in a food processor or blender, they also help to create a pourable, more substantial consistency.

Add a generous bunch of roughly chopped fresh herbs to your oil and vinegar. If you are blending your dressing by hand, finely chop the herbs before you add them.

Plant-based dressing sweeteners:
Add a small dash to your oil, vinegar and herbs.

- Date syrup
- Coconut sugar
- Vegan honey
- Maple syrup
- Agave
- Molasses

TRY SOME SWEETNESS:
If you've used a sweeter vinegar such as balsamic, you may not need to add extra sweetness. However, if you've got a very acidic and salty dressing, a hint of sweetness can really round things out.

simple + optimum
core routines for extraordinary living

DOWNLOAD YOUR FREE BONUS:
simpleoptimum.com/bookbonus

PLANT-BASED HEALTH
5 TIPS FOR HOW TO USE HERBS, NUTS, VINEGARS AND OILS TO CREATE DRESSINGS AND DIPPING SAUCES

A PINCH OF SPICE:
This one is totally optional, but a hit of heat can be amazing when dealing with Asian-inspired cuisine such as cold rice noodle salads, rice paper rolls or Thai veggie salads.

DON'T FORGET TO SEASON:
Seasoning is very important for all dressings and sauces. A good pinch of salt will do the trick. Sea salt is great because it's easier to "pinch" than table salt, but regular table salt will do as well.

ADD YOUR CRUNCH:
Sometimes, a salad dressing or cold sauce can really be elevated with the addition of a crunchy ingredient. Crunch adds extra texture to your dish, without adding bulk or overpowering flavors. When you get a salad leaf on your fork coated in smooth oil, sharp vinegar, a tiny hum of heat and a hint of crunchy texture...that's a great mouthful.

BLEND OR PULSE:
Give your dressing a few quick pulses in your blender or food processor until you reach the desired consistency. Or, use some elbow grease and use your whisk and a bowl.

TASTE AND ADJUST:
Tasting is crucial to creating the perfect dressing or dipping sauce. Truly taste the mixture and search for any imbalances of flavor. If it's too oily, add a dash more vinegar or lemon juice. If it's too acidic, add a bit more oil. If it's not fresh enough or the herbs aren't coming through, add more. If it's not well seasoned, add more salt. Keep going until you have the perfect balance of flavors.

Ways to add spice to dressings and dipping sauces...
Start with a very small addition of spice, you can add more later.

- Finely chop and add fresh red chilies
- Add a pinch of cayenne pepper
- Add a dollop of hot mustard
- Add a pinch of ground chili powder or dried chili flakes

Ways to add crunchy texture to dressings and cold sauces:
You can add your nuts and/or seeds to your dressing before or after blending, depending on how large you want the pieces to be.

- Finely chop walnuts
- Finely chop macadamia nuts
- Toast pumpkin seeds or sesame seeds

Now you have a delicious, plant-based dressing or sauce to enhance your plant-based meal. Either serve right away or keep in the fridge in an airtight vessel.

simple + optimum
core routines for extraordinary living

DOWNLOAD YOUR FREE BONUS:
simpleoptimum.com/bookbonus

PLANT-BASED HEALTH
7 TIPS FOR MAKING THE TRANSITION

These tips are for you if you're making the change from a meat-eating diet to a full plant-based diet and lifestyle.

Start slowly

You don't need to make all of the changes at once. You could take a month to ease yourself into the transition. One week, stop eating red meat. The next week, cut fish and poultry. The next week, go dairy-free, and end with removing processed sugars and processed grains. If you start all at once, the change may be too drastic, leaving you feeling tired, overwhelmed and deprived.

Research and read

Before you get started on your plant-based journey, be as equipped with knowledge as you can. Read about which plant-based foods are best for certain health requirements and cater your diet to your own personal health needs. Read about the benefits of a plant-based diet, it will only motivate you further. Read about the best ways to combine plant-based foods for the most balanced and nutritious diet.

Write lists

Shopping lists, recipe lists, meal planning lists and seasonal produce lists will help you to be as prepared as possible. Eating according to any specific diet or lifestyle philosophy works best when you're prepared. That way, you'll always have the ingredients you need to create well-rounded, balanced plant-based meals.

Be clear on your "why"

To make a drastic change to your diet and/or lifestyle, you must be clear on your reasons. If not, you might waver and fall back into your old lifestyle. It might be for general health and longevity reasons, for ethical reasons or for medical reasons as advised by a professional. You might have simply realized that a plant-based diet makes you feel happier and healthier in all ways. Whatever the reason is, keep it in your mind when you're first making the transition. It will help if you have any temptations put in your path.

Investigate your local produce suppliers

Do some research to seek out all of the local produce suppliers in your area. You may find that there's a greengrocer with exceptional prices or the freshest produce. You may find that there's a produce delivery service which brings your fruit and veggie order straight to your door at a low cost. Having the best produce available, and as accessible as possible will ensure you always have a fresh, abundant supply of plant-based foods at your fingertips. Look for farmers markets in your area and make the most of locally-grown produce.

Treat yourself to cookbooks

Buy yourself a couple of plant-based cookbooks to turn to whenever you need ideas and inspiration. It can be hard to continuously think of meal ideas, especially after a long, tiresome day. Have a few cookbooks handy to flick through for inspiration and guidance.

Stock up on staple ingredients

Keep plenty of spices, oils and vinegars in your cupboard so you can always add and adjust different flavors to customize each dish. Have a constant supply of dried gluten-free grains in the pantry, as well as frozen vegetables in the freezer. This will ensure that you have ample ingredients to create a plant-based meal even when your fresh produce supplies are lacking.

QUICK-FIRE TIPS

- Join with a friend or family member who wants to adopt a plant-based diet too. You can share recipes and motivate each other
- Get creative at home and plant your own herbs and even veggies if you have time and space
- Give yourself a challenge to source and try a new vegetable, fruit or grain each week. You'll find there's a vast array of plant-based foods you haven't tried or perhaps haven't heard of yet
- Keep adding to your collection of spices, gluten-free plant flours and specialty plant oils to create a full and varied store of flavors and ingredients
- Make the most of seasonal fruits and freeze them. When fruits such as mangoes and berries are in season, abundant and cheap, stock up on them and freeze them for when they are scarce later in the year

simple + optimum
core routines for extraordinary living

DOWNLOAD YOUR FREE BONUS:
simpleoptimum.com/bookbonus

PLANT-BASED HEALTH
6 WAYS HOW TO USE COOKED LEFTOVERS AND OFFCUTS TO AVOID WASTE

Even when we have the best intentions to eat all of our leftovers, there's often something that falls by the wayside and ends up being thrown out. If you've got lots of cooked food left over, get creative with it and see it as a whole new meal, or an ingredient for a future meal.

Don't underestimate the stir-fry

Sometimes, the best way to treat leftovers is to simply sauté them on a hot skillet or wok with a dash of oil. Treat it as a basis for adding new flavor to yesterday's meal. Layer with vinegars, spices, oils and herbs to create a hot, fast, flavorsome dish with minimal effort. If your leftovers are all light vegetables, add some brown rice to bulk it out. If your leftovers are heavy on the grains or legumes, add some fresh leafy greens to lighten it up.

Combine leftovers with freshness

If you've got leftovers but not quite enough for a full meal, don't disregard them or leave them sitting in the fridge sadly. Use them as a base for your next meal. You could use cooked veggies as a basis for a salad with fresh arugula. Leftover cooked quinoa can be mixed with black beans and herbs to create patties. View your leftovers as ingredients, not as an old meal which needs to be eaten alone.

Utilize the freezer

Let's say you made a delicious vegetable soup and you've made too much. You don't think you'll get a chance to eat it in the next few days. So, get some freezer-safe containers and pack the soup away into individual portions. Pop them into the freezer and you've got a homemade, plant-based meal to save you next time you find yourself in a pinch.

The same applies to little bits and bobs of leftover ingredients as you're cooking. Perhaps you peeled too much fresh ginger, picked too many hot chilies or peeled too many bananas for your needs. Pop them into airtight bags, label and put them in the freezer to use next time. This saves them from shriveling up in the fridge and being forgotten about.

Get the blender out

Let's say you have a bowl of leftover roasted pumpkin sitting in the fridge. You could reheat it or add it to a salad. Or, you could blend it with garlic, spices, chickpeas and olive oil to create a roasted pumpkin hummus. Or, you could add it to hot vegetable stock and blend with a stick blender to create roasted pumpkin soup.

Make stocks and broths

Extra veggies such as onions, carrots and celery which are in danger of going beyond edible are the best veggies for stocks. If you've got some veggies and herbs which you won't get a chance to use before they turn bad, pop them into a stock pot and boil with water and salt. Drain and freeze the stock and keep for next time you need a homemade vegetable stock.

Treat your pets

If worse comes to worst and you end up with too much leftover food to handle, and it's past the point of being desirable to eat, make pet food. You can mash and cook leftover veggies and grains to create homemade dog food your pets will love. Just make sure each ingredient is pet-safe. You'll save money on pet food, nothing with go to waste, and your pets will be very happy indeed.

simple + optimum — core routines for extraordinary living

DOWNLOAD YOUR FREE BONUS:
simpleoptimum.com/bookbonus

PLANT-BASED HEALTH
8 TIPS HOW TO PREPARE AND FREEZE FRESH PRODUCE YOURSELF

If there's a particular seasonal veggie or fruit you really love, you can buy lots of it and freeze it to use during the off season. You can also do this for your abundant homegrown produce you can't manage to eat while ripe. Here's how to prepare and freeze fresh produce at home.

Wash and dry

Gather your fresh produce and give all of the pieces a good wash. If they're delicate fruits or veggies such as berries, put them in a colander and run water over them. If they're sturdy and strong, such as stone fruits or carrots, give them a scrub with your hands or a light scrubbing brush.

Dry your washed produce with tea towels.

Chop

Chop your produce any way you like. Think about what you might be using your frozen produce for in the future, it will help you to decide the shape and size to chop them. Chopping your produce makes it easier to store as you can pack the bags of produce into smaller spaces. It also makes it easier for you to use the amount you require, without having to take out whole fruits and veggies when you may only need a handful of pieces.

Blanch

Most veggies should be blanched before they're frozen. This helps to lock the nutrients into the produce and helps to keep the vibrant color. There are little enzymes in your veggies which munch away at the produce, resulting in the breaking down of nutrients. Boiling water will stop the enzymes in their tracks. Blanching is kind of like halting the produce in time, keeping them at their prime. Plunge your cut produce into boiling water and allow to boil for around 2 minutes, but it does depend on the veggie you are blanching. Harder veggies need a longer blanche time than soft or leafy veggies.

Transfer the blanched veggies into a bowl of ice water until cold. This stops them from cooking any further. We don't want to fully cook the veggies, just give them a good shock with boiling water.

Note: you don't need to blanch most fruits, just veggies.

Initial freeze

Place the blanched produce onto a baking tray lined with baking paper. Pop the trays into the freezer and allow to freeze completely.

The reason we freeze our produce on trays first is so that they don't stick together in one big clump. Once they are frozen individually, they tend to remain unstuck and are easy to separate when you come to use them.

Pack

Transfer the frozen produce into airtight freezer bags. You can keep them separated by type, or create your own frozen produce mixes. You could have a mixture of berries and mango, or stone fruits and bananas, or peas, carrots and corn.

Label

It's a good idea to label any food you put into the freezer as it lets you know how long it's been in there. Write down what's in the bag and the date it was blanched and frozen.

Store

Now you're ready to pop your frozen veggies and fruits into the freezer. It can be very handy to flatten out your bags of frozen produce as opposed to bunching them up. This allows you to lay the bags on top of each other saving space and creating a tidy freezer.

Dry

Dry the blanched veggies. Laying them onto a tea towel and patting them down with another tea towel works well.

PLANT-BASED HEALTH | 7 EASY WAYS TO USE AN EXCESS OF STONE FRUITS DURING A GENEROUS HARVEST

Plums, peaches and nectarines are delicious when eaten fresh, raw and juicy. However, when you've got a huge amount of stone fruits hanging around in your kitchen or on a fruit tree in your yard, there's only so many you can eat! Here are some easy tips for making good use of excess stone fruits.

Stew

Stewed fruits can be spooned over homemade granola for breakfast, or eaten with a dollop of coconut yogurt for a fresh dessert. Stone fruits lend themselves exceptionally well to stewing as they have sweetness and tartness, as well as a texture which becomes soft but not completely soup-like. Halve the fruit, take the stones out, and simmer with a few cups of water, vanilla beans and a pinch of stevia.

Bake

Use your stone fruits to make desserts and baked goods. Coconut oil and ground almonds are great plant-based ingredients to make light cakes and bars, and stone fruits can add sweetness, tartness and moisture. Seek out some gluten-free, sugar-free, plant-based baking recipes and add stone fruits to the recipe.

Roast

Roasting your stone fruits brings out a whole new depth of flavor, and the heat caramelizes the natural sugars in the fruit. Place your halved stone fruits onto a baking tray, sprinkle with a little water, zested citrus peel and a few drops of vanilla extract. Roast them until they're soft and caramelized. Serve any way you like.

Dehydrate

If you have a dehydrator at home, use it to create dried stone fruits. Sliced stone fruits which have been dried to a chewy, candy-like texture can be a fantastic sweet treat without any added sugars.

Juice

If you have a heavy-duty juicer, you can juice your stone fruits which have gone a little soft. If you don't have a juicer, you could blend soft stone fruits in a blender or food processor and pass through a strainer.

Add to salads

Don't forget that fresh fruits can add incredible texture, sweetness, tartness and juiciness to all kinds of salads. Add fresh nectarine slices to green, leafy salads. Add fresh peaches to quinoa salads or a few grated plums to a red cabbage slaw. Get creative, there are no rights or wrongs!

Freeze

Frozen stone fruits are so handy to have in the freezer for when your fresh supplies have run out. Wash your stone fruits, chop them, freeze them on baking sheets then transfer into bags or containers. Blend frozen stone fruits with frozen banana to make a healthy, plant-based "ice cream", or simply add them to a pot with water and vanilla to stew them back to life.

simple + optimum
core routines for extraordinary living

DOWNLOAD YOUR FREE BONUS:
simpleoptimum.com/bookbonus

PLANT-BASED HEALTH
8 BEST WAYS TO MAKE THE MOST OF CITRUS

If you're lucky enough to have a citrus tree at home, or a family member who loves to shower you with their own abundant citrus, you'll know how hard it can be to keep up with it all. You may be at a loss as to what to do with it all, and fear you might let it go to waste. Fear not, here are some great ideas for making the most out of citrus fruits.

Preserve

Preserved lemons are incredibly easy to make, and very delicious. They provide fantastic flavor to all kinds of dishes, and they look great sitting on your shelf or counter. You just need a sterilized jar, lemons, salt and water. Use preserved lemons to flavor Moroccan-inspired dishes, salads, dressings, sauces, stews and curries.

Juice

This may seem obvious, but citrus juices offer so much flavor and punch to all kinds of foods and drinks. Juice your oranges, lemons, limes and grapefruits to make fresh, tart juices. Fresh citrus juice is a great way to enjoy a sweet drink without added refined sugar. You can also use fresh citrus juice to mix with plain soda water for a healthier take on fruit soda. Use a juicer if you have one, or use your muscles and do it by hand.

Dressings

Citrus juice, (especially lemon and lime) adds delicious acidity to salad dressings. Mix with olive oil and a pinch of salt and you've got a fresh dressing. You can even finely grate some of the zest into your dressing for a more intensified citrus flavor.

Special ice cubes

You can always turn to the freezer when you've got too much citrus to handle. Squeeze your citrus fruits and pour the juice into ice cube trays. Once the cubes are frozen, transfer them into an airtight bag and store in the freezer. Use them to flavor cold drinks or melt them down whenever you need citrus juice in a pinch.

Sweet and savory sauces

Plant-based desserts and baked goods can be elevated to higher heights with the addition of a citrus drizzle or sauce. Simmer freshly squeezed citrus juice with a little pinch of cornstarch to create a sticky sauce, free of refined sugar. Savory dishes such as roasted veggies can also be enhanced with a reduced citrus sauce. Drizzle simmered orange juice over roasted carrots or parsnips and you've got a simple yet very special side dish.

Teas

Citrus tea is energizing, refreshing and does wonders for the digestive system (especially lemon). Simply squeeze your fresh citrus into hot water with your favorite tea bag, or dry the peeled zest and make your own dried tea mixes.

Flavoring stocks

Older citrus can be roughly chopped and added to vegetable stocks. It adds a freshness and fragrance to your homemade stock.

Water flavorings

Fill some large jugs with ice cubes and water, add lots of sliced fresh citrus and a few cucumber slices. Now you've got a refreshing take on water with a whisper of flavor. This is a great way to drink more water throughout hot months or when you are unwell.

simple + optimum
core routines for extraordinary living

DOWNLOAD YOUR FREE BONUS:
simpleoptimum.com/bookbonus

PLANT-BASED HEALTH | 10 LOWER-CARB FRUITS

These fruits have a lower net-carb content per 100 grams than other fruits, and are all delicious and versatile. Add fruits to your diet to boost your intake of vitamins, fiber and antioxidants. Fruits can be the perfect answer to sweet cravings. Get yourself a little bowl of strawberries or a juicy slice of melon and enjoy the sweet freshness without refined sugars.

Watermelon
Total carbs per 100 grams: 8 grams
Net carbs per 100 grams: 7.6 grams

Honeydew melons
Total carbs per 100 grams: 9 grams
Net carbs per 100 grams: 8.2 grams

Avocados
Total carbs per 100 grams: 9 grams
Net carbs per 100 grams: 2 grams

Strawberries
Total carbs per 100 grams: 8 grams
Net carbs per 100 grams: 6 grams

Raspberries
Total carbs per 100 grams: 12 grams
Net carbs per 100 grams: 5 grams

Blackberries
Total carbs per 100 grams: 10 grams
Net carbs per 100 grams: 5 grams

Coconut flesh
Total carbs per 100 grams: 15 grams
Net carbs per 100 grams: 6 grams

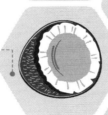

Plums
Total carbs per 100 grams: 11.4 grams
Net carbs per 100 grams: 10 grams

Oranges
Total carbs per 100 grams: 9.5 grams
Net carbs per 100 grams: 7.4 grams

Cherries
Total carbs per 100 grams: 12 grams
Net carbs per 100 grams: 10.4 grams

PLANT-BASED HEALTH
7 WAYS TO USE THE WHOLE VEGETABLE WITHOUT WASTAGE: STALKS, LEAVES AND FLOWERS

Most people overlook certain parts of fresh vegetables which can actually be used as tasty, nutritious ingredients. Most vegetables can be used in their entirety, from the fruit right down to the stalk. This decreases wastage, packs more nutrition into your diet and will eventually save you money.

Study the plant
Not all fruits and veggies have food-friendly leaves and stalks, so it's important to check before you eat them. A quick internet search will take seconds, so you can go ahead and eat your stalks, leaves and tops with confidence.

Blend the stalks
Not all stalks are tasty when eaten whole, but they can lend incredible flavor when blended and added to soups, sauces or dressings. Herbs which have tougher stalks which aren't as pleasant to eat as the leaves can be blended to harness the flavor. You can even pass your dressing or sauce through a sieve to remove any chunky pieces of stalk. Curry pastes and rubs for roasted veggies are also a great way to make use of tougher stalks and leaves. Blend them with other strong-flavored ingredients such as ginger and garlic.

Use to flavor your stocks and broths
Throw your rosemary stalks, celery leaves, older onions, overripe carrots and any other tasty vegetable "top" or leaf into your stock pot. Boil with water and salt to draw out the flavors, resulting in a tasty vegetable stock. Use any veggies which may be a little past their prime, or leaves and stalks you have no other use for. After making a salad or any other veggie dish, save the leftover parts of the veggies and set them aside for your stock.

Get your saute pan out
Tougher parts of popular veggies such as kale stalks, broccoli stalks, leek greens and beet greens are usually discarded. Instead of throwing away such wonderful sources of vitamins, minerals and fiber, make a stir-fry or veggie saute to serve as a side dish to accompany your main. Chop and saute the veggies on a hot skillet or saute pan with olive oil and sea salt.

Utilize your salad bowl
Zucchini flowers, carrot leaves, coriander stalks, fennel leaves, radish tops and borage flowers are all fantastic examples of forgotten parts of vegetables which are actually delicious. Toss them all into your salad bowl, drizzle over some olive oil and apple cider vinegar, add a sprinkle of pumpkin seeds and you have an exceptional and surprising salad.

Make ice cubes
If you have an overload of herbs and you can't possibly eat them all fresh, you can freeze them. Take the woodier, tougher herb stalks and blend them with water or vegetable stock. Pour them into ice cube trays and freeze. Next time you're making a stew, soup or sauce, pop an ice cube into the mix. It will melt away and enhance your dish with extra herby flavor without any chopping or fussing involved.

Trust your taste buds
Once you've ensured that your vegetable flower, stalk or leaf is safe to eat, let your taste buds decide on what the best use for it is. Have a taste of it raw. Do you like it? Is it nice just as it is or do you think it would be best cooked? Would it work in a salad with a touch of oil and vinegar? Does it have a strong flavor which would add life to a broth or stock? Is it too tough to enjoy whole or does it need to be blended and strained? There are no rules, so go with your culinary instincts!

simple + optimum
core routines for extraordinary living

DOWNLOAD YOUR FREE BONUS:
simpleoptimum.com/bookbonus

PLANT-BASED HEALTH
7 TIPS FOR MAINTAINING YOUR PLANT-BASED DIET DURING THE FESTIVE SEASON AND HOLIDAYS

When family and friends gather during the holiday season, there tends to be food around constantly. It's often rich food filled with dairy, meat, processed carbohydrates and refined sugars. It can be very tempting to give in, especially if you're unprepared and the easier route is to abandon your plant-based diet. There's nothing wrong with this, but you may end up feeling sick and fatigued if you have an aversion to meats, dairy, sugars and gluten-rich carbs. Here are some easy tips toward maintaining your plant-based diet during the festive season.

Make a plan

Plan your holiday food layout well in advance. Figure out when you'll be at home and when you'll be dining or staying with friends and family. This will give you a better idea of how to go ahead and write shopping lists and make cooking plans. If you're hosting most of the festivities at your house, you'll have more control over your plant-based diet. But if you're going to be with friends and family elsewhere, you'll have to be a little more strategic. Jot down on a calendar where you will be and if you need to come prepared with food.

Write lists

Lists are your best friends during the busy holiday season, especially when trying to upkeep a particular eating plan. Write detailed meal lists if you're hosting at your place, and shopping lists to make sure you've covered all of the required ingredients. Write lists of meals you'd like to take with you to contribute to dinners, parties and celebrations. Write your shopping lists in sequence to ensure you get your timing right.

Offer to help with the cooking

If you're going to be dining at a friend or family member's home for your holiday celebration, offer to help with the cooking. Instead of just hoping that there will be enough plant-based food for you to eat, make sure there is. Offer to bring a range of salads, sides and vegetarian mains to contribute to the day. This will not only take pressure off the hosts, but it will ease your mind to know you'll be well fed.

Get organized early

Don't leave your shopping till the last minute. If you head to the supermarket or greengrocer on Christmas Eve, you risk finding a serious lack of fresh produce and plant-based staples. Start shopping a couple of weeks before the holiday starts. Buy non-perishable items first and stash them away. Start to buy fresh produce a few days before the holiday and keep them refrigerated. Alternatively, you could find a fresh produce delivery service in your area and make an order which will be delivered as close to the holiday as possible. That way, you don't need to worry about braving the holiday rush.

Make plant-based treat alternatives

Don't feel left out of the festive feast. You can create your own plant-based traditional treats with a twist. Make a trifle made from coconut vegan custard, almond-flour sponge, fresh berries and whipped vanilla coconut cream. Make a "cheese" platter with gluten-free crackers, homemade hummus, homemade artichoke and spinach dip, toasted nuts, chutneys and relish. Make a pumpkin pie with coconut cream and a hazelnut base. You get the idea! You can still have decadent, luxurious foods while still staying true to your plant-based lifestyle.

Eat before you go out

If you're heading out for Christmas drinks, make sure you eat before you go so that you remain satiated. If you go out hungry, you'll likely be in a position where the only food around is non plant-based. Have a good meal before you go so that you can enjoy a drink or two without being led astray by hunger pangs and "banned" foods.

Allocate one treat

If you're on a flexible plant-based diet then there's no reason why you can't loosen the reins over the holidays and eat whatever you fancy. Take a couple of days to enjoy all that the festive season has to offer, then get back into your plant-based life afterward. If you're on a strict plant-based diet you could give yourself one treat allowance. Perhaps there's a special dish or treat you love but have given up due to your plant-based diet. Perhaps you're a milk chocolate addict or you can't resist roasted turkey. Go ahead and give yourself a treat meal or two.

simple + optimum
core routines for extraordinary living

PLANT-BASED HEALTH

WHAT ARE NIGHTSHADES? CONCERNS AND BENEFITS

Nightshades can be confusing as there are various opinions and concerns about eating them. But for most people, they're a nutritious and tasty plant group to enjoy.

WHAT ARE NIGHTSHADES?

Nightshades are a family of vegetables which includes eggplants, tomatoes, bell peppers, chili peppers, paprika, potatoes, goji berries, tobacco and okra.

Tomatoes
Benefits: tomatoes supply us with plenty of lycopene.

Total carbs per 100 grams: 4 grams
Net carbs per 100 grams: 3 grams

Okra
Total carbs per 100 grams: 7 grams
Net carbs per 100 grams: 3.8 grams

Goji berries
Total carbs per 100 grams: 51 grams
Net carbs per 100 grams: 30 grams

Eggplants
Benefits: eggplants are a tasty way to increase our Vitamin K intake.

Total carbs per 100 grams: 6 grams
Net carbs per 100 grams: 3 grams

White potatoes
Benefits: potatoes are a great source of potassium

Total carbs per 100 grams: 17 grams
Net carbs per 100 grams: 14.8 grams

Green chili peppers
Benefits: peppers are a strong source of vital Vitamin C

Total carbs per 100 grams: 9.5 grams
Net carbs per 100 grams: 8 grams

Bell peppers
Benefits: peppers are a strong source of vital Vitamin C

Total carbs per 100 grams: 6.7 grams
Net carbs per 100 grams: 5.5 grams

Benefits: there are plenty of reasons to keep nightshades in your diet! The pros far outweigh the cons, for most people.

Fiber: fiber is crucial to a healthy bowel, healthy blood sugar levels and a smooth digestive system. Nightshades offer plenty of fiber.

Low-carb: nightshades (apart from white potatoes) are low in carbs and won't give you an energy spike and sluggish crash.

Low-calorie: most nightshades are low in calories and can be eaten in abundance without overloading your daily calorie intake.

CONCERNS:

The famous poisonous plant "deadly nightshade" is a direct sibling of our favorite nightshade fruits and veggies. Some people have concerns that the same poisonous effects from deadly nightshades apply to the nightshades we eat.

Nightshades have a compound in them called alkaloids which are used by the nightshades to protect themselves against pests and viruses. When humans eat a high enough dose of alkaloids, they can experience vomiting, headaches and even hallucinations. However, the alkaloid content in nightshades is so little that alkaloid poisoning is really nothing to worry about.

The main concern about nightshades is that they can cause people with arthritis and autoimmune diseases such as rheumatism to have painful flare-ups. The research is still quite limited, but plenty of people with arthritis have found that cutting nightshades does help to soothe symptoms.

SHOULD YOU EAT THEM?

Yes, you should still continue to eat nightshades as they are full of fantastic health benefits. Just avoid green potatoes, green tomatoes and make sure to cook your eggplant and potatoes thoroughly. Avoid eating the stalks and leaves of nightshade fruits and veggies too.

The exception is if you suspect you have an aversion to nightshades. You may find that nightshades cause stomach issues such as IBS to flare up. If so, remove them and see if it helps with your symptoms and pain. Of course, the best thing to do concerning any food aversion or health issue is to speak with your doctor.

If you have arthritis or rheumatism which is causing you regular pain, you could try a nightshade elimination diet. You might find that it helps with your pain, which would be great. Or, it may not make a difference and you can go back to enjoying nightshades as part of your plant-based diet.

PLANT-BASED HEALTH
7 CABBAGES - THE UNDERRATED BENEFITS OF THE HUMBLE BRASSICAS

WHAT ARE BRASSICAS?

Brassicas are a group of vegetables which grow above ground in wintry, cold conditions. They are leafy, green and often tightly packed. The most common brassicas you will know are cabbage, broccoli and cauliflower. Brassicas are an extremely nutritious group of veggies, with many of them considered "superfoods" such as kale and broccoli.

THE BENEFITS OF BRASSICAS

Full of fiber: brassicas are a fantastic source of dietary fiber. Fiber helps to keep your digestive system smooth and regular. It also helps to keep blood sugar stable, and is great for reducing the risk of colorectal cancer. Fiber keeps you full, helping to prevent overeating and therefore helping to keep you at a healthy weight.

Great source of Vitamin K: Vitamin K is a great supporter of our bones, helping to keep them dense and strong. Eat lots of brassicas to reduce your chance of osteoporosis. Vitamin K helps to keep our heart healthy and our arteries clear, as well as promoting healthy, clot-free blood flow.

Lots of Vitamin A: Vitamin A protects our eyes and helps to keep our sight strong as we age, it might also reduce your risk of cancer. Vitamin A is a great vitamin to dose up on if you're after clear skin and reduced acne. The bones and the immune system are also supported and cared for by Vitamin A.

Packed with Vitamin C: Vitamin C is vital to us for many reasons and we must get it from food sources. Vitamin C is an antioxidant which protects us from diseases and age-related issues. Vitamin C protects the heart by helping to regulate cholesterol levels. Vitamin C helps our bodies to absorb iron, another very important mineral. Vitamin C supports our immunity and helps to keep us healthy year round.

Low-calorie: like most veggies, brassicas are low in calories. You can eat lots of brassicas without going over your recommended caloric intake, making them a great veggie to turn to for a steady weight.

Low-carb: brassicas are very low in carbohydrates, especially net carbs as they have a high fiber content. They won't spike your blood sugar or give you energy highs and lows.

Cancer-fighting abilities: brassicas contain a powerful set of compounds called glucosinolates which have been proven to reduce the risk of cancer, especially lung cancer.

COMMON BRASSICAS TO ENJOY WITH ABANDON:

Broccoli
Total carbs per 100 grams: 7 grams
Net carbs per 100 grams: 4.4 grams

Cauliflower
Total carbs per 100 grams: 5 grams
Net carbs per 100 grams: 3 grams

Cabbage
Total carbs per 100 grams: 6 grams
Net carbs per 100 grams: 3.5 grams

Brussel sprouts
Total carbs per 100 grams: 9 grams
Net carbs per 100 grams: 5.2 grams

Kale
Total carbs per 100 grams: 8.8 grams
Net carbs per 100 grams: 5.2 grams

Bok choy
Total carbs per 100 grams: 2 grams
Net carbs per 100 grams: 1 gram

Collard greens
Total carbs per 100 grams: 5 grams
Net carbs per 100 grams: 1 gram

A FEW TIPS FOR COOKING AND ENJOYING BRASSICAS

- Buy seasonally to enjoy the freshest brassicas in their prime
- Make cauliflower soup with spices and coconut cream
- Lightly sauté broccoli with fresh chili and garlic
- Finely shred cabbage to make a crunchy slaw
- Steam bok choy and drizzle with sesame oil
- Roast Brussels sprouts with olive oil, sea salt and garlic

DOWNLOAD YOUR FREE BONUS:
simpleoptimum.com/bookbonus

PLANT-BASED HEALTH
4 TIPS FOR HOW TO USE THE PLANTS IN YOUR KITCHEN AND GARDEN TO MAKE YOUR OWN HERBAL TEAS

Making your own herbal teas at home is a fun and creative way to make the best out of your fruits, herbs and flowers. If you have a citrus tree, herb garden or edible flower garden at home, you can regularly make use of your plants to create and store tea mixes. They also make fabulous gifts for loved ones. Pack the herbal tea mixes into small glass jars and make sure to label them.

Ginger
Fresh ginger makes a delicious herbal tea which helps to soothe sore tummies. It goes very well with citrus and turmeric.

Turmeric
Fresh turmeric root makes a golden tea when simmered in water with other flavors such as ginger and lemon peel.

NUTRITIONAL VALUE:

When following a low-carb, plant-based diet you can drink herbal tea with abandon, as long as it's unsweetened. Pouring hot water over dried citrus rinds, dried fruits, herbs and flowers will not add calories to your diet. At the most, you might be consuming 3 or 4 grams of carbs, but barely even that with most teas.

Apples
Dehydrated apples make for a delicious, fruity tea. Lay apple slices out on a rack and place in a dry area. Or, use a dehydrator if you've got one.

Berries
You can dry an excess of fresh berries and add them to tea mixes for a vibrant color and flavor.

CITRUS RINDS AND JUICES

Lemon, lime, orange, mandarin, tangerine and grapefruit peel is full of tasty oils and citrus flavor. You can either use it fresh by peeling the rind and pouring boiling water over the top immediately. Or, you can dry them and use them later, in dried tea mixtures. Don't include the white pith in your peel, as it's quite bitter.

HERBS SUCH AS...

Herbs are the ideal tea ingredient as they provide beautiful aromas, flavors and calming abilities. Use fresh or dried. Some of the tastiest herbs for making homemade teas are mint, lemon, thyme, lemongrass, rosemary, lemon balm, fennel and basil.

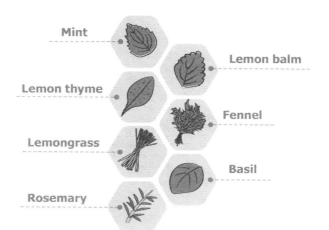

DOWNLOAD YOUR FREE BONUS:
simpleoptimum.com/bookbonus

PLANT-BASED HEALTH

5 TIPS FOR HOW TO USE THE PLANTS IN YOUR KITCHEN AND GARDEN TO MAKE YOUR OWN HERBAL TEAS

FRAGRANT EDIBLE FLOWERS SUCH AS...

Edible flowers lend their stunning aromas to teas, as well as adding subtle flavor. Like herbs, flowers have wonderful medicinal properties.

MAKE CONCENTRATE AND CORDIALS

You don't necessarily have to make dried tea mixes. You can also make concentrated liquids and cordials to mix with hot water for a homemade hot or cold drink. Simmer ingredients such as ginger, turmeric, citrus peel and juice until the mixture thickens and the flavor intensifies. You can also throw some tea bags into the mix as well. Pour into sterilized bottles, label and enjoy!

DRY YOUR INGREDIENTS

A dehydrator comes in very handy when making dried tea mixes. However, you can leave your herbs, citrus peels, fruits and flowers on a rack in a dry place until dried. With large bunches of herbs, tie them at the stalks and hang in a dry place. If you're in a pinch and you need tea fast, you can use the oven on a very low temperature to dry your fresh ingredients.

MAKE CUSTOM MIXES

Get creative and make any flavor combinations you like. Get all of your ingredients ready and lay them out. You could make a little "taster" platter of different combinations to find your signature combination. Make up different mixes with varied flavor profiles, mark clearly and store.

STORAGE

For liquid tea mixes such as cordials and concentrates, glass bottles with tight lids are best. You can use them over and over again, as they can be safely washed and sterilized. For dry tea mixes, glass jars or metal tins with airtight lids are best. Glass jars are great because you can see the tea through the jar, which is not only handy for selecting, but it's pretty too.

Flowers

Rose
Lavender

Jasmine
Chamomile

Nettles

Echinacea
Dandelion
Passionflower

simple + optimum
core routines for extraordinary living

DOWNLOAD YOUR FREE BONUS:
simpleoptimum.com/bookbonus

PLANT-BASED HEALTH
9 TIPS FOR STORING FRESH PRODUCT IN FRIDGE OR CUPBOARD

WHAT SHOULD GO IN THE FRIDGE?

There are many opinions and preferences about where to store certain fruits and veggies. At the end of the day, it does come down to what you prefer and what works best for you, but there are some helpful pointers backed by science to ensure you get the best out of your produce.

Leafy greens

Veggies such as lettuces and spinach must always be stored in the fridge, or else they'll wilt and rot very quickly.

Storage tip: one of the best ways to store leafy veggies is to give them a wash then spin or pat them dry. Wrap them in paper towels or tea towels and pop them in the fridge and they'll stay fresh and crunchy for longer.

Cruciferous veggies

Veggies such as cabbage, broccoli and cauliflower all need to be refrigerated or else they will wilt and become very unappealing. Pop them into your veggie drawer in the fridge and they'll last very well.

Mushrooms

Keep your mushrooms in a paper bag in the fridge and eat them as soon as possible or they tend to go a little hard and develop an odd smell.

Ripe tomatoes

If you've got some very ripe tomatoes which you don't want to ripen further, keep them in the fridge. However, be careful not to put them in the coldest area of the fridge as they can develop an unpleasant, grainy texture or hard, icy patches. The top of the fridge or in the door are great places.

Anything you want to stop from ripening

If you've got produce which usually sits on the counter or in the cupboard, pop it into the fridge once it has reached ripeness. For example, avocadoes, mangoes and tomatoes will all continue to ripen at room temperature but will be halted once they are chilled.

Tip: most veggies which are green, leafy or have a large water content should be in the fridge. Asparagus, kale, spinach, peas, green beans and bell peppers are all examples of veggies we instinctively know should be in the fridge. However, whole pumpkins, squash and sweet potatoes are dryer, harder and have a tougher outer layer which makes them fine to hang out in room temperature areas of the kitchen.

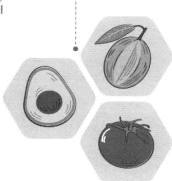

WHAT SHOULD SIT ON THE WINDOWSILL OR COUNTER?

Unripe fruits

Fruits which are still a bit green, hard and unripe can be put on the counter until they ripen to perfect softness. Once they're ripe, pop them into the fridge so they don't become overripe.

Live herbs

Herbs which are still alive and sitting in soil should be placed on the windowsill or sunny countertop. Give them a little water each day and chop them as you require them. With cut herbs, put them in a glass or vase of fresh water and keep them in the fridge.

simple + optimum
core routines for extraordinary living

DOWNLOAD YOUR FREE BONUS:
simpleoptimum.com/bookbonus

PLANT-BASED HEALTH: 5 TIPS FOR STORING FRESH PRODUCT IN FRIDGE OR CUPBOARD

WHAT SHOULD GO IN THE CUPBOARD?

There are many opinions and preferences about where to store certain fruits and veggies. At the end of the day, it does come down to what you prefer and what works best for you, but there are some helpful pointers backed by science to ensure you get the best out of your produce.

Potatoes

Keep your potatoes in a cool, dark place. This will stop them from going green and sprouting. Pack them into a paper bag and keep them on the bottom shelf of your pantry or cupboard. Keep your potatoes and onions separate as they can cause each other to turn bad when kept together.

Whole pumpkins and squash

Keep cut pumpkin and squash in the fridge, but whole, uncut pumpkins and squash can be kept in a cool area of the pantry or cupboard.

Onions and garlic

Keep your white and red onions and your garlic in a cool, dry place such as the bottom of your pantry. Keep them separate from your potatoes so they don't destroy each other!

Citrus

Citrus fruits can be kept in the fridge or at room temperature. Many people do prefer to keep them in a bowl on the counter as they are lovely to eat at room temperature. However, if you live in a very hot climate or you don't think you can eat them all in time, pop them into the fridge or they may grow mold.

Green or unripe tomatoes

Green tomatoes will ripen after they are cut from the vine. Put them into a paper bag and keep them at room temperature in your cupboard. You could put a ripe banana next to the tomatoes if you wish to speed the ripening process.

WHAT SHOULD BE SEPARATED?

The general rule to remember is that fruits and veggies aren't great partners when stored close together. Fruits tend to put off gasses such as ethylene into the atmosphere around them, causing nearby produce to ripen too quickly and ultimately rot. The most well-known example of this is bananas. When you put ripe bananas next to other fruits and veggies, they tend to ripen much faster. Keep your fruits and veggies in separate areas of the kitchen counter, and in different compartments in the fridge.

USING YOUR INSTINCTS

While there are a few rules you should follow, your own instincts are actually very valuable. If you think something needs to go in the fridge, go for it. If you feel it would be best left out for a little longer, follow that feeling. Your particular climate and temperature inside your home can influence how long your fruits and veggies should be left at room temperature or in the fridge. Go with your gut!

simple + optimum — core routines for extraordinary living

DOWNLOAD YOUR FREE BONUS: simpleoptimum.com/bookbonus

Chapter 8: The Two-Week Diet Plan and Grocery Shopping List

Antoine de Saint-Exupéry once said, "A goal without a plan is just a wish."

As such, starting a plant-based or low-carb diet without a well-researched plan can easily result in failure, so let's NOT do that. Remember all you've learned about replacing meat, keeping healthy fats, and keeping your carbs around 20%. If you follow our diet plan for two weeks you'll be doing just that.

You can also try out recipes from this diet plan as a way to move in the less-carbs, more plant-foods direction. We know that change can take time, but this is the ultimate goal!

We have crafted the following plan for all those who have weighed the challenges and benefits and decided that they are ready to follow a plant-based diet.

This includes new ideas for each meal, including snacks and desserts. However, if for any day you need to cook less, you have two options:

- Cook twice the amount for dinner and save half for the next day's lunch
- You can choose one breakfast and eat it for more than one day. If you are not hungry, skip breakfast and begin intermittent fasting

8.1 Breakfast Recipes

Let's start with breakfast options. Choose from some of these great recipes:

Low Carb Vegan Smoothie

Ingredients

- ¼ avocado
- 1 small wedge of cantaloupe
- ¼ cup kiwi fruit
- 1 tbs. chia seeds
- ¼ cup of coconut milk
- ¼ cup vegan vanilla protein powder
- ½ cup water
- ¼ cup ice cubes

Directions

- Peel the avocado and remove pit
- Put it in the blender with all other ingredients including peeled melon and kiwi
- Blend until smooth and serve

Nutritional values per serving

- total energy   457 calories
- net carbs   18.13g
- total fat   26.16g
- protein   41g

PLANT-BASED HEALTH: THE TWO-WEEK DIET PLAN AND GROCERY SHOPPING LIST

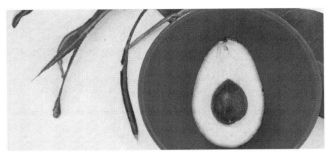

Avocado Smoothie with Ginger and Turmeric

Ingredients

- ¼ avocado
- 6 tbs. coconut milk
- 2 tbs. almond milk
- ½ tsp. grated ginger
- ½ tsp. turmeric
- ½ tsp. lemon juice
- ½ cup ice cubes

Directions

- add all the ingredients in a blender and blend until smooth and frothy
- enjoy

Nutritional values per serving

- Total energy   292 calories
- net carbs   5.8g
- total fat   28g
- protein   4g

Blackberry Cheesecake Smoothie

Ingredients

- ½ cup frozen blackberries
- ¼ cup creamed coconut milk
- ¼ cup coconut milk
- ½ cup water
- 1 tbs. extra-virgin coconut oil
- ½ tsp. vanilla extract (unsweetened)
- 2-4 fresh blackberries

Directions

- place all the ingredients in a blender and pulse until smooth and frothy
- empty into the serving glass. It's optional to garnish with fresh blackberries

Nutritional values per serving

- total energy   434 calories
- net carbs   25.75 g
- total fat   57.28 g
- protein   6.65 g

Healthy Green Smoothie

Ingredients

- 1 medium sized avocado
- ½ cup fresh spinach
- ½ cup coconut milk
- ½ cup water
- ½ cup ice cubes
- ½ tsp. vanilla extract (vegan)
- 1 tbs. extra-virgin coconut oil
- 1 tsp. matcha powder
- ¼ cup vegan chocolate

Directions

- remove avocado pit and scoop the flesh out
- add all the ingredients in a blender and pulse until smooth
- add ice cubes and blend again
- serve chilled

PLANT-BASED HEALTH : THE TWO-WEEK DIET PLAN AND GROCERY SHOPPING LIST

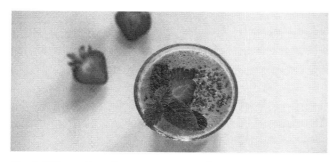

Nutritional values per serving

- total energy   878 calories
- net carbs   24.5 g
- total fat   81 g
- protein   11.4 g

Nutritional values per serving

- total energy   58 calories
- net carbs   3g
- total fat   4.2g
- protein   1g

Quick Strawberry Smoothie

Ingredients

- 1 cup coconut milk
- 1/3 cup strawberries
- ½ tsp. vanilla extract (vegan)

Directions

- put all the ingredients in a blender and blend until smooth
- serve and enjoy

Nutritional values per serving

- total energy   571 calories
- net carbs   5 g
- total fat   57.1 g
- protein   5.33 g

Berry Banana Smoothie

Ingredients

- 1 banana (fresh or frozen)
- ¼ cup frozen raspberries
- ¼ cup frozen strawberries
- ½ handful of fresh spinach
- ½ tsp. chia seeds
- ½ tbs. almond butter
- ½ cup ice cold water

Directions

- put all the ingredients in a blender and blend until smooth
- serve and enjoy

Nutritional values per serving

- total energy   222 calories
- net carbs   36.95 g
- total fat   9 g
- protein   8 g

Green Detox Smoothie

Ingredients

- 1 cup of water
- ¼ cup romaine lettuce
- ¼ cup freshly chopped cucumber
- ¼ bilse avocado (flesh scooped out)
- ¼ cup freshly chopped pineapple
- ¼ cup chopped kiwi fruit
- 1 tbs. fresh parsley
- ½ tbs. freshly chopped ginger
- ¼ cup crushed ice

Directions

- combine all the ingredients in a blender
- add crushed ice and stir well before serving

simple + optimum
core routines for extraordinary living

DOWNLOAD YOUR FREE BONUS:
simpleoptimum.com/bookbonus

THE TWO-WEEK DIET PLAN AND GROCERY SHOPPING LIST

Nutritional values per serving

- total energy   133 calories
- net carbs   12g
- total fat   10.9g
- protein   9g

Peanut Butter Chocolate Smoothie

Ingredients

- 1 cup coconut milk (unsweetened)
- 1 tbs. cocoa powder (unsweetened)
- 1 tbs. peanut butter (unsweetened)
- a pinch of sea salt

Directions

- place all the ingredients in blender
- pulse until frothy
- enjoy

Nutritional values per serving

- total energy   156 calories
- net carbs   4.63g
- total fat   13.24g
- protein   5g

Mexican Chocolate Shake

Ingredients

- 3 tbs. coconut cream
- 1 tbs. extra-virgin coconut oil
- ½ tbs. chia seeds (ground)
- 1 tbs. cocoa powder (unsweetened)
- ¼ tsp. vanilla extract (vegan)
- ¼ tsp. cayenne powder

- ¼ tsp. cinnamon powder
- ½ cup water
- ¼ cup ice cubes

Directions

- add all ingredients and blend for at least 30 seconds
- sprinkle some cinnamon powder over the top and serve

Nutritional Values per Serving

- total energy   327 calories
- net carbs   2.96 g
- total fat   36.1 g
- protein   2.75 g

Low Carb Blueberry Smoothie

Ingredients

- 1 cup coconut milk
- ¼ cup frozen blueberries
- ½ tbs. lemon juice
- ¼ tsp. vegan vanilla extract

Directions

- put all the ingredients in a blender and pulse until frothy
- empty in serving glass and enjoy

Nutritional values per serving

- total energy   575.5 calories
- net carbs   12 g
- total fat   57 g
- protein   6 g

PLANT-BASED HEALTH : THE TWO-WEEK DIET PLAN AND GROCERY SHOPPING LIST

Healthy Green Smoothie

Ingredients

- 1 medium-sized avocado
- ½ cup fresh spinach
- ½ cup coconut milk
- ½ cup water
- ½ cup ice cubes
- ½ tsp. vanilla extract (vegan)
- 1 tbs. extra-virgin coconut oil
- 1 tsp. Matcha powder
- ¼ cup vegan chocolate

Directions

- remove the pit of the avocado and scoop out the green flesh
- add all the ingredients to blender and pulse until smooth
- add ice cubes and blend again
- serve chilled

Nutritional values per serving

- total energy   878 calories
- net carbs   24.5 g
- total fat   81 g
- protein   11.4 g

Cinnamon Smoothie

Ingredients

- 1 cup of almond milk
- ½ tsp. cinnamon powder
- 1 tsp. flaxseed meal
- ¼ tsp. vanilla extract (vegan)
- 1 cup crushed ice

Directions

- add all the ingredients in a blender except the ice and pulse until well combined and smooth
- add crushed ice and pulse once again. Serve chilled and enjoy

Nutritional values per serving

- total energy   58 calories
- net carbs   0.85 g
- total fat   4.68 g
- protein   2.06 g

Matcha Smoothie Bowl

Ingredients

- ¼ avocado
- 1 handful greens
- ½ tsp. matcha powder
- ½ cup almond milk
- 1 handful of strawberries
- 6 blackberries
- ½ tbs. coconut flakes
- ½ tsp. crushed pecans
- 1 tsp. chia seeds
- ¼ cup ice cubes

Directions

- add almond milk, avocado, matcha powder and greens to a blender and pulse until smooth
- add ice cubes and blend again
- pour into a large serving bowl. Top with pecans, chia seeds, coconut flakes and berries
- enjoy

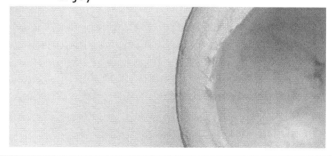

PLANT-BASED HEALTH: THE TWO-WEEK DIET PLAN AND GROCERY SHOPPING LIST

Nutritional values per serving

- total energy   250 calories
- net carbs   8g
- total fat   23g
- protein   17g

Raspberry Avocado Smoothie

Ingredients

- 1/2 medium-sized avocado with pit removed
- ½ cup water
- 1.5 tbs. fresh lemon juice
- ½ cup frozen raspberries (unsweetened)
- ¼ cup crushed ice

Directions

- put all the ingredients in a blender and blend until smooth and frothy
- empty in serving glasses and enjoy

Nutritional values per serving

- total energy   229.5 calories
- net carbs   10.3g
- total fat   15.8g
- protein   3.5g

Blackcurrant Smoothie

Ingredients

- ½ cup fresh black currants
- A handful of fresh strawberries
- ¼ cup coconut milk
- ½ cup water

- 2 tbs. chia seeds
- ¼ cup crushed ice
- ½ tsp vanilla extract (vegan)

Directions

- put all the ingredients in a blender
- pulse until smooth and serve

Nutritional values per serving

- total energy   323 calories
- net carbs   25g
- total fat   24g
- protein   8g

8.2 Lunch Recipes

Lunch can be just as satisfying and healthy as breakfast. Try these recipes:

Low Carb Coconut Granola

Ingredients

- ¼ cup unsweetened coconut flakes
- 3 tbs. unsweetened coconut milk
- 3 tbs. cup water
- 1 tbs. coconut flour
- 1 tsp. chia seeds
- ½ tsp. cinnamon
- handful of mixed berries

Directions

- toast coconut flakes carefully in a cooking pot on a medium-high heat until golden

THE TWO-WEEK DIET PLAN AND GROCERY SHOPPING LIST

- add coconut milk and water. Stir well
- cover and simmer for a while. Bring it to a boil
- empty into a bowl and add chia seeds. Mix well
- garnish with cinnamon and berries

Nutritional values per serving

- total energy   214 calories
- net carbs   13.07g
- total fat   16.09g
- protein   4.63g

Summer Cucumber Salad with Tahini

Ingredients

- 1 English cucumber
- ¼ tsp. salt
- 1 tsp. lemon juice
- ¼ tsp. ground pepper
- ¼ tsp. ground cumin
- 1 tsp. extra-virgin olive oil
- 3 tbs. sesame tahini

Directions

- cut the cucumber into thirds and sprinkle with some salt. Set aside
- in a bowl, combine lemon juice, ground pepper, cumin and olive oil. Mix well
- dry the cucumbers before adding them to the bowl
- mix well with the dressing and serve

Nutritional values per serving

- total energy   577 calories
- net carbs   7g

- total fat   5.2 g
- protein   2.35 g

Cheesy Broccoli Patties

Ingredients

- ½ tbs. flax seeds
- 1.5 tbs. warm water
- ½ cup broccoli florets (chopped)
- 1/3 cup chickpea flour
- 1 tbs. nutritional yeast
- ½ tsp. sea salt
- ¼ tsp. garlic powder
- Olive oil for frying

Directions

- mix flax seeds with warm water and set aside. This works as an egg replacement
- chop broccoli florets into small pieces with a knife and steam until fork-tender
- in a bowl, add garlic powder, salt, nutritional yeast and chickpea flour and mix well Add the flaxseed mixture and then the broccoli. Mix until well combined
- make 6 patties out of this mixture
- place these fritters in the skillet and cook each side for about 3 minutes or until golden brown. Empty into a serving dish and enjoy

Nutritional values per serving

- total energy   224 calories
- net carbs   17g
- total fat   13g
- protein   14g

PLANT-BASED HEALTH: THE TWO-WEEK DIET PLAN AND GROCERY SHOPPING LIST

Warm Cauliflower Salad

Ingredients

- ½ head cauliflower, cut into florets
- ½ mashed garlic clove
- 1 tbs. chopped capers
- 2 tbs. lemon juice
- 2 tbs. olive oil
- salt and black pepper to taste
- a handful of freshly chopped parsley
- olive oil for brushing

Directions

- preheat the oven to 425 □
- brush the cauliflower with olive oil and roast in the oven until golden
- take a small bowl and add the mashed garlic, chopped capers, salt, pepper, olive oil, and lemon juice. Whisk together until well combined
- toss the cauliflower in this dressing and sprinkle some parsley before serving

Nutritional values per serving

- total energy   355 calories
- net carbs   7g
- total fat   29g
- protein   7g

Grilled Vegetable Salad

Ingredients

- 1 corn on cob (husked)
- ½ bell pepper (quartered)

- ½ cup baby zucchini
- 1 tbs. extra-virgin olive oil
- salt and ground pepper to taste
- ¼ tbs. fresh lemon juice
- ½ tbs. freshly chopped oregano

Directions

- preheat barbeque grill to medium-high
- add corn, bell peppers, zucchini, 2 tbs. oil, salt and pepper to a bowl and toss well
- oil the grill rack, and grill the vegetables until tender (around 6 minutes for both zucchini and bell peppers and about 8 minutes for the corn)
- chop the bell peppers and zucchini into bite-size pieces and cut the corn kernels from cobs
- transfer the grilled vegetables to a bowl and garnish with oregano, lemon juice, and the remaining oil

Nutritional values per serving

- total energy   285 calories
- net carbs   32.7 g
- total fat   9 g
- protein   4.9 g

Spaghetti Squash and Pesto

Ingredients

- 1/2 small spaghetti squash
- 1.5 tbs. sun-dried tomatoes
- 1 handful of raw cashews
- 1 handful of toasted pine nuts

PLANT-BASED HEALTH: THE TWO-WEEK DIET PLAN AND GROCERY SHOPPING LIST

- 1 tbs. nutritional yeast
- ¼ tsp. sea salt
- 1 cup fresh basil
- 1 minced garlic clove
- extra-virgin olive oil for brushing
- red pepper flakes (optional)
- vegan parmesan cheese (optional)

Directions

- preheat oven to 400 ☐ and place foil on the baking sheet
- halve spaghetti squash along the length using a sharp knife
- use an ice cream scoop to scrape out the seeds
- brush the inside with oil and salt. Place cut-side down on baking sheet and bake for 40-50 minutes
- meanwhile, add pine nuts, cashews, nutritional yeast and salt to a food processor and pulse until well combined
- add basil, sun-dried tomatoes, garlic and olive oil into this mixture and combine. Add some water (2-3 tbs.)
- scoop out spaghetti squash, forming fine strings using a fork. Top it with pesto and toss lightly
- sprinkle with vegan parmesan cheese and red pepper flakes. Enjoy

Nutritional values per serving

- energy   426 calories
- net carbs   18.59g
- total fat   28.06g
- protein   14.16g

Vegetable Tahini Salad

Ingredients

- 1 tbs. olive oil
- 1 pickle-size Persian cucumber
- ½ large tomato (diced)
- 2 radishes (diced)
- ½ scallion (diced)
- ¼ bunch parsley (chopped)
- 1 mashed garlic clove
- 5 mint leaves (chopped)
- ¼ cup tahini
- 2 tbs. lemon juice
- salt to taste

Directions

- combine the cucumber, green onion, tomato, mint, radish, and parsley in a small bowl
- whisk together the tahini, garlic, lemon juice, salt, and olive oil until smooth
- drizzle the dressing over the vegetables and mix well. Refrigerate for 30 minutes
- serve chilled and enjoy

Nutritional values per serving

- total energy   502 calories
- net carbs   14g
- total fat   31g
- protein   7g

Summer Cucumber Salad with Tahini

Ingredients

- 1 English cucumbers

PLANT-BASED HEALTH: THE TWO-WEEK DIET PLAN AND GROCERY SHOPPING LIST

- ¼ tsp. salt
- 1 tsp. lemon juice
- ¼ tsp. ground pepper
- ¼ tsp. ground cumin
- 1 tsp. extra-virgin olive oil
- 3 tbs. tahini

Directions

- cut the cucumber into thirds and sprinkle with some salt. Set aside
- in a bowl, mix lemon juice, ground pepper, cumin and olive oil
- dry the cucumbers before adding them to the bowl
- mix well and serve

Nutritional values per serving

- total energy   577 calories
- net carbs   7g
- total fat   5.2 g
- protein   2.35 g

Russian Slaw

Ingredients

- ½ cup medium green cabbage
- ½ cup small red cabbage
- ½ cup medium celeriac, grated
- ½ fennel medium bulb

For Russian dressing

- 2 tbs. coconut milk
- 1 tbs. hot chili sauce
- 1 pickled cucumber
- 2 tbs. fresh lemon juice
- 1 tsp. freshly grated horseradish
- 2 tbs. freshly chopped chives
- 2 tbs. freshly chopped parsley
- Salt and black pepper to taste

Directions

- shred both green and red cabbage using a food processor, put in a bowl
- add the grated celeriac and shredded fennel to the bowl
- mix all the ingredients for the Russian dressing in a separate bowl
- add this dressing to the vegetables and mix well
- it's ready to eat

Nutritional values per serving

- total energy 261 calories
- net carbs 18g

Bok Choy Salad and 1 Cup of Almonds

Ingredients

- ½ tbs. peanut oil
- 1 cup fresh bok choy (tough ends removed)
- ½ cup fresh spinach leaves (tough stems removed)
- ½ tomato, finely diced
- 3 tbs. cashew nuts
- 1 tsp. mustard seeds
- 1 tsp. cumin seeds
- ¼ tsp. cayenne pepper
- ¼ cup water
- ¼ tsp. turmeric
- salt to taste

PLANT-BASED HEALTH: THE TWO-WEEK DIET PLAN AND GROCERY SHOPPING LIST

Directions

- preheat oven to 325 ☐ and bake cashew nuts until lightly golden
- heat the peanut oil in a medium pan over medium-high heat. Add cumin seeds and cook for 30 seconds, stirring continuously
- add the diced tomato, turmeric, mustard seeds, salt, and cayenne pepper. Cover with lid and cook for about 5 minutes on reduced heat
- add water and bring to a boil. Keeping the heat low, add bok choy and spinach and cook for 3-5 minutes
- put into a serving bowl and sprinkle with roasted cashew nuts

Nutritional values per serving

- total energy   345 calories
- net carbs   16.55g
- total fat   26.98
- protein   10g

Almonds (1 Cup)

Nutritional value per cup

- total energy   739 calories
- total fat   64 g
- net carbs   24 g
- total proteins 26 g

Grilled Eggplant with Parsley, Red Pepper, and Mint

Ingredients

- 1 long Asian eggplant
- olive oil for grilling
- ½ tbs. chopped parsley
- ½ tbs. chopped mint
- 1 tbsp. olive oil
- 1 tsp. red wine vinegar
- 1 tsp. fresh lemon juice
- ½ tsp. ground garlic
- ½ tsp. hot paprika
- ½ tsp. Spike seasoning (optional)

Directions

- mix olive oil, lemon juice, garlic, Spike seasoning (optional), chopped mint and parsley, red wine vinegar, and paprika in a bowl, and set aside
- wash eggplant thoroughly, let it dry and cut into even slices. You do not need to salt the eggplant
- preheat barbecue grill to medium-high
- brush both sides of eggplants with olive oil
- place eggplant on grill and cook for about 5 minutes per side, until you get nice brown grill marks
- empty into a tray in single layer, and apply the spicy sauce on each side of the eggplant slices. Wait 10 minutes
- sprinkle some mint and parsley over the eggplant slices and serve at room temperature

Nutritional values per serving

- total energy   250 calories
- net carbs   8 g
- total fat   24 g
- protein   3.6 g

PLANT-BASED HEALTH: THE TWO-WEEK DIET PLAN AND GROCERY SHOPPING LIST

Sweetcorn, Avocado and Quinoa Salad

Ingredients

- ½ tbs. extra-virgin olive oil
- ¼ cup uncooked quinoa
- ¼ cup diced cherry tomatoes
- 1 finely chopped spring onion
- ¼ cup frozen sweetcorn
- ½ ripe avocado
- ½ small pack fresh coriander (chopped)
- ½ tbs. finely grated lemon zest
- ½ tbs. lemon juice
- ½ long finely chopped red chili

Directions

- half fill a medium pan with water and bring it to boil. Add quinoa and simmer for about 12 minutes
- meanwhile, add sweetcorn to a fry pan and cook for 5 minutes. When lightly toasted, turn off the flame and set aside
- empty cooked quinoa into a sieve and press hard to remove excess water
- transfer the quinoa to a bowl and add olive oil, diced tomatoes, chopped coriander, spring onions, lime zest, and toasted sweetcorn
- season with black pepper and lemon juice. Serve

Nutritional values per serving

- total energy   547.75 calories
- net carbs   39.81g
- total fat   32.6g
- protein   5.3g

Low Carb Potato Salad

Ingredients

- 250 gram pack of new potatoes
- 1 tbs. vegan Dijon mustard
- 1 tbs. finely grated lemon zest
- 1 tbs. lemon juice
- 2.5 tbs. extra-virgin olive oil
- ¼ cup roughly chopped flat leaf parsley
- 1 sliced spring onion

Directions

- boil the potatoes in salted water until tender
- meanwhile, take a small bowl and add Dijon mustard, olive oil, lemon juice and zest. Whisk together the ingredients
- drain the potatoes and empty into a large bowl. Add the dressing to the potatoes and gently mix. Set aside for 15 minutes
- finally, add parsley and spring onions. Enjoy

Nutritional values per serving

- total energy   527 calories
- net carbs   39 g
- total fat   36.27 g
- protein   6.5 g

Lentils

For recipes in both the lunch and dinner sections calling for "cooked lentils" we recommend using whole dried lentils and cooking them before you begin the rest of the recipe. To cook whole dried

PLANT-BASED HEALTH: THE TWO-WEEK DIET PLAN AND GROCERY SHOPPING LIST

lentils, use 3 cups of water per 1 cup of dried lentils and simmer in a covered pot until soft! It generally takes no longer than 20 minutes, depending on quantities. If time is a real pinch for you, there is the option of using canned lentils if you need to cook in a rush. The same goes for chickpeas, we recommend using dried chickpeas and soaking them overnight before boiling them to softness.

Beans and lentils often require only 10 minutes of your time to prepare.

Red Dahl with Cauliflower Rice

Red lentils cooked to soft perfection with gentle spices and vegetable stock. Dolloped on a bed of cauliflower rice, this dish is warming, satisfying and full of fiber.

Serves: 4

Time: approximately 30 minutes

Ingredients

- 1 cup dried red lentils, rinsed (don't precook)
- 1 onion, finely chopped
- garlic cloves, finely chopped
- cups vegetable stock
- 1 tsp ground turmeric
- 1 tsp chili powder
- 2 tsp curry powder or garam masala
- Salt and pepper
- Fresh coriander to garnish

- 1 head cauliflower, blitzed in a food processor until the size of rice granules
- Tbsp olive oil
- Salt and pepper

Directions

- Place the lentils, onion, garlic, stock, turmeric, chili, curry powder/garam masala, salt and pepper into a saucepan and bring to a boil
- Once the pot is boiling, reduce the temperature to achieve a gentle simmer with the lid on, simmer for about 30 minutes, stirring occasionally
- As the dahl simmers, prepare the cauliflower rice: heat the olive oil in a large frying pan
- Add the cauliflower to the hot pan and stir as it cooks, add salt and pepper to taste
- Once the dahl is thick and the lentils are soft, you're ready to serve
- Garnish with lots of fresh coriander

Nutritional values per serving

- Calories: 285
- Fat: 7 grams
- Total carbs: 37 grams
- Net carbs: 29 grams
- Protein: 14 grams

Brown Lentil, Lemon and Pumpkin Seed Salad

This salad couldn't be easier. There is barely any cooking involved, apart from boiling the lentils

PLANT-BASED HEALTH: THE TWO-WEEK DIET PLAN AND GROCERY SHOPPING LIST

and quickly toasting the pumpkin seeds. Fresh parsley and lemon juice bring freshness and flavor to the dish.

Serves: 4

Time: approximately 10 minutes plus time to cook the lentils first

Ingredients

- cups cooked brown lentils
- 1 garlic clove, minced or crushed
- Tbsp pumpkin seeds, toasted on a dry pan
- ½ cup fresh parsley, finely chopped
- Juice and zest of 1 lemon
- 2 Tbsp olive oil
- Salt and pepper

Directions

- Place the lentils, garlic, pumpkin seeds, parsley, lemon juice and zest, olive oil, salt and pepper into a large bowl and stir to combine
- Serve immediately or keep in an airtight container in the fridge until needed

Nutritional values per serving

- Calories: 295
- Fat: 13 grams
- Total carbs: 32 grams
- Net carbs: 19 grams
- Protein: 17 grams

Lentil and Cashew "Meatballs"

These meatballs are of course, completely meat-free. They contain a base of lentils, cashews, ground almonds and spices. The balls are drenched in a simple tomato and coconut sauce.

Serves: 4

Time: approximately 30 minutes plus time to cook the lentils first

Ingredients

- 2 Tbsp olive oil
- ½ onion, finely chopped
- 2 garlic cloves, finely chopped
- 2 cups cooked brown lentils
- ½ cup raw cashew nuts, chopped
- ½ cup ground almonds
- ½ tsp ground cumin
- ½ tst chili powder
- Salt and pepper
- 1 ½ cups fresh tomatoes, blitzed in the food processor until smooth
- ¾ cup coconut cream
- Salt and pepper

Directions

- Preheat the oven to 400 degrees Fahrenheit and line a baking tray with baking paper
- Drizzle the olive oil into a frying pan and place over a medium heat

PLANT-BASED HEALTH: THE TWO-WEEK DIET PLAN AND GROCERY SHOPPING LIST

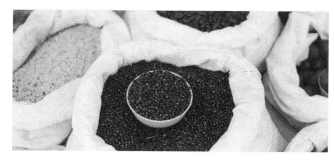

- Add the onion, garlic and cashews to the hot pan and stir as the onions become soft and translucent
- Take the pan off the heat and add the lentils, almonds, cumin, chili, salt and pepper, stir to combine thoroughly
- Roll the mixture into balls and place onto the lined baking tray, leave the pan aside and don't wash it yet, you want all the leftover flavors to go into the sauce
- Bake the balls in the oven for about 20 minutes or until golden
- While the balls cook, make the sauce: pour the tomato puree and coconut cream into the same pan you used for the balls, season with salt and pepper. Let the sauce come to a gentle simmer and allow it to thicken and become rich
- Once the balls are cooked, pop them back into the pan with the sauce before serving

Nutritional values per serving

- Calories: 370
- Fat: 20 grams
- Total carbs: 37 grams
- Net carbs: 25.5 grams
- Protein: 17 grams

Lentil, Chickpea and Radish Salad with Balsamic Vinaigrette

Another cooling, refreshing salad with no cooking required. This salad contains chickpeas as well as lentils for extra texture and nutrition. If cooking dried chickpeas, it's a good idea to get them soaking the night before, so they boil more easily.

Serves: 5

Time: approximately 10 minutes plus time to cook the lentils and chickpeas first

Ingredients

- 2 cups cooked lentils (use any color you have or prefer)
- 1 cup cooked chickpeas
- 4 radishes, thinly sliced
- ½ cucumber, sliced
- 3 cups baby spinach
- ¼ cup fresh mint, finely chopped
- 3 Tbsp olive oil
- 2 Tbsp balsamic vinegar
- Salt and pepper

Directions

- Place the lentils, chickpeas, radishes, cucumber, spinach and mint into a large bowl and stir to combine
- Combine the olive oil, balsamic vinegar, salt and pepper and pour over the salad, gently toss
- Serve immediately or store in an airtight container in the fridge

Nutritional values per serving

- Calories: 250
- Fat: 10 grams
- Total carbs: 30 grams
- Net carbs: 19 grams
- Protein: 11 grams

PLANT-BASED HEALTH: THE TWO-WEEK DIET PLAN AND GROCERY SHOPPING LIST

Spicy Black Bean Soup

Ingredients

- 1 tbs. olive oil
- ½ cup of rinsed black beans
- 1 small chopped yellow onion
- 1 small chopped carrot
- 1 chopped celery rib
- 2 medium chopped garlic cloves
- 2 cups of low sodium vegetable broth
- ½ tablespoon lime juice
- ½ tablespoon apple cider vinegar
- 1 handful of fresh cilantro leaves
- ½ tbs. ground cumin
- kosher salt to taste
- ½ chili pepper
- ½ finely diced jalapeno chili
- A pinch of ground black pepper
- red pepper

Directions

- heat olive oil in a cooking pot and add the chopped onion, celery, jalapeno, carrot and garlic
- sauté until the vegetables soften
- now add cumin, beans, and vegetable stock and cook on low flame for 30 minutes
- add lime juice, finely chopped cilantro leaves, and apple cider vinegar. Stir to mix well
- blend the soup using a hand blender for a lumpy texture
- add salt and pepper to taste and empty into a bowl
- garnish with diced jalapeno and diced red pepper

Nutritional values per serving

- total energy 678 calories
- total fat 28 g
- net carbs 51 g
- protein 22.6 g

Cold Lentil and Walnut Salad with Apple and Scallions

Apples and walnuts are a fantastic combination, especially in a cold salad like this one.

Serves: 4

Time: approximately 10 minutes plus time to cook the lentils first

Ingredients

- 2 cups cooked brown lentils
- 1 large apple, cut into small pieces (keep the skin on but discard the core and seeds)
- ½ cup walnuts, roughly chopped
- 4 Tbsp scallions
- 4 cups shredded iceberg lettuce
- 1 carrot, grated
- 2 Tbsp olive oil
- 1 Tbsp apple cider vinegar
- Salt and pepper

Directions

- Place all ingredients into a large bowl and gently toss to combine and coat with olive oil and apple cider vinegar

PLANT-BASED HEALTH: THE TWO-WEEK DIET PLAN AND GROCERY SHOPPING LIST

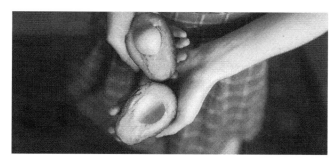

- This salad is best eaten fresh to ensure the apples don't go brown

Nutritional values per serving

- Calories: 315
- Fat: 17 grams
- Total carbs: 30 grams
- Net carbs: 19 grams
- Protein: 12.5 grams

"Sushi" Bowls with Lentils, Nori and Avocado

These bowls take inspiration from sushi as they contain nori sheets (dried seaweed), avocado and a dash of rice wine vinegar.

Serves: 4

Time: 20 minutes plus time to cook the lentils first

Ingredients

- 2 cups cooked brown lentils
- 2 nori sheets, cut into squares
- 2 avocados, flesh sliced
- 1 carrot, cut into strips
- ½ cucumber, peeled into ribbons with a potato peeler
- 4 Tbsp sesame seeds, lightly toasted on a dry pan
- 2 Tbsp coconut aminos (optional, but they're a soy-free substitute for soy sauce)
- 2 Tbsp rice wine vinegar
- 2 Tbsp olive oil

Directions

- Divide the lentils between the bowls to create a base
- Divide the nori squares and place them at the edge of the bowl
- Arrange the avocado, carrot and cucumber around the sides of the bowl
- Sprinkle the toasted sesame seeds onto the veggies
- Mix together the coconut aminos (if using), rice wine vinegar and olive oil and drizzle over the bowls before serving

Nutritional values per serving

- Calories: 365
- Fat: 22 grams
- Total carbs: 32 grams
- Net carbs: 16.5 grams
- Protein: 13 grams

Tomato-Based Warming Lentil Soup

This soup is so easy and requires simple ingredients most people have in their cupboard at all times.

Serves: 4

Time: approximately 30 minutes

Ingredients

- 2 Tbsp olive oil
- ½ onion, finely chopped
- 4 garlic cloves, finely chopped

PLANT-BASED HEALTH: THE TWO-WEEK DIET PLAN AND GROCERY SHOPPING LIST

- 1 fresh red chili, finely chopped
- 4 cups chopped fresh tomatoes
- 1 cup vegetable stock
- 1 cup dried red lentils
- Salt and pepper

Directions

- Drizzle the olive oil into a large saucepan and place over a medium heat
- Add the onion, garlic and chili to the hot pot and stir as the onions soften
- Add the fresh tomatoes, stock, lentils, salt and pepper to the pot and stir to combine
- Allow the soup to come to the boil before reducing to a simmer
- Simmer for approximately 20-25 minutes or until the lentils are soft
- Serve immediately

Nutritional values per serving

- Calories: 300
- Fat: 7 grams
- Total carbs: 36 grams
- Net carbs: 21.5 grams
- Protein: 14 grams

Red Cabbage, Mango and Lentil Slaw with Lime Dressing

Fresh mango gives this salad a fresh sweetness to offset the savory lentils. Great for Summertime dinners.

Serves: 4

Time: approximately 15 minutes plus time to cook the lentils first

Ingredients

- 4 cups shredded red cabbage
- 2 Tbsp chopped scallions
- 1 mango, flesh cut into small pieces
- 2 cups cooked brown lentils
- Juice of 1 lime
- 2 Tbsp olive oil
- Salt and pepper

Directions

- Combine all ingredients in a large bowl and serve immediately or store in the fridge in a covered container

Nutritional values per serving

- Calories: 240
- Fat: 8 grams
- Total carbs: 35 grams
- Net carbs: 25 grams
- Protein: 11 grams

Lentil, Barley and Kale Salad

A small amount of barley gives a chewy nuttiness, while seeds give crunch and cucumber provides freshness.

THE TWO-WEEK DIET PLAN AND GROCERY SHOPPING LIST

Serves: 4

Time: approximately 30 minutes plus time to cook the lentils first

Ingredients

- 1 cup cooked brown lentils
- ½ cup dried barley
- 2 cups finely shredded kale
- 2 Tbsp pumpkin seeds
- 2 Tbsp sunflower seeds
- 1 Tbsp sesame seeds
- 2 tomatoes, cut into chunks
- ½ cucumber, cut into chunks
- ½ cup fresh parsley, finely chopped
- Salt and pepper

Dressing:

- 3 Tbsp olive oil
- Juice of 1 orange
- 2 tsp dijon mustard

Directions

- Rinse the raw barley and place it into a saucepan with 1 and a half cups of water and a pinch of salt, cover and allow to simmer until the water evaporates and the barley is soft to bite
- Stir the lentils into the cooked barley and season with more salt and pepper if necessary
- Transfer the barley and lentil mixture to a large bowl and add all of the remaining salad ingredients (not including the dressing ingredients), gently toss to combine
- Combine the dressing ingredients in a small bowl and pour over the salad, gently fold through
- Serve cold or warm

Nutritional values per serving

- Calories: 350
- Fat: 17 grams
- Total carbs: 40 grams
- Net carbs: 29.5 grams
- Protein: 12 grams

Leek, Mushroom and Lentil Dry Curry

This curry is drier than other curries, letting the leeks, mushrooms and lentils shine through. Make sure you find a vegan curry paste.

Serves: 4

Time: approximately 30 minutes plus time to cook the lentils first

Ingredients

- 3 Tbsp olive oil
- 1 onion, finely chopped
- 3 garlic cloves, finely chopped
- 3 Tbsp curry paste, a good-quality authentic store bought vegan paste is fine, or you can make your own if you have a favorite recipe
- Two leeks, green parts removed, sliced
- 2 cups mixed mushrooms, sliced

- 2 cups cooked brown lentils
- 1 cup coconut cream

Directions

- Drizzle the olive oil into a large frying pan or saucepan and place over a medium heat
- Add the onion, garlic, curry paste, leeks and mushrooms and stir as they cook and soften together
- Add the lentils and stir to combine with the curry paste and veggies
- Stir the coconut cream through and allow to simmer for about 15-20 minutes
- Serve hot with cauliflower rice if desired

Nutritional values per serving

- Calories: 425
- Fat: 24 grams
- Total carbs: 43 grams
- Net carbs: 32 grams
- Protein: 14 grams

Roasted Lentil-Stuffed Capsicums

Capsicums are great for stuffing, and these ones are stuffed with lentils and spices.

Serves: 4

Time: 35 minutes plus time to cook the lentils first

Ingredients

- 4 red capsicums, seeds removed, cut in half
- 2 Tbsp olive oil
- 3 garlic cloves, finely chopped
- 1 onion, finely chopped
- 2 cups cooked brown lentils
- 1 tsp ground cumin
- 1 tsp ground coriander seeds
- ½ cup fresh coriander, finely chopped
- Salt and pepper

Directions

- Preheat the oven to 400 degrees Fahrenheit and line a baking tray with baking paper
- Place the capsicum halves onto the line baking tray
- In a bowl, combine the olive oil, garlic, onion, lentils, cumin, coriander seeds, fresh coriander, salt and pepper
- Spoon the lentil mixture into the capsicum halves
- Bake the stuffed capsicums in the preheated oven for approximately 25-30 minutes or until golden and soft
- Serve hot, warm or cold

Nutritional values per serving

- Calories: 260
- Fat: 11 grams
- Total carbs: 30 grams
- Net carbs: 18 grams
- Protein: 12 grams

Fresh Strawberry, Lentil and Citrus Salad

Fresh strawberries can be used in so many ways, like this unique lentil salad dotted with fresh orange and baby spinach.

PLANT-BASED HEALTH: THE TWO-WEEK DIET PLAN AND GROCERY SHOPPING LIST

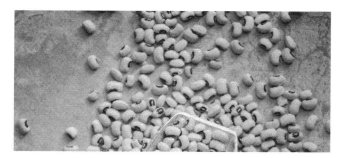

Serves: 4

Time: 15 minutes plus time to cook the lentils first

Ingredients

- 12 strawberries, chopped into quarters
- 2 cups cooked brown lentils
- 1 orange, peeled and cut into small pieces
- 2 garlic cloves, minced
- 3 cups baby spinach leaves, roughly chopped
- 4 Tbsp pumpkin seeds
- 2 Tbsp olive oil
- Salt and pepper

Directions

- Place all ingredients into a large salad bowl and toss to combine
- Serve immediately to enjoy the freshness of the strawberries

Nutritional values per serving

- Calories: 275
- Fat: 13 grams
  Total carbs: 30 grams
- Net carbs: 20 grams
  Protein: 14 grams

Beans

Preparing dried beans is simple. All you need to do is soak the beans overnight in plenty of cold water, then boil them the next day until soft.

The general rule for soaking dried beans is 10 cups of cold water per 2 cups of dried beans or chickpeas. If you're completely blindsided and need a quick meal ASAP, there is always the option of using a good-quality canned bean without any added sugars or flavors.

Tomato, Basil and Bean Salad

Kind of like a caprese salad without the cheese, this salad utilizes the sweet juiciness of fresh tomatoes and the fragrance of fresh basil.

Serves: 4

Time: approximately 10 minutes plus time to soak and cook the beans

Ingredients

- 4 large, ripe tomatoes, sliced
- 12 fresh basil leaves, torn
- 1 cup cooked chickpeas
- 1 cup cooked black beans
- 2 Tbsp olive oil
- Salt and pepper
- ½ tsp dried chili flakes

Directions

- Layer the tomato slices and basil leaves onto a large serving platter
- Place the chickpeas, black beans, olive oil, salt, pepper and chili flakes into a bowl and stir to combine
- Scatter the chickpea-bean mixture over the tomatoes and basil

- Serve immediately, with an extra drizzle of olive oil if desired

Nutritional values per serving

- Calories: 185
- Fat: 9 grams
- Total carbs: 25 grams
- Net carbs: 19 grams
- Protein: 8 grams

Cannellini Bean and Capsicum Soup

Cannellini beans are great for soups because of their soft, creamy texture. Capsicum adds color and depth of flavor to this easy soup.

Serves: 4

Time: approximately 35 minutes plus time to soak and cook the beans

Ingredients

- 2 Tbsp olive oil
- 1 onion, finely chopped
- 2 garlic cloves, finely chopped
- 4 red capsicums, seeds removed, flesh cut into chunks
- 1 tsp ground paprika
- 2 cups cooked cannellini beans
- 3 cups vegetable stock
- Salt and pepper

Directions

- Place all ingredients into a large saucepan and place over a medium-high heat, bring to a boil

- Reduce to a simmer and simmer for approximately 30 minutes
- Use a hand-held stick blender to blend until smooth and creamy
- Serve hot

Nutritional values per serving

- Calories: 190
- Fat: 8 grams
- Total carbs: 29 grams
- Net carbs: 19 grams
- Protein: 7.5 grams

Bean and Apricot Stew

Apricots are fantastic additions to vegetarian stews as they provide sweetness and a hint of tang.

Serves: 4

Time: approximately 30 minutes plus time to soak and cook the beans

Ingredients

- 2 Tbsp olive oil
- 1 onion, finely chopped
- 4 garlic cloves, finely chopped
- 1 tsp dried rosemary
- 2 cups cooked cannellini beans
- 2 cups chopped fresh tomatoes
- 4 ripe apricots, stones removed, flesh chopped into chunks
- Salt and pepper

THE TWO-WEEK DIET PLAN AND GROCERY SHOPPING LIST

Directions

- Drizzle the olive oil into a large saucepan and place over a medium heat
- Add the onion, garlic and rosemary and stir as the onion softens
- Add the beans, tomatoes, apricots, salt and pepper and stir to combine
- Allow the stew to simmer for about 20-25 minutes, adding water if you feel it's becoming dry at any point
- Serve hot

Nutritional values per serving

- Calories: 203
- Fat: 7 grams
- Total carbs: 30 grams
- Net carbs: 20.5 grams
- Protein: 8 grams

Kidney Bean and Walnut Balls

These are a great substitute for meatballs, with the crunch of walnuts and freshness of parsley. Serve alone or with a simple tomato sauce.

Serves: 4

Time: approximately 30 minutes plus time to soak and cook the beans

Ingredients

- 2 cups cooked kidney beans
- ½ onion, finely chopped
- 2 garlic cloves, finely chopped

- ½ cup walnuts, chopped
- ½ cup fresh parsley, finely chopped
- Salt and pepper

Directions

- Preheat the oven to 400 degrees Fahrenheit and line a baking tray with baking paper
- Place all ingredients into a large bowl and use a potato masher or a large fork to mash together until a combined mixture forms
- Roll the mixture into balls and place them onto the baking tray
- Bake the balls for approximately 20-25 minutes or until golden
- Serve alone or on top of a simple salad

Nutritional values per serving

- Calories: 170
- Fat: 11 grams
- Total carbs: 14.5 grams
- Net carbs: 9 grams
- Protein: 6.5 grams

Black Bean Guacamole with Roasted Butternut Squash

Guacamole dotted with glossy black beans, served with soft-roasted butternut squash.

Serves: 4

Time: approximately 40 minutes plus time to soak and cook the beans

THE TWO-WEEK DIET PLAN AND GROCERY SHOPPING LIST

Ingredients

- 2 cups cooked black beans
- 2 avocados, flesh removed
- ½ red onion, finely chopped
- Juice of 1 lime
- ½ cup fresh coriander
- Salt and pepper
- 3 cups butternut squash, cut into chunks
- 2 Tbsp olive oil
- 1 tsp ground paprika

Directions

- Preheat the oven to 400 degrees Fahrenheit and line a baking tray with baking paper
- Place the butternut squash onto the tray and rub with the olive oil, paprika and a sprinkle of salt and pepper
- Place the tray into the oven and roast for approximately 30 minutes or until soft
- Prepare the guacamole as the squash roasts: place the black beans, avocados, onion, lime, coriander, salt and pepper into a bowl and mash together until combined but still chunky
- Serve the hot, soft butternut squash with a big spoonful of bean guacamole

Nutritional values per serving

- Calories: 350
- Fat: 18 grams
- Total carbs: 40 grams
- Net carbs: 25.5 grams
- Protein: 11 grams

Leafy Green Salad with Orange-Glazed Cannellini Beans

A fresh salad with plenty of greens and cannellini beans sweetened with the bright taste of just-squeezed orange juice.

Serves: 4

Time: approximately 20 minutes plus time to soak and cook the beans

Ingredients

- 4 cups shredded lettuce
- 2 cups arugula (rocket)
- 3 Tbsp finely chopped scallions
- 2 tomatoes, cut into wedges
- ½ cucumber, cut into chunks
- 1 avocado, sliced
- 2 Tbsp olive oil
- 2 cups cooked cannellini beans
- Juice of 1 orange
- Salt and pepper

Directions

- Place the lettuce, arugula, scallions, tomato, cucumber and avocado into a large salad bowl and toss to combine
- Drizzle the olive oil into a frying pan and place over a medium heat
- Add the beans, orange juice, salt and pepper and stir as the beans become hot and the orange juice reduces
- Scatter the hot beans over the prepared salad and toss gently to combine
- Serve immediately

PLANT-BASED HEALTH: THE TWO-WEEK DIET PLAN AND GROCERY SHOPPING LIST

Nutritional values per serving

- Calories: 260
- Fat: 12 grams
- Total carbs: 29 grams
- Net carbs:
- Protein: 8.5 grams

3-Bean Chili

Chili is a classic dish which can be made without any meat or animal products at all. This chili has 3 kinds of beans and lots of spices to fill your kitchen with aroma.

Serves: 4

Time: approximately 30 minutes plus time to soak and cook the beans

Ingredients

- 2 Tbsp olive oil
- 1 onion, finely chopped
- 4 garlic cloves, finely chopped
- 1 tsp ground paprika
- 1 tsp ground chili
- 1 tsp ground cumin
- 1 tsp ground coriander
- 1 cup cooked kidney beans
- 1 cup cooked black beans
- 1 cup cooked cannellini beans
- 2 cups chopped fresh tomatoes
- 1 Tbsp balsamic vinegar
- Salt and pepper

Directions

- Drizzle the olive oil into a large saucepan and place over a medium heat
- Add the onion, garlic, paprika, chili, cumin and coriander and stir as the spices become fragrant and the onions soften
- Add the kidney beans, black beans, cannellini beans, tomatoes, balsamic vinegar, salt and pepper and stir to combine
- Allow the chili to come to the boil before reducing to a simmer
- Allow to simmer for about 20-25 minutes or until thick and rich
- Serve immediately or store in the fridge

Nutritional values per serving

- Calories: 260
- Fat: 8 grams
- Total carbs: 37 grams
- Net carbs: 24.5 grams
- Protein: 12.5 grams

Creamy White Bean Soup

A creamy soup without any dairy products to be seen. Coconut cream provides richness to the velvety cannellini beans.

Serves: 4

Time: approximately 30 minutes plus time to soak and cook the beans

Ingredients

- 2 Tbsp olive oil

PLANT-BASED HEALTH: THE TWO-WEEK DIET PLAN AND GROCERY SHOPPING LIST

- 5 garlic cloves, finely chopped
- 1 onion, finely chopped
- 4 cups cooked cannellini beans
- 4 cups vegetable stock
- 1 cup coconut cream
- 2 Tbsp fresh thyme, chopped
- Salt and pepper

Directions

- Place all ingredients into a large saucepan and stir to combine
- Allow to come to the boil before reducing to a simmer
- Allow to simmer for about 25 minutes
- Use a hand-held stick blender to blend the soup until smooth and creamy
- Serve hot

Nutritional values per serving

- Calories: 380
- Fat: 17 grams
- Total carbs: 44 grams
- Net carbs: 31 grams
- Protein: 14 grams

8.3 Dinner Recipes

Try these delicious and filling recipes for dinner:

Grilled Vegetable Salad

Ingredients

- 1 corn on cob (husked)
- ½ bell pepper (quartered)
- ½ cup baby zucchini
- 1 tbs. extra-virgin olive oil
- salt and ground pepper to taste
- ¼ tbs. fresh lemon juice
- ½ tbs. freshly chopped oregano
- 2 tbs. tahini sauce

Directions

- preheat barbeque grill to medium-high
- add corn, bell peppers, zucchini, 2 tbs. oil, salt and pepper together in a bowl and toss well
- oil the grill rack and grill the vegetables until tender (around 6 minutes for both zucchini and bell peppers and about 8 minutes for the corn)
- chop the bell peppers and zucchini into bite-size pieces and cut the corn kernels from the stems
- transfer the grilled vegetables to a bowl and garnish with oregano, lemon juice, and the remaining oil

Nutritional values per serving

- total energy   469 calories
- net carbs   32.7 g
- total fat   9 g
- protein   4.9 g

Maple Roasted Brussels Sprouts and Kale with Sautéed Pistachios and Chickpeas

100% pure maple syrup used in small quantities is a great way to add sweetness to your dishes without using processed sugars. These Brussels sprouts will convert any sprout hater.

THE TWO-WEEK DIET PLAN AND GROCERY SHOPPING LIST

PLANT-BASED HEALTH

Serves: 4

Time: approximately 30 minutes plus time to soak and cook the chickpeas

Ingredients

- 16 Brussels sprouts
- 2 cups chopped kale
- 2 Tbsp olive oil
- 2 Tbsp pure maple syrup
- Salt and pepper
- 1 ½ cups cooked chickpeas
- ☐ cup pistachio nuts

Directions

- Preheat the oven to 400 degrees Fahrenheit and line a baking tray with baking paper
- Place the Brussels sprouts, kale, olive oil, maple syrup, salt and pepper onto the tray and mix with your hands to combine and coat everything with oil and maple syrup
- Place the tray into the preheated oven and roast for about 20 minutes or until the sprouts begin to turn golden
- While the sprouts are cooking, prepare the chickpeas: drizzle a little olive oil into a pan and place over a medium heat, add the chickpeas, pistachios and a pinch of salt and pepper, stir as the chickpeas and pistachios become hot and golden
- Serve the roasted Brussels sprouts and kale with a side of hot chickpeas and pistachios

Nutritional values per serving

- Calories: 306
  Fat: 15.5 grams
- Total carbs: 34 grams
- Net carbs: 24 grams
  Protein: 10 grams

Bean Bolognese with Zucchini Noodles

Zucchinis are fantastic when made into noodles and topped with a rich, 3-bean bolognese with dried herbs.

Serves: 4

Time: approximately 40 minutes plus time to soak and cook the beans

Ingredients

- 2 Tbsp olive oil
- 2 garlic cloves, finely chopped
- 1 onion, finely chopped
- 1 cup cooked cannellini beans
- 1 cup cooked black beans
- 1 cup cooked kidney beans
- 3 cups chopped fresh tomatoes
- 2 Tbsp balsamic vinegar
- Salt and pepper
- 1 tsp dried rosemary
- 1 tsp dried thyme
- ¼ cup walnuts, chopped
- 4 zucchinis, made into noodles with a "spiralizer"

Directions

- Drizzle the olive oil into a large saucepan and place over a medium heat
- Add the garlic, onion, cannellini beans, black beans, kidney beans, tomatoes, balsamic vinegar, salt, pepper, rosemary, thyme and walnuts, stir to combine
- Allow the bolognese to come to the boil before reducing to a simmer
- Simmer for about 30 minutes until thick
- As the bolognese simmers, prepare the zoodles: place the zoodles into a microwave-safe bowl and cook in the microwave on high for 1-2 minutes or until just soft but still slightly crunchy
- Serve the bolognese over a bed of just-cooked zoodles

Nutritional values per serving

- Calories: 320
- Fat: 13 grams
- Total carbs: 40 grams
- Net carbs: 25 grams
- Protein: 13 grams

Kidney Beans Sautéed with Fresh Chili, Brussels Sprouts and Macadamia Nuts

Brussels sprouts appear once again, this time pan-fried with kidney beans, macadamia nuts and garlic.

Serves: 4

Time: approximately 20 minutes plus time to soak and cook the beans

Ingredients

- 2 Tbsp olive oil
- 1 onion, finely chopped
- 3 garlic cloves, finely chopped
- 2 cups cooked kidney beans
- 12 Brussels sprouts, cut in half
- ½ cup macadamia nuts, roughly chopped
- 1 fresh red chili, finely chopped
- Salt and pepper

Directions

- Drizzle the olive oil into a large pan and place over a medium heat
- Add the onion, garlic, beans, Brussels sprouts, macadamia nuts, chili, salt and pepper and stir to combine
- Stir occasionally as the Brussels sprouts cook and the beans become hot
- Serve immediately

Nutritional values per serving

- Calories: 330
- Fat: 20 grams
- Total carbs: 30 grams
- Net carbs: 18 grams
- Protein: 12 grams

Bean and Corn Salad with Roasted Asparagus

When asparagus spears are roasted they become soft, gooey and full of flavor. They are even better when served with corn and bean salad with fresh lemon juice.

THE TWO-WEEK DIET PLAN AND GROCERY SHOPPING LIST

Serves: 4

Time: approximately 30 minutes plus time to soak and cook the beans

Ingredients

- 16 asparagus spears
- 2 Tbsp olive oil
- Salt and pepper
- 1 cup cooked black beans
- 1 cup cooked kidney beans
- 1 cup fresh corn kernels
- ½ cup fresh parsley, finely chopped
- Juice of 1 lemon

Directions

- Preheat the oven to 400 degrees Fahrenheit and line a baking tray with baking paper
- Place the asparagus, olive oil, salt and pepper onto the tray and mix with your hands to coat the asparagus with oil and seasoning
- Place into the oven to bake for about 20 minutes or until the asparagus is soft
- While the asparagus spears are cooking, prepare the salad: place the black beans, kidney beans, corn, parsley and lemon juice into a salad bowl and toss to combine
- Add the cooked asparagus to the salad and toss through
- Serve immediately

Nutritional values per serving

- Calories: 210
- Fat: 8 grams
- Total carbs: 27 grams
- Net carbs: 17 grams
- Protein: 8 grams

Ginger, Turmeric and Tomato 2-Bean Soup

Ginger and turmeric are wonderful for the digestive system, and they provide amazing flavor to this tomato and bean soup.

Serves: 4

Time: approximately 30 minutes plus time to soak and cook the beans

Ingredients

- 2 Tbsp olive oil
- 1 onion, finely chopped
- 3 garlic cloves, finely chopped
- 2 Tbsp grated fresh ginger
- 1 tsp ground turmeric
- 4 cups chopped fresh tomatoes
- 2 cups cooked cannellini beans
- 1 cup cooked black beans
- Salt and pepper

Directions

- Place all ingredients into a large saucepan and place over a medium heat
- Allow the soup to come to the boil before reducing to a simmer

PLANT-BASED HEALTH: THE TWO-WEEK DIET PLAN AND GROCERY SHOPPING LIST

- Allow to simmer, stirring occasionally, for about 25 minutes
- Serve immediately (no need to blend, this soup is nice when left chunky)

Nutritional values per serving

- Calories: 275
- Fat: 8 grams
- Total carbs: 44 grams
- Net carbs: 32 grams
- Protein: 12 grams

Green Beans and Chickpeas with Lemon Garlic Sauce

Green beans and chickpeas are a great pair, especially when drizzled with a lemony-garlic sauce. Great as a light meal or side dish.

Serves: 4

Time: approximately 20 minutes plus time to soak and cook the beans

Ingredients

- 3 Tbsp olive oil
- 3 cups fresh green beans, ends cut off
- 2 cups cooked chickpeas
- Juice of 2 lemons
- 2 garlic cloves, finely chopped
- Salt and pepper

Directions

- Drizzle the olive oil into a frying pan and place over a medium heat
- Add the green beans, chickpeas, lemon juice, garlic, salt and pepper and stir to combine
- Stir occasionally as the green beans cook and the sauce thickens
- Serve immediately

Nutritional values per serving

- Calories: 245
- Fat: 12 grams
- Total carbs: 26 grams
- Net carbs: 17 grams
- Protein: 8 grams

Caramelized Onion and Black Bean Open Burgers with Mushroom Buns

These burger patties are simple to make and have a fantastic flavor. Serve on a "bun" of mushroom, with fresh tomato and a sprinkle of dried thyme.

Serves: 4

Time: approximately 30 minutes plus time to soak and cook the beans

Ingredients

- 2 Tbsp olive oil
- 2 red onions, finely sliced
- 2 cups cooked black beans
- Salt and pepper
- 4 large Portobello mushrooms
- 1 tsp dried thyme
- 1 tomato, sliced

PLANT-BASED HEALTH: THE TWO-WEEK DIET PLAN AND GROCERY SHOPPING LIST

Directions

- Drizzle the olive oil into a frying pan and place over a medium-high heat
- Add the onions and stir as they soften and caramelize
- Add the black beans to the onion and season with salt and pepper
- Take the pan off the heat and transfer the onion and beans to a bowl
- Use a potato masher to mash the beans and onions together
- Shape the bean mixture into patties and place them back onto the frying pan with a drizzle of olive oil, and place over a medium-high heat
- Cook the patties on both sides until golden
- Set the patties aside and place the mushrooms onto the hot frying pan to cook on both sides
- Lay a patty onto each cooked mushroom, place a tomato slice on top, then sprinkle with the dried thyme and a little drizzle of olive oil
- Serve immediately

Nutritional values per serving

- Calories: 235
- Fat: 8 grams
- Total carbs: 32 grams
- Net carbs: 21.5 grams
- Protein: 10 grams

Slow-Cooked Leek, Pea and Bean Stew

Use your slow cooker for this recipe if you have one, otherwise just use a pot on the stove and cook for an hour as opposed to 8 hours. A perfect stew for Winter nights.

Serves: 4

Time: approximately 8 hours if you have a slow cooker or 1 hour if not, plus time to soak and cook the beans

Ingredients

- 3 Tbsp olive oil
- 1 onion, finely chopped
- 4 garlic cloves, finely chopped
- 2 leeks, green parts removed, the rest cut into chunks
- 2 cups fresh peas
- 1 cup cooked cannellini beans
- 1 cup cooked kidney beans
- 4 cups vegetable stock
- 1 fresh sprig rosemary
- Salt and pepper

Directions

- Place all ingredients into a slow cooker and set the time to 8 hours and the temperature to "low"
- If you don't have a slow cooker, place all ingredients into a large saucepan and place over a low-medium heat, allow to simmer for about an hour or until the leeks are soft
- Serve hot

PLANT-BASED HEALTH: THE TWO-WEEK DIET PLAN AND GROCERY SHOPPING LIST

Nutritional values per serving

- Calories: 395
- Fat: 12 grams
- Total carbs: 57 grams
- Net carbs: 42 grams
- Protein: 16 grams

4-Bean Salad with Toasted Mixed Seeds and Fresh Arugula

An incredibly simple salad of four different beans, peppery arugula and mixed seeds.

Serves: 5

Time: approximately 15 minutes plus time to soak and cook the beans and chickpeas

Ingredients

- 1 cup cooked cannellini beans
- 1 cup cooked black beans
- 1 cup cooked kidney beans
- 1 cup cooked chickpeas
- 5 cups fresh arugula
- 3 Tbsp pumpkin seeds
- 2 Tbsp sunflower seeds
- 4 Tbsp olive oil
- Juice of 1 lemon
- Salt and pepper

Directions

- Place the cannellini beans, black beans, kidney beans, chickpeas and arugula into a large salad bowl and toss to combine
- Place the pumpkin seeds and sunflower seeds into a dry frying pan and place over a high heat
- Keep the seeds moving as they toast and become golden
- Immediately transfer the seeds into the bowl with the beans
- Add the olive oil, lemon juice, salt and pepper to the bowl and toss to combine
- Serve immediately or store in the fridge

Nutritional values per serving

- Calories: 375
- Fat: 19 grams
- Total carbs: 42 grams
- Net carbs: 26 grams
- Protein: 16 grams

Black Bean, Lime and Pumpkin Seed Patties

Black beans, lime juice and chili combine with the nutty crunch of pumpkin seeds for a light meal or side dish.

Serves: 4

Time: approximately 20 minutes plus time to soak and cook the beans

Ingredients

- 2 cups cooked black beans
- ½ onion, finely chopped
- 3 garlic cloves, finely chopped
- 1 fresh red chili, finely chopped or minced

PLANT-BASED HEALTH: THE TWO-WEEK DIET PLAN AND GROCERY SHOPPING LIST

- Juice and zest of 1 lime
- 4 Tbsp pumpkin seeds
- Salt and pepper

Directions

- Preheat the oven to 400 degrees Fahrenheit and line a baking tray with baking paper
- Combine all ingredients in a large bowl and mash with a potato masher
- Shape the mixture into patties and lay them on the baking tray
- Bake for about 15 minutes or until golden on both sides, you can turn the patties halfway through if necessary

Nutritional values per serving

- Calories: 185
- Fat: 6 grams
- Total carbs: 24 grams
- Net carbs: 15.5 grams
- Protein: 11 grams

Bean and Cauliflower Curry

Cauliflower is great in curries as it soaks up flavors really well. I use a vegan Thai green curry paste for this recipe and it works a treat.

Serves: 4

Time: approximately 20 minutes plus time to soak and cook the beans

Ingredients

- 2 Tbsp olive oil
- 1 onion, finely chopped
- 3 Tbsp curry paste
- 2 cups cooked cannellini beans
- 1 cup cooked chickpeas
- 1 cauliflower head, cut into florets
- 2 cups coconut cream
- 1 cup vegetable stock
- Salt and pepper

Directions

- Drizzle the olive oil into a large saucepan and place over a medium heat
- Add the onion and curry paste and stir as the onions soften
- Add the cannellini beans, chickpeas, cauliflower, coconut cream, stock, salt and pepper and stir to combine
- Allow the curry to come to the boil before reducing to a simmer
- Cook for approximately 15 minutes or until the cauliflower is just beginning to soften
- Serve immediately

Nutritional values per serving

- Calories: 430
- Fat: 30 grams
- Total carbs: 45 grams
- Net carbs: 34 grams
- Protein: 11 grams

Roasted Leek, Mushroom, Bean and Thyme One-Tray Dinner

A very comforting dish which only requires one tray. Mushrooms and leeks provide a deep, earthy and rich flavor to this easy dinner.

PLANT-BASED HEALTH : THE TWO-WEEK DIET PLAN AND GROCERY SHOPPING LIST

Serves: 4

Time: approximately 35 minutes plus time to soak and cook the beans

Ingredients

- 2 leeks, green part removed, the rest cut into chunks
- 2 cups mixed mushrooms, larger ones cut to achieve even sizing if necessary
- 2 cups cooked kidney beans
- 1 cup cooked chickpeas
- 1 red onion, cut into chunks
- 3 Tbsp olive oil
- Salt and pepper
- 2 sprigs fresh thyme

Directions

- Preheat the oven to 400 degrees Fahrenheit and line a baking tray with baking paper
- Place all ingredients onto the tray and combine with your hands to coat everything with olive oil and seasoning
- Roast in the oven for about 30 minutes or until the veggies are soft
- Serve hot, warm or cold

Nutritional values per serving

- Calories: 315
- Fat: 12 grams
- Total carbs: 41 grams
- Net carbs: 30 grams
- Protein: 14 grams

Cannellini Beans and Silverbeet (Swiss chard) with Garlic, Chili and Olive Oil

Sometimes, the best way to cook beans and greens is to simply sauté them in a hot pan with garlic, chili and olive oil.

Serves: 4

Time: approximately 15 minutes plus time to soak and cook the beans

Ingredients

- 2 Tbsp olive oil
- 4 garlic cloves, finely chopped
- 1 fresh red chilli, finely chopped
- 2 cups cooked cannellini beans
- 4 cups silverbeet (Swiss chard), woody stalks removed, leaves roughly chopped
- Salt and pepper

Directions

- Drizzle the olive oil into a large frying pan and place over a medium heat
- Add the garlic, chili, beans, silverbeet, salt and pepper
- Stir occasionally as the silverbeet wilts and cooks
- Serve immediately, with an extra drizzle of olive oil if desired

Nutritional values per serving

- Calories: 175
- Fat: 7 grams
- Total carbs: 22 grams
- Net carbs: 14 grams
- Protein: 10 grams

PLANT-BASED HEALTH | THE TWO-WEEK DIET PLAN AND GROCERY SHOPPING LIST

Ginger, Lime and Coconut Chickpea Patties

These patties have flavors reminiscent of Thai cuisine with the addition of ginger and coconut. Serve with lettuce buns for a quick burger, or eat alone as a light meal or snack.

Serves: 4

Time: approximately 30 minutes plus time to soak and cook the chickpeas

Ingredients

- 2 Tbsp grated fresh ginger
- 5 garlic cloves, finely chopped
- Zest and juice of 1 lime
- ½ cup coconut cream
- 2 cups cooked chickpeas
- ½ cup ground almonds
- Salt and pepper

Directions

- Preheat the oven to 400 degrees Fahrenheit and line a baking tray with baking paper
- Combine all ingredients into a bowl and mash with a potato masher so that some of the chickpeas are crushed while some remain chunky
- Shape the mixture into patties and place onto the baking tray
- Bake for approximately 20 minutes or until golden on both sides, you can turn them halfway through if necessary

Nutritional values per serving

- Calories: 320
- Fat: 19 grams
- Total carbs: 30 grams
- Net carbs: 23.5 grams
- Protein: 11 grams

Green Bean, Black Bean, Kidney Bean and Green Pea Bowls

Green beans and peas join kidney and black beans for a fiber-filled bowl of nutrition and great flavors.

Serves: 4

Time: approximately 20 minutes plus time to soak and cook the beans

Ingredients

- 2 Tbsp olive oil
- 4 garlic cloves, finely chopped
- 1 tsp dried chili flakes
- 2 cups fresh green beans, ends cut off
- 1 cup cooked black beans
- 1 cup cooked kidney beans
- 1 ½ cups fresh peas
- 4 cups baby spinach leaves
- 4 cups shredded lettuce
- 4 Tbsp sunflower seeds

Directions

- Drizzle the olive oil into a large saucepan and place over a medium heat
- Add the garlic, chili, green beans, black beans, kidney beans and peas to the pan

PLANT-BASED HEALTH: THE TWO-WEEK DIET PLAN AND GROCERY SHOPPING LIST

and stir to combine, stir occasionally as the beans cook together and become hot
- Toss the spinach, lettuce and sunflower seeds into a large salad bowl
- Scatter the hot bean mixture over the salad leaves just before serving

Nutritional values per serving

- Calories: 365
- Fat: 13 grams
- Total carbs: 42 grams
- Net carbs: 28 grams
- Protein: 20 grams

Roasted Broccoli with Pesto-Coated Cannellini Bean

Broccoli takes on a wonderful flavor when roasted, and is even better when served with cannellini beans tossed in homemade pesto.

Serves: 4

Time: approximately 30 minutes plus time to soak and cook the beans

Ingredients

- 1 broccoli head, cut into florets
- 2 Tbsp olive oil
- 1 red onion, cut into chunks
- Salt and pepper
- 2 cups cooked cannellini beans

Pesto:

- 1 cup fresh basil leaves and stalks
- ½ cup pine nuts
- ☐ cup olive oil
- Salt and pepper

Directions

- Preheat the oven to 400 degrees Fahrenheit and line a baking tray with baking paper
- Lay the broccoli and onion onto the tray and drizzle with olive oil, salt and pepper
- Roast the broccoli and onion in the preheated oven for about 20 minutes or until the onions are soft and the broccoli is just beginning to turn darker in color
- While the broccoli is roasting, prepare the pesto: place all pesto ingredients into a small blender or food processor and pulse until a sauce forms, with a few chunks of pine nuts and basil still remaining
- Combine the pesto and beans in a bowl and serve with the roasted broccoli and onions while they're still hot

Nutritional values per serving

- Calories: 450
- Fat: 37 grams
- Total carbs: 28 grams
- Net carbs: 18 grams
- Protein: 11 grams

Stuffed Cheese Eggplant Rolls

Ingredients:

- 1 large eggplant, sliced lengthwise ¼ inch thick
- 1 chopped red bell pepper

PLANT-BASED HEALTH : THE TWO-WEEK DIET PLAN AND GROCERY SHOPPING LIST

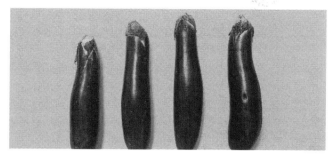

- ½ chopped onion
- ½ cup chopped carrots
- ¼ cup chopped celery
- 2 cloves garlic, finely chopped
- 4 ounces baby spinach, chopped
- ½ tbs. no-salt seasoning blend
- ½ cup low sodium pasta sauce, divided
- 1-ounce non-dairy mozzarella-type cheese
- 1 tbs. water
- olive oil for brushing
- 1 tbs. roasted peanuts (optional)

Directions

- preheat the oven to 350 ☐
- brush a non-stick baking pan with olive oil. Arrange the eggplant slices in a single layer in the pan and bake until the eggplant is flexible enough to roll up easily
- in a large pan, heat 2 tablespoons of water and add the onion, carrots, bell pepper, celery, and garlic. Sauté until the vegetables are tender
- add the spinach and no-salt seasoning and cook until spinach is wilted
- transfer vegetables to a mixing bowl and add 2 tbs. of low sodium vegan pasta sauce and the shredded cheese. Combine well
- put this vegetable mixture on each eggplant slice and roll
- spread ¼ cup of pasta sauce in the baking pan and place the eggplant rolls in it
- pour the remaining pasta sauce over the rolls and bake for about 25 minutes
- serve and enjoy

Nutritional values per serving

- total energy   537 calories
- net carbs   48.75g
- total fat   14.82g
- protein   36g

Grilled Summer Vegetable Salad with Tahini

Ingredients

- 1 ear of corn
- 1 small green bell pepper
- 2 ozs. baby zucchini
- 1 tbs. extra virgin olive oil
- salt and ground pepper to taste
- ½ tbs. red wine vinegar
- ½ tbs. fresh oregano
- 2 tbs. tahini sauce

Directions

- preheat grill on medium high
- add 2 tablespoons of oil, salt and pepper and mix with the corn, zucchini, and bell pepper in a bowl
- oil the grill rack and grill vegetables
- transfer vegetables to serving dish and drizzle with vinegar, oregano, and one tablespoon of oil

Nutritional values per serving

- total calories   493
- total carbs   26g

PLANT-BASED HEALTH: THE TWO-WEEK DIET PLAN AND GROCERY SHOPPING LIST

- total fat   18g
- total protein   7g

Creamy Walnut-Stuffed Eggplant Rolls

Ingredients

- extra-virgin olive oil cooking spray
- 1 medium-sized eggplant
- ½ cup walnuts
- ¼ cup hot water
- 1 garlic clove
- ½ tsp. ground coriander
- ½ tsp. khmeli suneli (a ground mixture of savory, coriander, fenugreek seeds, celery, dill, black peppercorns, parsley, and basil)
- 1 tsp. white wine vinegar
- Salt and black pepper to taste
- 1 tbs. pomegranate seeds

Directions

- preheat the oven to 350 ☐
- slice the eggplants lengthwise with a sharp knife. Brush the baking tray with olive oil and arrange eggplant slices on it
- season the eggplants with salt, black pepper, and olive oil spray. Bake on each side for 15 minutes
- add walnuts, garlic cloves, khmeli suneli, salt and pepper, white wine vinegar and ground coriander to a food processor and process until well combined
- empty in a bowl with the help of a spatula and add hot water slowly, constantly stirring, to mix everything
- now fill each eggplant slice with 2 heaped tsp. of this mixture and roll
- sprinkle with pomegranate seeds and serve

Nutritional values per serving

- total energy   302 calories
- net carbs   18g
- total fat   23g
- protein   10g

Bok Choy Salad

Ingredients

- ½ tbs. peanut oil
- 1 cup fresh bok choy (tough ends removed)
- ½ cup fresh spinach leaves (tough stems removed)
- ½ finely diced tomato
- 3 tbs. cashew nuts
- 1 tsp. mustard seeds
- 1 tsp. cumin seeds
- ¼ tsp. cayenne pepper
- ¼ cup water
- ¼ tsp. turmeric
- salt to taste

Directions

- preheat oven to 325 ☐ and bake cashew nuts until lightly golden
- heat the peanut oil in a medium pan over medium-high heat. Add cumin seeds and cook for 30 seconds while stirring continuously

THE TWO-WEEK DIET PLAN AND GROCERY SHOPPING LIST

- add the diced tomato, turmeric, mustard seeds, salt and cayenne pepper. Cover with lid and cook for about 5 minutes on reduced heat
- add water and bring to a boil. Keeping the heat low, add bok choy and spinach and cook for 3-5 minutes
- empty into a serving bowl and sprinkle with roasted cashew nuts

Nutritional values per serving

- total energy   345 calories
- net carbs   16.55g
- total fat   26.98
- protein   10g

Zucchini Noodles with Pecans

Ingredients

- 1 medium-sized zucchini
- 2 medium-sized cherry tomatoes
- ½ cup fresh basil
- ¼ cup of walnuts
- 1 tbs. pesto
- salt and pepper to taste

Directions

- use a spiral maker to make zucchini noodles or simply slice it into threads
- heat a pan with olive oil and set the heat to low
- add walnuts and diced cherry tomatoes to the pan
- cook for around 10 minutes and then add pesto
- sauté for some time before emptying into a dish
- garnish with basil leaves and pepper

Nutritional values per serving

- total energy 163 calories
- total fat 21.8 g
- net carbs 7.4 g
- protein 5.9 g

Pecans

Nutritional values per 50 g of pecans

- total calories   395
- total fat   36 g
- net carbs   7 g
- protein   4.5 g

Roasted Vegetable Lasagna with Spinach Pesto

Ingredients

- ½ tsp. olive oil
- 1 cup fresh spinach
- ½ medium-sized zucchini
- ½ small sweet potato
- 1 tomato (sliced)
- ¼ small butternut squash
- 1 oz. cashews soaked for 2 hours and drained
- 1 mashed clove of garlic
- 1 tsp. nutritional yeast
- ¼ cup water
- ¼ tsp. garlic powder
- 1 tbs. lemon juice

- 2 tbs. olive oil
- pinch of salt and pepper

Directions

- preheat the oven to 450 ☐ and line baking sheets with parchment paper
- add the drained cashews to a blender along with ½ cup water, salt, garlic powder, lemon juice and 1 tsp. of nutritional yeast. Blend until well combined
- empty into a small bowl and set aside
- wash the blender and dry thoroughly. Now add the spinach, garlic cloves, 2 tsp. nutritional yeast, salt, pepper, and 1/3 cup olive oil
- peel and remove seeds from butternut squash. Cut the sweet potato and butternut squash into ¼ inch thick slices. Slice zucchini lengthwise
- place these vegetables on the baking sheet and season with olive oil, salt, and pepper
- bake for 20 minutes
- let them cool for 10 minutes
- grease the baking dish and begin to arrange the lasagna. First, layer the bottom with sweet potato slices, then add pesto and then the cashew mixture
- add layers of each vegetable and use the same amount of pesto and cashew mixture between the vegetable layers
- spread the remaining pesto and cashew cheese mixture over the top and bake for 30 minutes
- serve and enjoy

Nutritional values per serving

- total energy   581 calories
- net carbs   36.8g
- total fat   43.6g
- protein   10.38g

Black Bean Stuffed Portobello Mushrooms (Serves 2)

Ingredients

- 2 large portobello mushroom caps
- 1.5 tsp. olive oil
- ½ onion finely diced
- 2 minced garlic cloves
- ½ cup cooked black beans
- 1 tsp. ground cumin
- ½ tsp. chili powder
- 1 tsp. lime juice
- salt and black pepper to taste

Directions

- preheat oven to 400 ☐
- brush the mushrooms caps with olive oil and place on a baking sheet. Bake for 10 minutes on each side
- heat oil in a skillet over medium heat. Sauté onion and garlic together for 5 minutes. Add cooked beans, chili powder, cumin, lime juice, salt and pepper and sauté for a further 2 minutes, stirring continuously
- fill the caps with the bean mixture and top with chopped scallions, diced tomato and cilantro

THE TWO-WEEK DIET PLAN AND GROCERY SHOPPING LIST

PLANT-BASED HEALTH

Nutritional values per serving

- total energy   397 calories
- net carbs   29g
- total fat   19g
- protein   20g

Cauliflower Risotto

Ingredients

- ¼ medium-sized cauliflower
- 100 grams mushrooms
- ½ medium-sized onion
- 1.5 tbs. olive oil
- 1 finely chopped garlic clove
- 3 tbs. pine nuts
- ¼ cup vegetable broth
- 1 tbs. nutritional yeast
- salt and black pepper to taste
- 1 tbs. vegan margarine
- truffle oil

Directions

- heat olive oil in a frying pan and sauté mushrooms until tender. Empty into a bowl
- cook onions and garlic in the frying pan until color changes
- add cauliflower and cook for about 5 minutes, until tender
- lower the flame, add the broth, and cook for a few minutes
- pulse the pine nuts, salt, and nutritional yeast in a food processor
- mix the pine nut mixture with cauliflower
- garnish with mushrooms and some truffle oil

Nutritional values per serving

- total energy   787 calories
- net carbs   17.7 g
- total fat   76.3 g
- protein   13 g

Mixed Green Bowl with Garlicky Lentils

These bowls are full of greens, with a scattering of lentils cooked with garlic.

Serves: 4

Time: approximately 15 minutes plus time to cook the lentils first

Ingredients

- 1 broccoli, cut into florets
- 4 cups baby spinach
- 2 cups watercress
- 2 Tbsp olive oil
- 1 ½ cups cooked brown lentils
- 3 garlic cloves, crushed
- Salt and pepper

Directions

- Steam the broccoli in a microwave-safe bowl, covered, with a dash of water for about 1 - 1 ½ minutes or until just cooked but still crispy
- As the broccoli cools, prepare the lentils: drizzle the olive oil into a frying pan and place over a medium heat. Add the

lentils, garlic, salt and pepper and stir as they cook
- Place the broccoli, spinach and watercress into a large bowl and toss to combine
- Scatter the garlic lentils over the top and add another drizzle of olive oil if desired
- Serve immediately

Nutritional values per serving

- Calories: 180
- Fat: 8 grams
- Total carbs: 21 grams
- Net carbs: 12.5 grams
- Protein: 10 grams

Lentil Chili with Guacamole

A spicy, rich chili made with lentils and tomatoes. Served with a creamy guacamole spiked with lime juice.

Serves: 4

Time: approximately 30 minutes plus time to cook the lentils first

Ingredients

- 2 Tbsp olive oil
- 1 onion, finely chopped
- 3 garlic cloves, finely chopped
- 1 ½ cups cooked brown lentils
- 2 cups chopped fresh tomatoes
- 2 tsp balsamic vinegar
- 1 tsp ground paprika
- 1 tsp ground chili
- Salt and pepper
- 2 avocados, flesh scooped out
- 2 Tbsp chopped scallions
- ½ fresh red chili, finely chopped
- Juice of 1 lime
- Salt and pepper
- 1 Tbsp olive oil

Directions

- Drizzle the olive oil into a large saucepan and place over a medium heat
- Add the onion and garlic and stir as the onion softens
- Add the lentils, tomatoes, balsamic vinegar, paprika, chili, salt and pepper and stir to combine
- Allow the mixture to come to the boil before reducing to a simmer
- Leave to simmer for about 25 minutes or until slightly thickened and some of the tomato liquid has evaporated
- While the chili simmers, prepare the guacamole: place all ingredients into a bowl and mash with a fork
- Serve the chili hot with a big dollop of guacamole

Nutritional values per serving

- Calories: 340
- Fat: 21 grams
- Total carbs: 27 grams
- Net carbs: 14 grams
- Protein: 10 grams

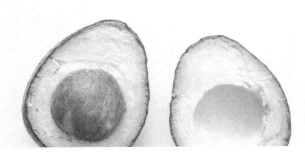

PLANT-BASED HEALTH | THE TWO-WEEK DIET PLAN AND GROCERY SHOPPING LIST

Lentil, Black Bean and Sunflower Seed Burrito Bowls

A flurry of lentils, black beans, sunflower seeds, fresh salad greens and fresh coriander.

Remember to soak the black beans the night before making this dish.

Serves: 4

Time: 15 minutes plus time to cook the lentils and beans first

Ingredients

- 2 Tbsp olive oil
- 2 garlic cloves, crushed
- 1 cup cooked brown lentils
- 1 cup cooked black beans
- 4 Tbsp sunflower seeds
- 4 cups shredded lettuce
- 1 carrot, grated
- 1 medium-large tomato, sliced
- 1 cup roughly chopped coriander (cilantro)
- 1 avocado, sliced

Directions

- Drizzle the olive oil into a saucepan and place over a medium heat
- Add the garlic, lentils and black beans and stir as they heat
- Once hot and combined, divide the lentil-bean mixture between your four bowls
- Arrange the sunflower seeds, lettuce, carrot, coriander and avocado in the bowls whichever way looks best to you, there are no rules, just pile everything in!

Nutritional values per serving

- Calories: 320
- Fat: 17 grams
- Total carbs: 30 grams
- Net carbs: 17 grams
- Protein: 12 grams

Lentil and Carrot Soup

An easy soup with a base of lentils, carrots and a hum of garlic.

Serves: 4

Time: approximately 40 minutes

Ingredients

- 3 Tbsp olive oil
- 2 onions, finely chopped
- 4 garlic cloves, finely chopped
- 5 carrots, peeled and chopped into chunks
- 5 cups vegetable stock
- 1 cup dried red lentils
- Salt and pepper

Directions

- Place all ingredients into a large saucepan and place over a medium heat, bring to the boil before reducing to a simmer

simple + optimum
core routines for extraordinary living

DOWNLOAD YOUR FREE BONUS:
simpleoptimum.com/bookbonus

- Allow to simmer for approximately 35 minutes or until the lentils and carrots are soft
- Use a hand-held stick blender to blend the soup until smooth and creamy
- Serve hot

Nutritional values per serving

- Calories: 340
- Fat: 11 grams
- Total carbs: 46 grams
- Net carbs: 38 grams
- Protein: 13 grams

Mushroom, Lentil and Coconut "Porridge"

This is called "porridge" because it has a similar texture and consistency. It isn't quite a stew and not quite a soup. Mushrooms provide earthiness and coconut adds creaminess.

Serves: 5

Time: approximately 20 minutes plus time to cook the lentils first

Ingredients

- 2 Tbsp olive oil
- 2 cups mixed mushrooms, sliced
- 1 onion, finely chopped
- 3 garlic cloves, finely chopped
- 3 cups cooked brown lentils
- 2 cups vegetable stock
- 1 cup coconut cream
- Salt and pepper

Directions

- Add the olive oil to a large saucepan or deep-sided frying pan and place over a medium heat
- Add the mushrooms, onion and garlic and stir as the onions and mushrooms soften
- Add the lentils, vegetable stock, coconut cream, salt and pepper and stir as the mixture comes to the boil
- Reduce the temperature and allow to simmer until thick
- Serve hot

Nutritional values per serving

- Calories: 300
- Fat: 12.5 grams
- Total carbs: 35 grams
- Net carbs: 24 grams
- Protein: 13.5 grams

Roasted Veggie Salad with Spiced Lentils and Mixed Seeds

Roasted veggies are the star of this dish, with lentils scattered throughout. The mixed seeds add extra crunchiness and nutty flavor.

Serves: 5

Time: approximately 35 minutes plus time to cook the lentils first

Ingredients

- 1 cup raw beetroot cubes
- 1 cup parsnip cubes

PLANT-BASED HEALTH: THE TWO-WEEK DIET PLAN AND GROCERY SHOPPING LIST

- 1 cup zucchini, cut into chunks
- 1 cup carrots, cut into chunks
- 2 Tbsp olive oil
- Salt and pepper
- 1 cup cooked brown lentils
- 2 Tbsp pumpkin seeds
- 2 Tbsp sunflower seeds
- 1 Tbsp sesame seeds
- ☐ cup fresh parsley, chopped
- Juice of 1 lemon

Directions

- Preheat the oven to 400 degrees Fahrenheit and line a baking tray with baking paper
- Place the beetroot, parsnip, zucchini and carrots onto the baking tray and drizzle the olive oil, salt and pepper over the top and ensure the veggies are all coated
- Bake the veggies in the preheated oven for about 30 minutes or until soft and beginning to turn golden
- Transfer the cooked veggies into a large bowl and add the lentils, seeds, parsley and lemon, toss to combine
- Serve warm

Nutritional values per serving

- Calories: 195
- Fat: 10.5 grams
- Total carbs: 20 grams
- Net carbs: 13 grams
- Protein: 8 grams

Toasted Almond, Avocado and Lentil Bowls

These bowls are filled with creamy avocado, crunchy almonds and soft lentils. Great for a filling and nutritious midweek lunch or dinner. They're all about arranging and not about cooking. You just need to place the ingredients into a bowl and that's it.

Serves: 5

Time: approximately 10 minutes plus time to cook the lentils first

Ingredients

- 3 cups cooked brown lentils
- ½ cup chopped raw almonds
- 2 ripe avocados, flesh sliced
- 1 red capsicum (bell pepper), seeds removed, chopped
- 3 Tbsp scallions, chopped
- 2 Tbsp olive oil
- Juice of 1 lime
- Salt and pepper

Directions

- Place a base of lentils into the bottom of each bowl
- Sprinkle the almonds into each bowl
- Lay the avocado along the edge of the bowls
- Sprinkle the bell pepper and scallions over the top
- Drizzle the olive oil, lime juice, salt and pepper over the bowls

PLANT-BASED HEALTH: THE TWO-WEEK DIET PLAN AND GROCERY SHOPPING LIST

- Enjoy cold immediately, or keep in the fridge until needed

Nutritional values per serving

- Calories: 370
- Fat: 22
- Total carbs: 33 grams
- Net carbs: 17 grams
- Protein: 15 grams

Slow-Cooked Lentil Curry with Butternut Squash and Spinach

If you don't have a slow cooker you can just use the stove and a saucepan and simmer the curry for about an hour. The butternut squash becomes soft and sweet as the curry cooks.

Serves: 5

Time: approximately 8 hours

Ingredients

- 2 Tbsp olive oil
- 1 onion, finely chopped
- 4 garlic cloves, finely chopped
- 3 Tbsp curry paste, a good-quality, authentic store bought vegan paste is fine, or you can make your own if you have a favorite recipe
- 1 ½ cups dried red lentils
- 2 cups butternut squash, cut into cubes
- 2 cups chopped spinach
- 3 cups vegetable stock
- 2 cups coconut cream
- Salt and pepper

Directions

- Place all ingredients into a slow cooker and set the time to 8 hours and the temperature to "low"
- If you don't have a slow cooker, just simmer all ingredients in a large saucepan over a low heat for about 1 ½ hours
- Serve hot

Nutritional values per serving

- Calories: 427
- Fat: 24.3 grams
- Total carbs: 44 grams
- Net carbs: 32 grams
- Protein: 12 grams

Fresh Herb and Lentil Salad with Toasted Chili Seeds

The fresh herbs in this salad create a symphony of fresh, aromatic flavors to compliment the soft lentils. Chili-toasted seeds add saltiness and crunch.

Serves: 4

Time: approximately 10 minutes plus time to cook the lentils first

Ingredients

- 2 cups cooked lentils (any kind)
- ½ cup fresh parsley, chopped
- ½ cup fresh coriander (cilantro), chopped

PLANT-BASED HEALTH
THE TWO-WEEK DIET PLAN AND GROCERY SHOPPING LIST

- ½ cup fresh mint, chopped
- ¼ cup fresh chives, chopped
- ☐ cup pumpkin seeds
- 1 tsp chili powder
- 2 Tbsp olive oil
- Salt and pepper

Directions

- Start by preparing the seeds: place the pumpkin seeds into a dry pan over a medium heat. Once the seeds are hot and beginning to toast, add the chili powder and a dash of olive oil and quickly stir as the oil dries. Take the pan off the heat and leave to cool as you prepare the rest of the salad
- Place the lentils, parsley, coriander, mint and chives into a large bowl and toss to combine
- Add the chili seeds, olive oil, salt and pepper
- Serve immediately

Nutritional values per serving

- Calories: 235
- Fat: 11 grams
- Total carbs: 23 grams
- Net carbs: 14 grams
- Protein: 13.5 grams

Eggplant and Lentil Bake

Soft, spongy eggplant baked with lentils and a tomato-oregano sauce.

Serves: 6

Time: 40 minutes plus time to cook the lentils first

Ingredients

- 3 Tbsp olive oil
- 1 onion, finely chopped
- 3 garlic cloves, finely chopped
- 1 large eggplant, cut into thin rounds
- 2 cups cooked lentils
- 2 cups chopped fresh tomatoes
- 1 tsp dried oregano (substitute for other dry herbs you like better)
- Salt and pepper

Directions

- Preheat the oven to 400 degrees Fahrenheit and grease a casserole dish
- Drizzle the olive oil into a frying pan and place over a medium-high heat
- Add the onion, garlic and eggplant, fry the eggplant on both sides until golden
- Transfer the eggplant, onion and garlic to the casserole dish, laying the eggplant slices in one layer
- Add the lentils, tomato, oregano, salt and pepper to the frying pan and place back onto a medium heat, stir as the mixture becomes hot and bubbly
- Pour the hot lentil mixture over the eggplant slices and place the dish into the oven
- Bake in the oven for approximately 25 minutes or until bubbling
- Serve hot with a simple green salad

PLANT-BASED HEALTH: THE TWO-WEEK DIET PLAN AND GROCERY SHOPPING LIST

Nutritional values per serving

- Calories: 190
- Fat: 7 grams
- Total carbs: 24 grams
- Net carbs: 17.5 grams
- Protein: 8 grams

Roasted Beetroot, Almond and Lentil Tray Bake

Roasted beetroot has an amazing color and earthy taste. This is an unusual yet very tasty one-tray meal.

Serves: 4

Time: approximately 35 minutes plus time to cook the lentils first

Ingredients

- 2 raw beets, cut into chunks
- 2 large red onions, cut into chunks
- 2 zucchinis, cut into chunks
- 2 cups cooked brown lentils
- ½ cup almonds, roughly chopped
- 1 sprig fresh thyme
- 2 Tbsp olive oil
- Salt and pepper

Directions

- Preheat the oven to 400 degrees Fahrenheit and line a baking tray with baking paper
- Place all ingredients onto the tray and mix with your hands so that everything is coated and combined with olive oil, salt and pepper
- Roast in the preheated oven for about 30 minutes or until the beetroot is soft
- Serve warm, hot or cold

Nutritional values per serving

- Calories: 335
- Fat: 16 grams
- Total carbs: 36 grams
- Net carbs: 24 grams
- Protein: 14 grams

Fresh Herb and Pine Nut Relish with Onion-Lentil Bed

Fresh herbs and pine nuts are placed on top of a caramelized onion and lentil base. The lemon gives a refreshing bite of sourness.

Serves: 4

Time: 15 minutes plus time to cook the lentils first

Ingredients

- 2 Tbsp olive oil
- 2 red onions, sliced
- 2 cups cooked brown lentils
- ☐ cup pine nuts
- ½ cup fresh parsley, finely chopped
- ¼ cup fresh mint, finely chopped
- ☐ cup fresh basil, finely chopped
- Juice of 1 lemon
- Salt and pepper

PLANT-BASED HEALTH: THE TWO-WEEK DIET PLAN AND GROCERY SHOPPING LIST

Directions

- Drizzle the olive oil into a large frying pan and place over a medium-high heat
- Add the onions and lentils and stir to combine, keep stirring every now and then as the onions caramelize and the lentils become hot, season with salt and pepper
- Combine the pine nuts, parsley, mint, basil, lemon, salt and pepper in a small bowl
- Spoon the lentil-onion mixture onto your four plates and top with fresh herb and pine nut relish
- Serve immediately or store in the fridge

Nutritional values per serving

- Calories: 280
- Fat: 16 grams
- Total carbs: 28 grams
- Net carbs: 18 grams
- Protein: 12 grams

Crispy Raw Broccoli and Lentil Bowls with Coconut Cream Dressing

Raw broccoli is crunchy and delicious, especially when served with lentils and a creamy coconut dressing.

Serves: 4

Time: approximately 15 minutes plus time to cook the lentils first

Ingredients

- 1 broccoli head, cut into small pieces
- 2 cups cooked brown lentils
- ½ red onion, finely chopped
- Juice of 1 lemon
- 1 Tbsp olive oil
- ☐ cup coconut cream
- ½ tsp ground chili
- Salt and pepper

Directions

- Combine the broccoli, lentils and onion in a large bowl
- In a small bowl, combine the lemon juice, olive oil, coconut cream, chili, salt and pepper until smooth
- Pour the coconut cream mixture over the broccoli and lentils and stir to coat and combine
- Serve immediately

Nutritional values per serving

- Calories: 200
- Fat: 7 grams
- Total carbs: 27 grams
- Net carbs: 17 grams
- Protein: 11 grams

Vegetable Shirataki Noodles

Ingredients

- 4oz. packet of shirataki noodles
- ½ cup freshly chopped broccoli

- ¼ cup freshly chopped celery
- ¼ cup freshly chopped onion
- ½ cup diced bell peppers (red, yellow, and green)
- 2 mashed cloves of garlic
- salt and fresh ground pepper to taste
- ½ tsp. chili powder
- 1 tbs. extra-virgin olive oil

Directions

- rinse the noodles and put them in a dry skillet over medium heat
- stir to dry for about 4 minutes and put aside
- heat the olive oil in a pan and sauté all the vegetables until tender
- add noodles to the vegetables and mix well. Serve and enjoy

Nutritional values per serving

- total energy   204.5 calories
- net carbs   14.69g
- total fat   14.62g
- protein   4.6g

Zucchini Noodles

Ingredients

- 1 medium-sized zucchini
- 2 medium-sized cherry tomatoes
- ½ cup fresh basil
- 1 cup of walnuts
- 1 tbs. pesto
- Salt and pepper to taste

Directions

- use a spiralizer to make zucchini noodles, or simply slice in threads
- heat a pan with olive oil and set the heat to low
- add walnuts and diced cherry tomatoes to the pan
- cook for around 10 minutes and add pesto
- sauté for some time before emptying into a dish
- garnish with basil leaves and pepper

Nutritional values per serving of zucchini noodles

- total energy 772
- total fat 73.8
- net carbs 9.9
- proteins 17.9

Spaghetti Squash and Pesto

Ingredients

- 1/2 small spaghetti squash
- 1.5 tbs. sun-dried tomatoes
- 1 handful of raw cashews
- 1 handful of toasted pine nuts
- 1 tbs. nutritional yeast
- ¼ tsp. sea salt
- 1 cup fresh basil
- 1 minced garlic clove
- extra-virgin olive oil for brushing
- red pepper flakes (optional)
- vegan parmesan cheese (optional)

PLANT-BASED HEALTH: THE TWO-WEEK DIET PLAN AND GROCERY SHOPPING LIST

Directions

- preheat oven to 400 ☐ and place foil on the baking sheet
- halve spaghetti squash along the length using a sharp knife
- use an ice cream scoop to scrape out the seeds
- brush the inside with oil and salt. Place, cut-side down, on baking sheet and bake for 40-50 minutes
- meanwhile, add pine nuts, cashews, nutritional yeast, and salt to a food processor and pulse until well combined
- add basil, sun-dried tomatoes, garlic and olive oil into this mixture and combine. Add some water (2-3 tbs.) to make it smooth
- scoop out spaghetti squash, forming fine strings using a fork. Top it with pesto and toss lightly
- sprinkle with vegan parmesan cheese and red pepper flakes. Enjoy

Nutritional values per serving

- energy   426 calories
- net carbs   18.59g
- total fat   28.06g
- protein   14.16g

Raw Kale and Brussels Sprout Salad with Tahini Dressing

Ingredients

- ½ bunch of curly green kale
- 3 Brussels sprouts
- 1.5 tbs. sliced almonds
- ¼ cup shaved vegan parmesan cheese
- a pinch of sea salt

Tahini dressing

- 3 tbs. tahini
- ½ tbs. white wine vinegar
- ½ tsp. sesame paste
- dash of red pepper flakes
- ¼ cup water

Directions

- remove the ribs of the kale leaves and chop into bite-sized pieces. Sprinkle with some salt and use your hands to squeeze them a little until it becomes more fragrant
- discard the ends of the Brussels sprouts and shred the sprouts using food processor
- Add them to a bowl along with kale
- in a small bowl, whisk together the ingredients for the tahini dressing until the mixture is creamy and smooth
- pour this tahini dressing over the kale and sprouts and mix until well absorbed
- in a frying pan, toast the almonds until fragrant and golden
- toss the toasted almonds and vegan parmesan shavings with the salad and serve

Nutritional values

- total energy   393.5 calories
- net carbs   14.7g
- total fat   31g
- protein   14g

simple + optimum
core routines for extraordinary living

DOWNLOAD YOUR FREE BONUS:
simpleoptimum.com/bookbonus

8.4 Dessert Recipes

Believe it or not, even dessert can be healthy! Try one of the recipes that follow:

Chocolate Fudge (10 Squares)

Ingredients

- ½ cup of peanut butter
- 1 tsp. vanilla extract
- ¼ cup coconut oil
- ¼ cup coconut or almond milk
- 1 tbs. cocoa powder

Directions

- spread parchment paper in a flat baking dish
- add peanut butter, and vanilla extract in a bowl. Mix and set aside
- mix coconut oil, coconut milk, and cocoa in a saucepan and bring to a boil
- pour this hot mixture over peanut butter mixture in the bowl. Mix until well combined
- pour this in the container and place in refrigerator to cool for 2-3 hours
- cut into squares and enjoy

Nutritional values per square

- total energy   164.4 calories
- net carbs   2.13g
- total fat   13.445g
- protein   3.4g

Peanut Butter Protein Balls (5 Balls)

Ingredients

- ¼ cup natural peanut butter
- 1 tsp. vanilla extract (vegan)
- ¼ cup gluten-free oats
- ¼ cup shredded coconut
- a pinch of salt
- ¼ cup mini chocolate chips
- 1 tsp. water

Directions

- in a bowl, mix the peanut butter and vanilla extract
- add the oats, shredded coconut, and salt until well combined
- add the chocolate chips and mix again
- add water or vanilla extract if the mixture does not hold together
- form about 15 medium equal sized balls (2 inches in diameter)
- you can store in refrigerator up to 1 week
- optionally, coat the balls with dry cocoa powder before serving

Nutritional values per ball

- total energy   112 calories
- net carbs   9.56 g
- total fat   10.7 g
- protein   4.3 g

Low Carb Chocolate Pudding

Ingredients

- 1 cup almond milk (unsweetened)

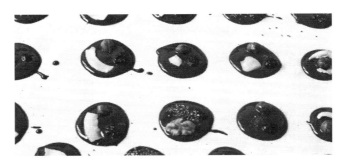

PLANT-BASED HEALTH : THE TWO-WEEK DIET PLAN AND GROCERY SHOPPING LIST

- 1 tbs. unsweetened cocoa powder
- 2 tbs. chia seeds

Directions

- put all the ingredients in a medium bowl and whisk well
- cover and place in refrigerator for 5-6 hours
- enjoy

Nutritional values per serving

- total energy   190 calories
- net carbs   6.33 g
- total fat   13.3 g
- protein   7.2 g

Strawberry Popsicle

Ingredients

- 2 cups sliced strawberries
- 2 tbs. lemon juice
- 4 cups water
- popsicle molds

Directions

- in a small saucepan, heat the strawberries on low heat for 10 minutes
- pour this and the lemon juice into blender and blend until smooth
- combine with water in large bowl. Whisk well
- pour this liquid into the popsicle molds and freeze until hard
- take out from the molds and enjoy

Nutritional values per serving

- total energy   23.4 calories
- net carbs   4.4g
- total fat   0.22g
- protein 2.3g

Chocolate Avocado Pudding

Ingredients

- ¼ cup cocoa powder
- 1 avocado
- 1 tsp. pink salt
- ½ tsp

Directions

- remove avocado pit and scoop flesh into a mixing bowl
- add cocoa powder and vanilla extract and mix until a pudding is formed
- top with pink salt and enjoy

Nutritional values per serving

- total energy   329 calories
- net carbs   9.4g
- total fat   30g
- protein 13g

Total for the day

- total calories   2177
- total carbs   91 g
- total protein   67 g
- total fat   161 g

PLANT-BASED HEALTH | THE TWO-WEEK DIET PLAN AND GROCERY SHOPPING LIST

Matcha Smoothie Bowl

Ingredients

- ¼ avocado
- 1 handful of greens
- ½ tsp. matcha powder
- ½ cup almond milk
- 1 handful of strawberries
- 6 blackberries
- ½ tbs. coconut flakes
- ½ tsp. crushed pecans
- 1 tsp. chia seeds
- ¼ cup ice cubes

Directions

- put almond milk, avocado, matcha powder, and greens together in a blender and pulse until smooth. Add ice cubes and blend again
- pour into a large serving bowl. Top with pecans, chia seeds, coconut flakes, and berries
- enjoy

Nutritional values per serving

- total energy   250 calories
- net carbs   8g
- total fat   23g
- protein   17g

Cookie Dough Bites (6 Bites)

Ingredients

- ½ cup fresh almond pulp (dried)
- 2 tbs. coconut oil
- 2 tbs. almond butter
- 1 tsp. vanilla extract
- salt to taste
- ¼ cup of chocolate chips

Directions

- combine the dried almond pulp flour with the almond butter, coconut oil, vanilla extract and salt in a food processor and pulse until a smooth batter forms
- empty into a bowl and add chocolate chips to the batter. Combine well with a spoon
- make bite-sized balls from the batter. Roll between your hands for a smooth ball, and press a little to a form cookie shape
- place the cookies on parchment paper on a baking tray and place in refrigerator
- wait for 30 minutes or until the texture is suitable to serve

Nutritional values

- total energy   97 calories
- net carbs   4 g
- total fat   10.4 g
- protein   2g

Peanut Butter Protein Balls (5 Balls)

Ingredients

- ¼ cup natural peanut butter
- 1 tsp. vanilla extract
- ¼ cup gluten-free oats
- ¼ cup shredded coconut
- a pinch of salt
- ¼ cup mini chocolate chips
- 1 tsp. water

PLANT-BASED HEALTH: THE TWO-WEEK DIET PLAN AND GROCERY SHOPPING LIST

Directions

- in a bowl, mix the peanut butter and vanilla extract
- mix the oats, shredded coconut, and salt until well combined
- add the chocolate chips and mix again
- add water or vanilla extract if the mixture does not hold together well
- form about 15 medium equal sized balls (2 inches in diameter)
- you can store in refrigerator up to 1 week
- it's optional to coat the balls with dry cocoa powder before serving

Nutritional values per ball

- total energy   112.1 calories
- net carbs   9.56 g
- total fat   10.7 g
- protein   4.3 g

Frozen Peppermint Hot Chocolate

Ingredients

- 1 cup almond milk (unsweetened)
- ¼ cup vegan dark chocolate
- ½ tsp. peppermint extract
- 1 cup ice cubes
- 1 tsp. freshly crushed peppermint

Directions

- add all the ingredients into a blender and pulse on high until frothy
- top with crushed peppermint and serve

Nutritional values per serving

- total energy   170 calories
- net carbs   5.9 g
- total fat   2.5 g
- protein   1 g

8.5 Snack Recipes

Spicy Bean Dip with Veggie Sticks

Beans make a perfect base for filling dips. Chop up carrot, capsicum and cucumber to use as dipping sticks to scoop up the tasty dip.

Serves: 4

Time: approximately 15 minutes plus time to soak and cook the beans

Ingredients

- 2 cups cooked kidney beans
- 2 garlic cloves, finely chopped
- 1 tsp dried chili flakes
- 4 Tbsp olive oil
- Juice of 1 lemon
- 1 carrot, cut into sticks
- ½ cucumber, cut into sticks
- 2 red capsicums, seeds removed, cut into sticks

Directions

- Place the beans, garlic, chili, olive oil and lemon juice into a food processor and pulse until thick and creamy

simple + optimum
core routines for extraordinary living

DOWNLOAD YOUR FREE BONUS:
simpleoptimum.com/bookbonus

PLANT-BASED HEALTH | THE TWO-WEEK DIET PLAN AND GROCERY SHOPPING LIST

- Serve on a platter with the fresh veggie sticks

Nutritional values per serving

Calories: 255
Fat: 15 grams
Total carbs: 25 grams
Net carbs: 15 grams
Protein: 8 grams

Spicy Zucchini Chips with Half Cup of Brazil Nuts

Ingredients

- 1 medium zucchini
- ½ tbs. coconut oil
- ½ tbs. lime juice
- ½ tbs. fresh lime zest
- ½ tsp. chili powder
- Salt to taste

Directions

- preheat oven to 230 ☐.
- mix lime juice, lime zest, salt and chili powder in a small bowl
- cut thin slices of zucchini and coat them with the lime mixture
- spread them on a baking tray and spray with some coconut oil and add some pepper
- bake for 40 minutes or until golden brown
- serve in a bowl and enjoy the crisps

Nutritional values per serving

- total energy 109.5 calories
- net carbs 4.7 g
- total fat 7.8 g
- protein 2.42 g

Pecans

Nutritional values per cup

- total energy 760 calories
- total fat 78 g
- net carbs 15 g
- protein 10 g

Baked Carrot Chips

Ingredients

- ½ pound carrots
- 2 tbs. coconut oil
- ½ tsp. sea salt
- ½ tsp. ground cumin
- ½ tsp. ground cinnamon

Directions

- preheat the oven to 425 ☐.
- line baking sheet with parchment paper and set aside
- trim the carrot tops and cut them in thin slices, you can even use a vegetable slicer to do this
- mix sliced carrots in a large bowl along oil, salt, cinnamon and cumin. Place on the baking sheet in single layers
- bake for 10 minutes until the edges crisp. Flip and bake for a further 7 minutes
- empty in a serving dish and serve

PLANT-BASED HEALTH : THE TWO-WEEK DIET PLAN AND GROCERY SHOPPING LIST

Nutritional values per serving

- total energy 347 calories
- net carbs 18.45 g
- total fat 29.6 g
- protein 3.25 g

Roasted Eggplant Dip with Whole Grain Crackers

Ingredients

- 1 medium eggplant
- 1 Tbs. olive oil
- ½ small finely chopped garlic clove
- ½ tbs. lemon juice
- 1 tbs. tahini paste
- 1 small hot chili pepper (optional)
- salt and black pepper to taste
- ½ cup finely chopped fresh mint leaves
- ¼ tsp. ground cumin
- 1 jalapeno

Directions

- preheat oven to 400 □
- cut the eggplant in two and apply olive oil and thyme with a brush
- place with the cut side down on foil and bake for 30 minutes
- use a spoon to scoop the soft portion from the baked eggplant, leaving the skin behind
- transfer the pulp to a food processor. Add garlic, tahini paste, lemon juice, cumin and chili pepper, and blend until smooth
- season with salt, pepper, and jalapenos and serve with whole grain crackers

Nutritional values per serving

- total energy 359 calories
- total fat 23.24g
- net carbs 27.52g
- protein 12.5g

8.6 Substitutes

If you don't like certain ingredients or are craving for old favorites, you can look for an alternative that is completely allowed on your plant-based keto diet.

Flavored Yogurt

To replace sugary flavored yogurt, you can mix coconut milk yogurt with fresh fruit of your choice and add spices.

Pasta

If you are missing pasta, you can have alternatives like Shirataki noodles or zucchini noodles.

Bread for Sandwiches

You can use lettuce wraps or flax seed wraps, or even psyllium husk wraps.

Cookies or Chips

Dehydrated vegetables or low carb vegan cookies.

THE TWO-WEEK DIET PLAN AND GROCERY SHOPPING LIST

Crackers

You can make your crackers using flaxseed or chia seed.

Soda and Juices

Instead of juices, have fresh fruits, and drink water, smoothies or tea.

Cappuccino and Frappe

Make your ketoproof coffee using coconut oil and butter.

Ice Creams

Have low carb sorbet.

Chewiness

Missing the chewiness of dense cakes? Add psyllium husk or flaxseed.

Rice

Rice, being starchy and carb heavy, is definitely not allowed on the keto diet, but you can instead create cauliflower rice. Cauliflower can be cut into smaller pieces that, when cooked, create a texture similar to rice.

Flour

Use almond flour.

Non-Vegan Medicines

It is important to mention here that more than 75% of medicines prescribed by doctors in the UK contain animal-derived products. As vegans, or someone on a plant-based diet, you need to be careful and avoid the use of medicines that are not vegan. Be sure to discuss your vegan lifestyle with your doctor before buying any medications.

All ingredients have a safer and healthier replacement. I have mentioned just a few above. Have fun with the ingredients, mix and match, and discover your substitutes. Experiment, put in a little effort, create your own recipes, and enjoy your healthy keto lifestyle.

8.7 Grocery Shopping List for the Two-Week Diet Plan

Be sure to have the following foods in your pantry if you are going to follow a plant-based keto diet. You need a good source of fats, proteins, vegetables, etc., readily available in your kitchen.

8.7.1 Fruits and Vegetables:

- Avocado - 5 -6 avocados
- Baby spinach - 4 ounces
- Asian eggplant -2 long
- Eggplant - 5-6
- Lemon - 6-7
- Pickle-sized Persian cucumbers - 2

PLANT-BASED HEALTH: THE TWO-WEEK DIET PLAN AND GROCERY SHOPPING LIST

- Tomatoes - 10 medium
- Radish - 2
- Mint - 1 bunch
- Brussels sprouts - 6
- Scallion - a bunch/ 7-8
- Potatoes - 250 grams
- Romaine lettuce - 1 bunch
- Butternut squash - 1 small
- Fresh basil leaves - 62.5 grams (about 2 ½ cups)
- Asparagus stalks - 2
- Bok choy - 70 grams (about three cups)
- Curly green kale - 1 bunch
- Coriander - 1 bunch
- Cucumber - 2
- Cauliflower - 1
- Zucchini - 4-5 medium
- Sweet potato - 1 large
- Pineapple - 1
- Banana - 2
- Cantaloupe - 1
- Kiwifruit - 1/4 kg
- Carrot - 1
- Green beans - 50 grams
- Blackcurrant - 50 grams
- Broccoli - 2 medium
- Celery - 2-3
- Parsley - 1 bunch
- Fresh thyme - 1 bunch
- Jalapeno chili - 2
- Onion - 5 medium sized
- Cherry tomatoes - 1/2 kgs
- Bell peppers red, yellow, green - 3-4 each
- Garlic- 500 grams
- Ginger - 250 grams
- Cilantro - 1 bunch
- Spring onions - 4
- Chives - 1 bunch
- Oregano - 1 bunch
- Hot chili pepper - 1
- English cucumbers - 2
- Baby zucchini - 4 ounces
- Strawberries - ½ kgs
- Spinach - 250 grams
- Blackberries - 250 grams

8.7.2 Frozen Food:

- Frozen raspberries - 1 can
- Frozen sweetcorn - 1 can
- Frozen blackberries - 1 can

8.7.3 Dairy Alternatives:

- Coconut milk - 1 can
- Coconut milk yogurt - 1 packet
- Creamed coconut milk - 1 can
- Coconut cream - 1 packet
- Almond milk - 1 can

8.7.4 Nuts and Seeds (1 packet of each):

- Almonds
- Walnuts
- Chia seeds
- Cumin seeds
- Pine nuts
- Cashews nuts
- Peanuts
- Hemp seeds
- Pomegranate seeds
- Mustard seeds
- Cumin seeds

PLANT-BASED HEALTH | THE TWO-WEEK DIET PLAN AND GROCERY SHOPPING LIST

- Sesame seeds
- Pumpkin seeds
- Sunflower seeds
- Flaxseed meal
- Mixed nuts: Brazil, almonds, hazelnuts, pecans, and walnuts
- Coconut flakes
- Ground golden flax meal

8.7.5 Flour:

- Chickpea flour - 30 grams
- Coconut flour - 1 small pack

8.7.6 Fats and Oils:

- Extra virgin olive oil - 1 bottle
- Coconut oil - 1 jar
- Vegan margarine - 1 packet
- Truffle oil - 1 bottle
- Peanut oil - 1 bottle

8.7.7 Spices and Natural Flavors:

- Turmeric - 1 packet
- Black pepper - 1 packet
- Dry thyme - 1 packet
- Black salt - 1 packet
- Khmeli suneli - 1 packet
- Sea salt - 1 packet
- Matcha powder - 1 packet
- Kosher salt -1 packet
- Vanilla powder - 1 packet
- Cinnamon powder - 1 packet
- Ground pepper - 1 packet
- Garlic powder - 1 packet
- Chili powder - 1 packet
- Cayenne pepper - 1 packet
- Rosemary - 1 packet
- Cinnamon - 1 packet
- Sweet paprika - 1 packet
- Organic cane sugar - 1 packet
- Cocoa powder - 1 packet
- Cayenne powder - 1 packet

8.7.8 Beans and Legumes:

- Black beans - 20 ounces
- Red kidney beans - 250 grams

8.7.9 Other Items:

- Apple cider vinegar - 1 bottle
- Tahini paste - 1 jar
- Vegan dark chocolate - One bar
- Peppermint extract - 1 bottle
- Dried cranberries - 1 can
- Low sodium vegan pasta sauce - 1 jar
- Portobello mushrooms - 2 large
- Mushrooms - 150 grams
- Brown rice miso paste - 1 packet
- Nutritional yeast - 1 packet
- Pesto - 1 small jar
- Hot chili sauce - 1 bottle
- Gluten-free bread slices - 5
- Rolled oats- gluten free - 1 packet
- Gluten-free oats - 1 packet
- Red wine vinegar - 1 bottle
- Spike seasoning sprite - 1
- Mini chocolate chips (vegan) - 1 packet
- Quinoa - 60 grams
- Vegan Dijon mustard - 1 bottle
- Gluten-free baking powder - 1 packet
- Capers - 1 jar

PLANT-BASED HEALTH: THE TWO-WEEK DIET PLAN AND GROCERY SHOPPING LIST

- Spaghetti squash - 1 large
- Vegan parmesan cheese – 1 small packet
- Vegan mozzarella cheese - 1 small packet
- Coleslaw mix-without dressing - 1 packet
- Cinnamon sticks - 1 packet
- Vegan bittersweet chocolate - 1 packet
- Cocoa powder - 1 packet
- Peanut butter - 1 jar
- Vanilla protein powder - 1 packet
- Vegan vanilla extract - 1 bottle
- Shirataki noodles - 1 packet
- Coconut aminos - 1 bottle
- Corn on the cob - 2

8.8 Saving Money While on the Vegan Keto Diet

Many people believe the vegan keto diet is more expensive than the Standard American Diet. However, with careful planning and by following the tips below, you can easily manage to follow plant-based keto diet while staying within your budget.

- Consider cooking meals in bulk to save time, energy, and money. If you have a membership to a big box store like Cost Co or Sam's, shop with a friend and split the savings.

- Look for offers, sales, coupons, and discounts to buy what you need at a discounted price. Ibotta, Retail-Me-Not and other apps can be helpful.

- Instead of buying pre-made food, try to make everything yourself to save money. Pre-made food is often more expensive.

- Don't think about diet soda. Switch to water, tea or coffee.

- Omit snacks and desserts. They cost more than real food and don't give you any nutrition.

- Always make a list before you go grocery shopping and stick to your shopping list. Without a list, you will end up buying a

Made in the USA
Middletown, DE
31 May 2019